LEARNING TO ROLEPLAY IN VIRTUAL WORLDS

LEARNING TO ROLEPLAY IN VIRTUAL WORLDS

Pannie Paniscus

First edition: 2021

ISBN paperback: 978-9942-38-725-7

ISBN hard cover: 978-9942-40-075-8

Cover design by IzabelaDesign

Cover photo "The Other Side" by Ooxooi (Uxui Resident)

Virtual India Map by Naoko Sakuri (RenaSakuri Resident)

Disclaimers: All roleplay transcripts are used with permission, but some character names have been changed to protect their anonymity.

To provide constructive feedback on the contents of this book, please contact Panpaniscus Resident in Second Life or visit www.panniepaniscus.com.

To all those dear friends who have already taken their flight to the great roleplay region in the sky.

Mamakie: "Why are you here, Arjun?
To have fun, right?"

Arjun: "In part, yes, but mostly to challenge
myself and others to learn and grow."

CONTENTS

FOREWORD BY DRAXTOR

I am honored to be asked to write a foreword for this important book. Why? Well, the fact of the matter is that I need all the help I can get to learn how to roleplay in Second Life.

And possibly become an expert?

I say this as a 14-year-old resident who has made well over 200 mini-documentaries/video reportages on quite a variety of virtual communities and creative individuals.

I happen to be one of those Second Lifers who feel they have merged with their avatar. My avatar is in fact me, at least in terms of everyday behavior and core personality.

And although I sometimes dress up differently to play other parts in my videos, I have never really roleplayed within a community in Second Life.

Often when I parachute into roleplaying communities—as a mere observer—I have felt mesmerized, yet left out. And not for offers to 'move in,' as of late I have been invited to become a centaur, a medieval king, a vampire, and an artiste.

Pannie's book is coming at the right time, and it seems to scream at me, "You can reinvent yourself Draxman, yes you can, and here is how!"

In my role [not much play to it] as a documentarian of virtualities, I get interviewed by mainstream media quite often and asked —provocatively— why I would waste my time with an escapist platform where nobody knows who anybody is, implying that SL facilitates "running away from oneself" and never confronting what truly matters.

I usually respond [and because I have done these interviews so many times I do it a lot more calmly than in the early days] that through roleplaying different parts of ourselves or exploring aspects that we feel may not be part of us, we actually run towards our true self, our essence. We learn to accept, integrate, become whole.

With Pannie's book read, highlighted, and the take-aways fully absorbed, I can now much more truthfully respond in upcoming interviews that I have gone through the 'program' and have become more than a bearded virtual journalist with flip-flops and a Pacman shirt.

Is this book coming at the right time as I suggest? Heck yes. The current global situation is terrible and terrifying, but this is also a time to reflect and run towards ourselves rather than away.

Let's explore worlds and identities, in all lives. Let's not only learn how to cope but to embrace all aspects of ourselves and those imagined (and therefore real) universes.

See you inworld!

Bernhard Drax, aka
Draxtor in Second Life

HOW TO USE THIS BOOK

"What? You mean I have to read this whole book to roleplay? No way!"

If this is you, fear not. Summaries are included at the end of each 'classroom' chapter, giving you enough to get started. You can also flip through the book and read the lift-out pull quotes scattered throughout the text. Then go out and start gaining experience. After all, you learn to roleplay by roleplaying, right?

Next, check the index at the back for areas to strengthen. Want to know what a roleplay term means? There is a glossary at the back. You can always go back and actually *read* the book to find out how Arjun learned all those lessons. It includes several insider tips and examples. Read just a chapter a day if you want, but don't let studying take priority over actually getting out and *doing* it.

"Nah, I don't need a book about roleplay. I have it pretty well down already."

This could be true if you are a seasoned roleplayer, but I've been studying and practicing roleplay for years now, and I still learn new things all the time. This book just might show you an approach you never thought of. Roleplaying in virtual worlds is an art, not a science, so there can be differing, even contrasting, approaches, opinions, and even terms used. I have tried to reflect this diversity through discussions among players who don't always see eye-to-eye.

Okay, now for a few disclaimers. First, it should be clear to most that roleplaying in virtual worlds is not the same as playing a pre-scripted videogame. Rather, it is a creative interaction among characters managed by actual people, not by a machine. Nobody decides beforehand what will happen.

This is not just a how-to manual, although I've tried to make it as complete as possible. Instead—like many works of fiction—it starts with a 'what if' proposal: WHAT IF a total newbie went to a virtual region with a tutoring system in place that taught people how to roleplay through mentoring, classes, and quests?

The story unfolds in Second Life—arguably the most popular virtual world to date—although its lessons should apply to any virtual world. It takes place in an imaginary region called Virtual India. I decided against setting it in any of the existing regions due to the fluid nature of virtual worlds. For a list of Second Life's current roleplay regions, sign up with WORP (World of Roleplay) inworld.

Virtual India's roleplay support system—both combat and economic—is also imaginary but combines several of those currently in use. I have added a few new features from my personal wishlist but left out some of the more complex elements (such as experience points) to keep it simple. The experiences described should adapt to most regions and their systems.

The book assumes that you, the reader, are familiar with the basics of Second Life. If not, several good resources are available, both inworld and on the Web. The technical tips the book offers are more advanced and based on the freeware Phoenix Firestorm viewer—the most commonly used—which can be downloaded from www.firestormviewer.org. For other viewers, please see their tutorials and help files.

I hope to show that roleplay can be much more than family life, where several people share a home, use voice chat, and play house without much of a plot or storyline. Of course, there is nothing wrong with that kind of roleplay *per se*, but this book goes beyond that. Roleplay is also more than just sex, although we will also address erotic roleplay in depth.

This book received valuable input from several experienced roleplayers in the form of classes, conversations, essays, and, most importantly, actual roleplay experience with them. The list is too long to mention here, covering several years and numerous roleplay regions, but you know who you are. A heartfelt thankyou to all who have selflessly enriched this book and my life in so many ways.

So, without further ado, join our dorky newbie in this adventure as he learns to roleplay in virtual worlds.

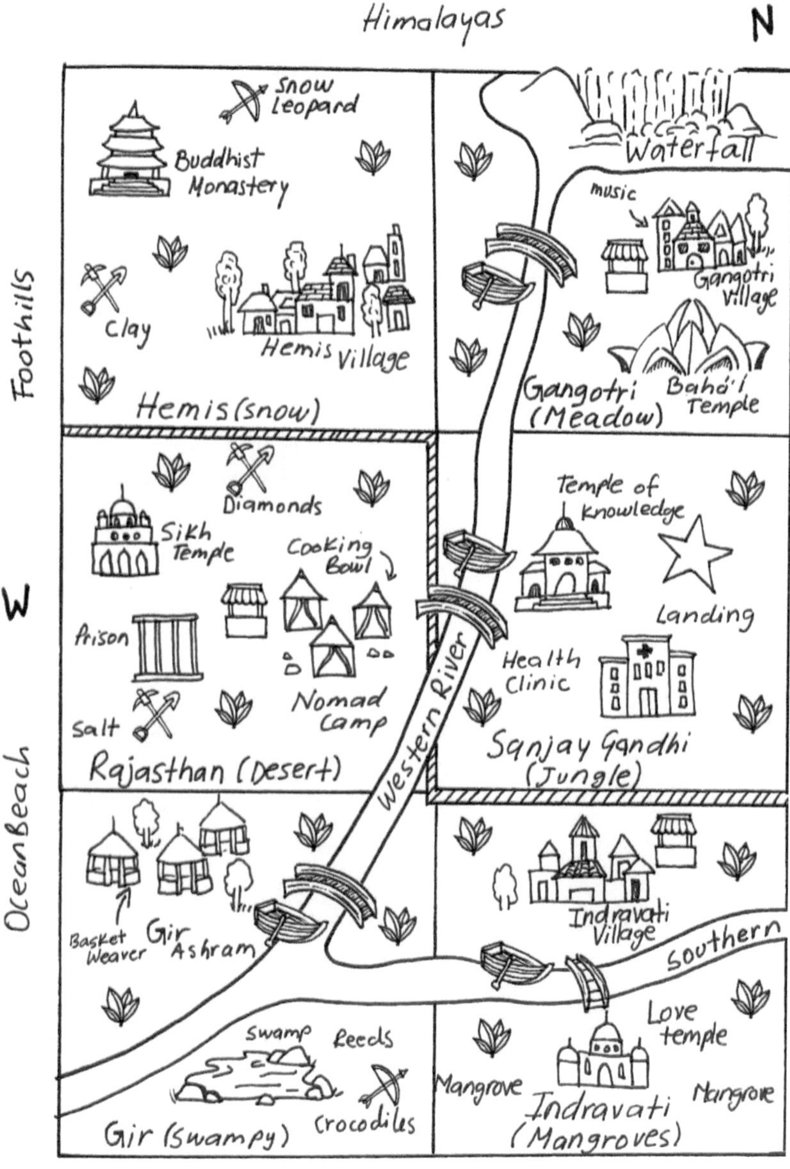
Himalayas
N
Snow Leopard
Buddhist Monastery
Waterfall
music
Gangotri Village
Foothills
Clay
Hemis Village
Hemis (snow)
Gangotri (Meadow)
Bahá'í Temple
Diamonds
Sikh Temple
Cooking Bowl
Temple of Knowledge
W
Prison
Landing
Health Clinic
Nomad Camp
Salt
Sanjay Gandhi (Jungle)
Rajasthan (Desert)
Western River
OceanBeach
Basket Weaver
Gir Ashram
Indravati Village
Southern
Love temple
Swamp
Reeds
Mangrove
Indravati (Mangroves)
Mangrove
Crocodiles
Gir (Swampy)
OceanBeach

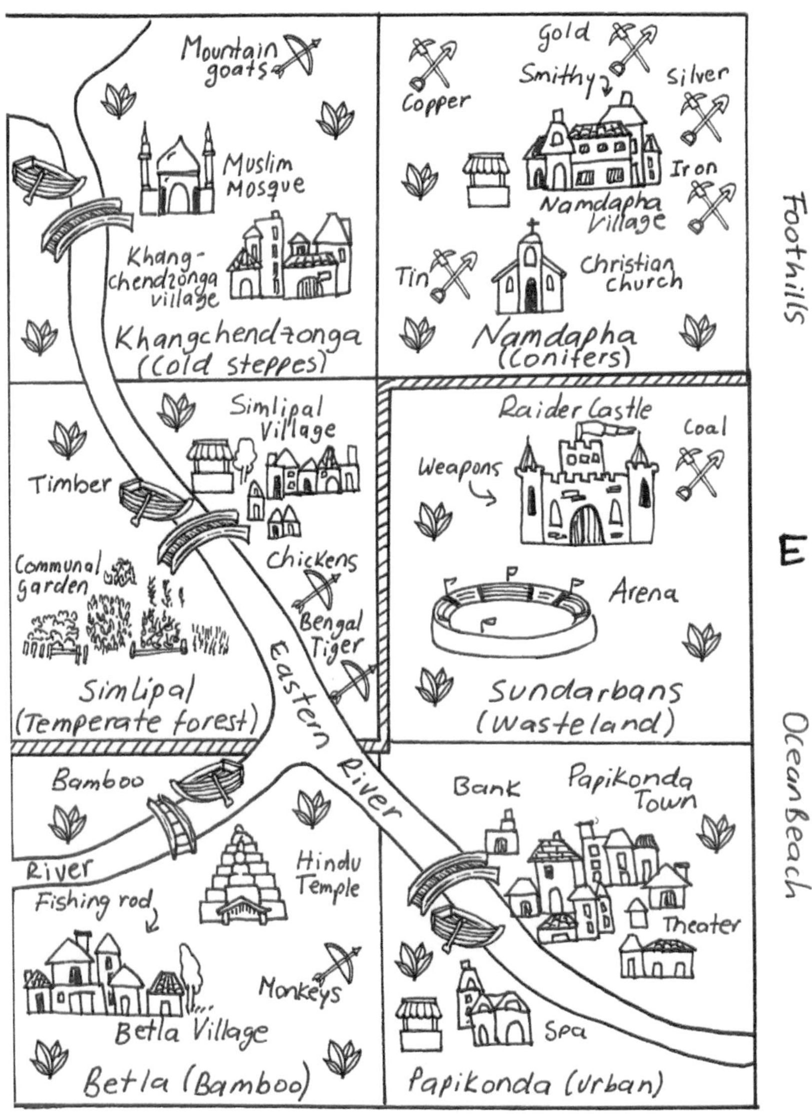
Himalayas
Mountain goats
Muslim Mosque
Khang-chendzonga village
Khangchendzonga (Cold steppes)
Gold
Smithy
Silver
Copper
Iron
Namdapha Village
Tin
Christian church
Namdapha (Conifers)
Foothills
Simlipal Village
Timber
Communal garden
Chickens
Bengal Tiger
Simlipal (Temperate forest)
Raider Castle
Coal
Weapons
Arena
Sundarbans (Wasteland)
E
Eastern River
Bamboo
River
Fishing rod
Hindu Temple
Monkeys
Betla Village
Betla (Bamboo)
Bank
Papikonda Town
Theater
Spa
Papikonda (Urban)
Ocean Beach
S
Ocean Beach

Part I:

Arjun Gets His Bearings

CHAPTER ONE

ARRIVING AT VIRTUAL INDIA

Detecting hardware...
Initializing texture cache...
Initializing VFS...
Grid Status: Online
Inworld: 43,164
SL Time: 10:07 am

Username: Arjun Tagore
Password: ********
Login: Virtual India

Logging in...
Initializing world...
Loading world...
Initializing communications...
Connecting to region...
Verifying cache files (can take 60 to 90 seconds) ...
Requesting region capabilities...
Waiting for simulator ack...
Waiting for region handshake...
Processing response...
Decoding images...

A small salmon-colored cloud billows in the middle of the large earthen plaza. It gradually congeals into the mesh body of a young man, seemingly in his late teens or early twenties, clad only in a flexi silk loincloth and sandals. Unkempt black waves of 'rigged mesh' hair frame his youthful Bento face as his dark brown eyes, penetrating and mischievous, brightly dart this way and that through long, curved lashes crowned by thick dark brows.

Prim by exquisitely textured prim, a misty jungle appears around him, its thick underbrush teeming with butterflies and buzzing insects. Above tower lofty trees draped with vines, alive with multicolored birds, whose cacophony of calls contrasts with the soft strains of a sitar, the rhythmic cadences of a tabla drum and the plaintive cries of a bansuri flute. A broad brown river, busy with boats, laps lazily beneath the foliage, and in the distance, the crashing of ocean surf on a rocky beach can be heard.

The boy's flared nostrils can almost smell the rich, humid earth and tropical flowers as his full lips curl in a satisfied smile. He squints up at the bright sun as it warms his bronze Omega skin and chuckles contentedly to himself. For reasons fathomable only by the one peering over his shoulder through a virtual reality headset on a far-distant world—a world our young friend will never know—this place feels like home. "Well, here goes nothing..." he murmurs to himself, then chuckles mirthlessly. "Then again, they say the third time's a charm."

Glancing around the plaza, the boy spies a tall, dark, muscular man dressed in a white cotton pajama a red silk Achkan jacket and a large white turban over straight black hair, sundry weapons on his back and waist. His tag announces him as a Mentor by the name of Mahir, and he stands to attention, a distant gaze in his brown eyes that seem to take in everything and nothing at once.

Approaching him hesitantly, the young man bows his head in respect and smiles, pressing his palms together at chest level in the customary Anjali mudra fashion, and says, "Excuse me, Mentor Mahir, sir. Could you help me?" Actually, he types this because the voice function is disabled in this region since—as he will learn—most roleplay is done via text in virtual worlds.

Mahir glances down and frowns, returning the gesture, pleased enough at the youth's deferential demeanor to overlook him breaking several roleplay conventions in one go. They were, after all, at the 'Landing' plaza, where the rules were relaxed. "Well, that depends, young man," he booms. "What do you need?"

Arjun Seeks His Purpose in Life

"Where am I? Who am I? What am I doing here?" the boy blurts out without thinking.

Mahir laughs in what could be perceived as either a humorous or scornful tone, or more likely both. "Well, the first two questions are easy. You're in the Virtual India region, and the tag above your head says your name is Arjun Tagore... As for your last question, this is a roleplay region, so I assume you're here to roleplay. But only you can decide what role you'll end up playing."

Glancing up at his tag, then at the address in the top bar, the young man hangs his head in chagrin at having asked not only one but three stupid questions in one go. "Oh, yes... of course..." he stammers, then looks up with renewed eagerness. "But... um... what are roles... and what roles are there?"

Mahir smiles at the bashful youth, a fatherly expression of compassion and willingness to help spreading across his otherwise stern face. "Well, Arjun, aside from 'who' you are—your name—your role says 'what' you are. Each roleplay region has different kinds of roles. For example, in a Wild West setting, you would expect to see cowboys and Indians, sheriffs and outlaws, farmer men and women. A medieval setting might have knights and ladies, kings and serfs, blacksmiths and tavern keepers, and so on.

"The setting pretty much determines the roles. You most likely wouldn't play a Viking in a futuristic sci-fi setting, for example. That's what's known as 'roleplay cross-over' or 'character cross-over'—transferring a character from one setting to another where it might not fit."

Arjun perks up, wagging his head from side to side in the characteristic Indian way of signaling understanding and agreement. "Oh, I see... and... what about here?"

Mahir casts a measured glance at a group that has started gathering around Arjun with expressions of interest. "Here in Virtual India, there are peasants and laborers, tradespeople and merchants, healers and warriors, village commissioners and guards, mentors and gurus...

"Most are natives, who should look, dress, and act like natives, but there are also foreigners, who tend to be more diverse. Characters can range from peaceful hunters, gatherers, and farmers to rogues who fight, steal, kidnap, and rape, and from wildlife to monks and gurus... Be realistic and choose a role that's right for you, your personality and interests, your aspirations and fantasies."

Be realistic and choose a role that's right for you, your personality, interests, aspirations, and fantasies.

Arjun's eyes sparkle with ideas as he listens, shifting from one foot to the other as though eager to start (or else just needing to pee), and muses as if to himself, "I like talking, so don't want to be an animal, but I really feel like I belong here, so maybe a native... I certainly don't like violence."

Mahir gazes sternly at some people clustering around them, then looks Arjun up and down appreciatively, doing the head bobble thing again. "Yes, that would work for you, but you'll find that some natives also have violent tendencies, so don't let that..."

"Don't think that a dark complexion makes you an 'authentic' native," a slender blonde woman with bright pink cheeks and a khaki safari outfit interrupts with the sharp, authoritarian tone characteristic of an academic. "Real-life Indian natives come in all shades, from white to black and everything in between. Actually, size is much more important. The average real-life Indian is only about five feet (152 cm) for women and 5.4 feet (165 cm) for men, like our friend Arjun here."

She sneers up at the seven-foot Mahir, "Besides, authentic native Indians don't usually look like they lift weights in a gym every day but tend to have less muscle mass and more body fat," she adds, jabbing a taunting finger at Mahir's muscular torso. The Mentor stiffens and scowls at her.

Airily ignoring his withering look, she proceeds nonchalantly with her incisive tirade. "Also, native penis sizes average about six inches erect, but some peckers around here are larger than a child's leg," she snorts, eyeing the tip of a dashing black man's massive cock visible below his long loincloth. "You really should see a doctor about that condition of yours, Urstud."

Some of those in the group giggle, glancing nervously around, while Urstud mumbles something about arrogant know-it-all anthropologists to a busty blonde on his arm whose tag identifies her as EyeCandey. Arjun surreptitiously pulls out the waist of his loincloth and glances down, relieved to see that his own member is within the scientifically-approved proportions.

"And what about native attitudes and behaviors?" continues the woman, tossing her golden locks defiantly, then quickly raising a hand to steady the round safari helmet on her head. "Most natives of India are gentle, kind, generous, community-oriented people. An aggressive, individualistic, competitive, neo-Darwinian approach to life will immediately give you away as a First-World Westerner, no matter how many embroidered silks you wear."

Mahir counters testily, obviously straining to remain even-tempered, "Well, that's your opinion, Ms. Margaret, but the owners of each roleplay region are free to set whatever rules they wish, and these are their rules." He then turns to Arjun with a softer tone. "It's up to you, son, so choose your role carefully, and decide for yourself how you'll play it out."

Lesson Number One

Mahir lays a large hand on the shoulder of a youth dressed in blue jeans and a plain black tee-shirt, a little older and taller but thinner than Arjun. He has milk-white skin and clear green eyes, and a shock of ginger hair frames his impish freckled face. "Why don't you show our newcomer around—teach him the ropes and help him get adjusted," Mahir says in what sounds more like a command than a question.

"Do I have to?" the youth frowns up at him, then whispers, "*He's such a noob.*"

Mahir scowls down at him, "You DO want to finish that quest, don't you?" he says sternly.

The boy sighs in resignation and shrugs, "Oh, alright, Mentor."

Mahir turns to Arjun and smiles. "Virtual India is an open roleplay region, meaning anyone is welcome to roleplay here, but we provide mentoring to help you adjust and advance through the various levels more quickly and easily."

Meanwhile, reviewing the youth's tag and profile, Arjun discovers he is at Level 29, his name is Christopher Eric, or Chris for short, and his father is a British businessman. "I'd really appreciate the help of a Level 29 player, Chris," he says, trying to sound ingratiating. "I see you're British. Is your father's business here in Virtual India?"

"How do you know so much about me?" Chris gripes.

"Well... it's in your tag... and... and your profile..." Arjun starts, a confused look on his face.

"That's METAgaming, KID," Chris interrupts in a haughty, impatient tone. "You're not supposed to KNOW that 'til somebody TELLS you."

Having heard of the peculiarly Western custom of bonding by testing each other's mettle, Arjun decides to confront Chris. Drawing himself up to his full five-foot-three stature, he scowls, clenches his fists, and growls, "Look here, Chris, I may be SHORTER than you, but I'm no KID. I'm eighteen years old, and my NAME is Arjun Tagore..." He deflates a little and quickly adds, "...although my FRIENDS call me Arjun..."

Chris relaxes visibly and grins. "Point taken, Arjun. Good to meet you. Name's Chris." He holds out his hand to shake Arjun's, then frowns. "But don't get your knickers in such a twist, mate... I mean, bloody hell. Don't you know ANYthing about roleplaying?"

Arjun, thrilled his strategy actually worked, shakes Chris's hand. "Oh, um... hi, Chris. Yeah, well... I got kicked out of one place because they said I was breaking some kind of rule, and then another place wouldn't take me because they said I had a crappy profile, so a friend said I should come here to learn." He shrugs, "I mean, you gotta start somewhere, right? So, um... what's that you said about 'meta'-whatever?"

> Metagaming means using information you couldn't have known in-game.

Chris relaxes further and sighs, "Fair enough... Well, metagaming means using information that you couldn't have known in-game, erm... I mean, that you got from outside the roleplay itself. For example, although you can see my nametag and profile, that's 'out-of-character' information because in a real-life situation, they wouldn't be there, so you can't use it in your roleplay until you learn it some other way 'in character.'"

Mahir breaks in, bobbling his head in agreement. "That's right, Arjun. You can't know a person's name until you've been introduced... unless, of course, you're roleplaying someone who should already know everyone's name and basic information, such as a long-time student in a school or the son or daughter of a family. Otherwise, you need to learn about people 'in character' as part of the roleplay. So get used to saying 'Hello, ma'am/sir' or something like that when you first meet someone. And remember—they won't know your name either until you introduce yourself."

A young man with multi-colored hair, whose hovertext says he is a techie named Chiptag, breaks in. "If you have a bad memory like me and don't remember who you know and don't know in character, you can add acquaintances to a 'Set' called 'Names I know' or some such. Just right-click their tag or name in chat and select Add – Set and create or select the set you want them in. Then you can assign a specific color to that set so that you will know right away who belongs to it. For Phoenix Firestorm, see the details at wiki.phoenixviewer.com/fs_contact_sets."

CHAPTER TWO

THE MENTORING STARTS

Arjun takes a deep breath. "Oookaaaay..." This was not going to be as easy-peasy as he had thought. But he was already well into his summer vacation, this being his third attempt, and he was determined to learn to roleplay or bust.

"If you ever have any other questions," Mahir adds, "just send an internal message (IM) to the Virtual India group, and we'll be glad to help."

The Temple of Knowledge

Chris grins and pats Arjun on the back, "Don't worry ki... er... I mean, Arjun—you'll get the hang of it. Come on; I'll show you a place that will answer many of your questions." He sets off across the plaza at a brisk pace. Arjun follows him to a large marble building fashioned roughly after the Taj Mahal, "Temple of Knowledge" etched above the tall arched doorway.

"Here you can learn all about the Virtual India region," Chris says as Arjun tries and fails to open the door. "Oh... zero-level 'Tourists' can't get in—just join the Virtual India group to get the key," he explains, pointing to a group-joiner sign to the right of the door. Arjun touches the sign and joins the group, accepting the system prompt. A message pops up in his Local Chat:

> Dharma Guide: Welcome to Virtual India. You are now Level 1 - Guest, with a capacity for 10 HP and access to the help chat. To begin your journey, please click on your Karma Tag and receive your first quest.

Arjun looks up and sees a green tag has appeared above his head:

Status:	Guest
Level:	1
HP:	10.0

"What does HP mean?" Arjun asks.

"HP can mean 'hit points' for fighters or 'health points' in our case," Chris answers. "That's how much health you have left until you die. You use HP just by being alive and even more when you're working, sick, or injured, so you need to 'buff up' or recover your health points by eating regularly. Some of your first quests will teach you how to collect food. When you reach higher levels, you will be allowed more HP."

"Okay... so now what should I do?"

"Click on your tag and then on 'Quests' to get the key to the temple." As Arjun does so, a menu appears:

> You have a new quest available: Temple of Knowledge [Accept] [Cancel]

Arjun clicks 'Accept,' and another message appears in Local Chat:

> Dharma Guide: You have accepted the "Temple of Knowledge" quest and received the key to enter. To complete the quest, please follow the arrows and touch each placard to read its contents. You will be given a test at the end, so study well. Good luck.

Arjun tries the door again, and it swings open, revealing a large courtyard, semi-circles of placards on either side. Centered in the middle is a brilliant white effigy of Hayagriva, the horse-headed, four-armed god of knowledge and wisdom, seated on a white lotus blossom. Following the blue arrows on the white marble-textured floor, Arjun reads each placard carefully, taking notes, while Chris adds details and answers his questions.

He learns the region's rules, the various functions of the 'Karma Tag' and the reasons for its different colors, and more about the roles Mahir had listed, including some exclusive ones assigned only to the leaders: District Guards, Village Commissioners, Builders, Techies, and Gurus.

About thirty basic quests are available, completed by following the 'Dharma System' instructions to 'level up' and gain new powers and abilities. They are not designed to be very difficult, like in an FPS videogame, but rather to familiarize him with the region and its economic/combat systems, put him in touch with other residents, and give him roleplay experience. "Wow, I had no idea roleplay regions had such complete mentoring programs for newcomers," Arjun says.

"Actually, this is the first roleplay region to implement such a program, so they are still trying out new things, seeing what works, what doesn't, and learning from experience," Chris replies. "It's also a great way for people to learn the region's rules in practice and not just as a long list of do's and don'ts."

Arjun scrunches up his face. "Why are there so many rules?"

Chris nods thoughtfully. "I had the same question until I realized that we're all guests of this region's owners, who pay monthly fees for it and have created or bought and installed most of what you see here. They are our Emperors, so to speak, our hosts. They have invested a lot of valuable time, effort, and money into realizing their dream of making this the best possible roleplay region for everyone, so they have the right to expect us to be well-behaved, polite guests.

The region's owners invest time, effort, and money to provide this roleplay opportunity, so they have a right to expect well-behaved, polite guests.

"They set down basic principles—like a country's constitution—in consultation with the Council of Leaders, which then crafts specific rules based on both need and experience, much like the region's legislature. Everyone has to follow the law or pay the consequences, just like in real life."

Arjun sways his head slowly from side to side. "Sounds reasonable."

"Punishment for breaking the law," Chris continues, "can be anything from a slap on the wrist to downtime in the Jail, losing levels and powers, and temporary banning from the region—or even permanent banning in the worst cases. But the Leaders don't want to have to punish people; they'd rather talk things out to solve problems. They are all here to help make our roleplay experience as enjoyable as possible. They know that people can always vote with their feet and leave the region if they're upset, so they try to be reasonable. But we have to follow their regulations, even if we disagree with them."

By this point, Arjun had finished reading all the placards and started on the test. He needed to check his notes for some of the questions and even returned to review a placard for a couple, but a message finally appears in Local Chat:

> Dharma Guide: Congratulations. You have passed the Temple of Wisdom test and advanced to Level 2 - Novice. You are encouraged to come back here any time. Please check your Karma Tag for your next quest.

Arjun looks up at his Karma Tag, which now reads:

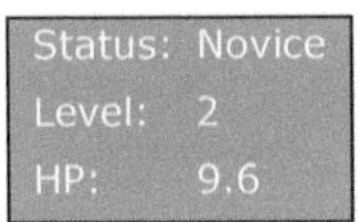

Swimming Lessons

Arjun clicks on 'Quests' again and reads, "You have a new quest available: Swimming." He clicks the 'Accept' button, and a message appears in Local Chat:

Dharma Guide: You have accepted the quest "Swimming." To complete it, you must take swimming lessons to keep from drowning. Good luck.

"Where do I take the swimming lessons?" Arjun asks.

"It's against the rules for me to tell you directly how to do your quests," Chris replies, "but I can give you a wee hint.... Where would you go to swim?"

Arjun laughs, a little chagrined, "To the river, of course." He had seen a river from the Landing, so he trots westward, a grinning Chris following. There he finds a dock with a sign saying 'Swimming Lessons' and, in smaller print, 'If you enter the water without knowing how to swim, you can drown.' Arjun clicks the sign, and a 'Swimming HUD' (heads-up display) enters his Inventory. He finds it, right-clicks 'Add,' and it appears as a little menu prompt at the bottom of his screen.

"Let's try it out," Arjun says. The two boys shed their clothes and jump into the water. Arjun practices the different swimming strokes, and soon, a message in Local Chat says:

Dharma Guide: Congratulations. You have successfully learned to swim and advanced to Level 3 - Swimmer. Wear the swimming HUD at all times, as you can drown without it. Please check your Karma Tag for your next quest.

Arjun's Karma Tag now says:

Status:	Swimmer
Level:	3
HP:	9.3

"Why are my health points going down?" Arjun asks, stopping to tread water near Chris as he saves his outfit to always have the Swimming HUD on.[1]

Chris hesitates a moment, then opens an internal message.

Chris: "Let's discuss this in IMs because we're outside the Landing, the only place you can be OOC."

Arjun: "Okay... What does OOC mean?"

Chris: "It's short for 'out of character'—anything you write that your character would normally not say or do. That can include talking and acting in a way your character wouldn't do—for example, if a courteous, respectful character suddenly starts talking and acting offensively. But it usually means discussing things outside of the roleplay, which can either relate to your roleplay, such as where the story should go, whose turn it is, and so on, or it can relate to real life.

[1] An 'outfit' is any clothing, HUDs, and other attachments an avatar is 'wearing.' Each outfit can be saved with a unique name to find and change outfits easily. In Firestorm, click on the 'Appearance' icon, go to 'Appearance' in the Avatar menu, or press Ctrl-O. Then click 'Save As' at the bottom of the window. While there, click on the "?" help button for further details.

"For example, out here in the river, you couldn't really say 'BRB — doorbell'[2] in character because there are no doorbells around... unless you happened to bring one along for the swim. Did you? ... No, I didn't think so. So to signal it's an OOC comment, you would put it in double brackets ((like this)).

"The opposite of OOC is 'in character' or IC, which is all the make-believe we create during roleplay. Being in character means taking on your character's 'persona' and speaking, acting, and responding as your character would. You should always be in character in Local Chat, except in OOC places like the Landing and at OOC events, such as classes. The basic rule is NEVER to mix OOC and IC in Local Chat."

Anything you write that your character wouldn't normally do or say is OOC (out of character).

Arjun: "Wow, I have a LOT to learn about roleplay. Can you give me more examples of OOC?"

Chris: "Well, let's see... RP-related OOC posts are things like 'BRB' and 'AFK,'[3] which should be kept to a minimum in Local Chat and always in double brackets ((like this)). If your RP-related message is longer than a few words, such as discussing the next step in an ongoing scene, don't use Local Chat. Instead, open a group chat or, if it's just one other person, a personal IM.

"The other type of OOC post is RL-related—for instance, telling others about your real life, which is why they are known as 'out-of-game' or OOG posts. They have nothing to do with roleplay, so they should be kept out of Local Chat entirely and limited to IMs, if at all."

Arjun: "Okay, so I could write something like ((BRB - doorbell)) in Local Chat, but not tell people who was at the door or what they wanted. Is that it?"

Chris: "Right, although even mentioning the doorbell borders on RL-related talk because it establishes that you have a doorbell, that people visit you, and you're able to answer it yourself, which is not the case with everyone."

Arjun: "What's wrong with that?"

Chris: "Well, as an immersionist, I see roleplaying like being an actor in a play. When you see a play or movie, you know it's not real, but you 'suspend disbelief' to immerse yourself in the story, and the actors also immerse themselves in their characters. That's what makes the theatre so magical.

"In the middle of Hamlet, Claudius wouldn't say, 'Hold on everybody, I'll be right back—I just remembered I didn't turn off the iron at home' because that would be totally out of character. If he did, he would ruin all the effort the actors made to get into character and the audience put into suspending disbelief and immersing themselves in the story.

"It's the same with roleplay. If you say ((BRB - doorbell)), your RP partners now imagine you sitting behind a computer, getting up from your chair, going to the door, answering it, and talking to whoever rang the bell. BAM! Some

---

[2] BRB = be right back.

[3] AFK = away from the keyboard.

of the RP magic has just been stripped from your character. You've reminded them you're not that Arjun character; that it's just fiction."

Arjun: "You mean we should NEVER say ANYTHING about our real life?"

Chris: "Right, well, at least not here, and DEFINITELY not in Local Chat. A roleplay region is not a social media hangout. We're here to roleplay. Period. If we DO want to discuss our real life with friends, we should keep it out of Local Chat, or better yet, go to a non-roleplay region to do it.

"Personally, I go one step further and use one account for my RP character... well, actually more than one... and another to just be myself and talk about my RL. I NEVER talk about RL in my roleplay accounts. That way, I keep the two completely separate.

"By the way, the easiest way to make the ((double brackets)) is to hold down the Alt key when you press Enter."

Arjun tries it and types, "Thank you ((BRB))," then holds down the Alt key. The message comes out "((Thank you ((BRB))))."

Chris: "Ok, but you wouldn't use Alt-Enter in that case, because you wrote the double brackets manually. If you're going to include OOC comments at the end of IC posts, it's a good idea to activate the 'Auto-close ((OOC)) parentheses' option in Preferences – Chat – Typing. That way, you only have to type the double brackets to open the OOC comment, and the brackets will automatically close for you at the end of the post."

Arjun adjusts his Preferences. "Got it. So... getting back to my question about my HP going down...?"

Chris: "Oh, yeah, you use about one HP per hour just by being in the region. And when you're sick, underwater, injured, or doing physical labour, it drops even faster."

Arjun: "How can I recover my HP?"

Chris: "That's your next quest. Check it out."

Emoting with a Frog

Arjun clicks his Karma Tag, then on 'Quests.' The prompt says, "You have a new quest available: Basketry." He clicks 'Accept' and reads the Local Chat message:

Dharma Guide: You have accepted the quest "Basketry." To complete it, collect 10 reeds and take them to the nearest village to make one collecting basket of each type. Good luck.

"I know you can't tell me outright," Arjun says, "but... how about another hint?"

"Well, where do reeds usually grow?"

Arjun thinks a while, chewing on his lip, then looks up, grinning. "In swamps!" he exclaims, then looks doubtful again. "But where do I find a swamp?" Chris doesn't answer but starts walking slowly back towards the Temple of Knowledge, clearing his throat pointedly.

Arjun remembers seeing a large map of the region there, and he passes Chris at a run into the Temple to study it again. It shows the region's twelve districts or 'sims'[4] and their main features. Two main rivers flow from the northern mountain range to the southeast and southwest, with a smaller river connecting them to the south. Almost every district has a village and main building, around which are mountains, forests, plains, deserts, beaches, and so on.

So many items are on the map that it's a little confusing, but Arjun knows swamps are usually found in lowlands near river deltas, so he inspects the southeastern and southwestern areas until he spots one near the western river delta. The nearest village is the 'Gir Ashram.' He checks his location with the 'You are here' star on the map to see which way to go.

Quickly taking a snapshot of the map for future reference, Arjun exits the Temple and sets off westward at an easy lope. Chris trots after him, grinning contentedly; this youngster is turning out to be not so dorky after all.

Back at the river, the boys turn left and run along the mossy eastern bank until they come to the cross-cutting Southern River, swimming across it and arriving at the swamp. Arjun wrinkles his nose at the smell of rotting things and swamp gasses bubbling up through the mud. The still, murky water is partially covered by some sort of floating plant with small green leaves, punctuated here and there by water lilies. Only the occasional whine of a mosquito, hum of a dragonfly, croak of a frog, or cry of a fishing bird breaks the eerie silence of the place.

"Mind the crocs," Chris calls out as Arjun steps into the water. Squinting through the haze covering the swamp, Arjun sees the ghostly forms of lone mangrove trees grasping the muddy bottom with their many-fingered roots and the whitened skeletons of long-dead trees towering over them like solemn sentinels. On an island at the center of the swamp, nestled among weeping willows, stand the remains of a rotting wooden shack, its front gutted, giving a clear view of the grungy old furnishings inside and what seems to be human bones on the floor. Around the shack, among tufts of pampas grass under huge fan-like gunnera leaves, a cluster of crocodiles lies in wait, some almost submerged like floating logs, others with gaping snouts showing rows of sharp teeth.

Shuddering, Arjun turns his attention to the edge of the swamp, strewn with the decaying remains of toppled trees. Patches of cattails grow along the banks, interspersed with small bamboo thickets. Among them, he spies the tall stems of reeds that change his cursor to a hand icon when passed over them. He collects the largest ones with mature flowers, which disappear and go into his Inventory. Soon, he has his ten reeds, plus a few more for good measure.

Croaky Frog: entered chat range (19.82 m)

---

[4] 'Sim' is an abbreviation of 'simulator,' the basic unit of a virtual world, which enables a virtual 'simulation.' In Second Life, each sim is 256m x 256m (65,536 m^2)—the size of each district in Virtual India.

Chris: /me walks along the edge of the swamp looking for basket reeds when suddenly he slips on a muddy part of the bank and falls in, spluttering and splashing around as he sinks into the goo and reaches out reflexively to grab on to an orangish rock lying nearby

Croaky Frog: /me chomps contentedly on a fly he has caught with his long, sticky tongue when he hears a loud splash and startles as a hand reaches out to grab him. Instinctively, he secretes a layer of toxin through the skin on his back before trying to jump away

Chris: /me turns to see that the rock wriggling under his hand is actually an enormous orange frog. He releases it with a frightened yelp, but too late. He watches in horror as his hand breaks out in hives that run up his arm and soon cover his torso as his mucous membranes swell, and he starts gasping for breath

Croaky Frog: /me quickly dives into the water and swims away to find a more peaceful place to catch flies

Chris: /me plunges his hand into the mud to clean off the toxin, then drags himself painfully up onto the bank, heaving and retching, until the effects of the poison gradually subside. He flops onto his back, clutching his chest and panting, "Gods, that was a close call. I thought I was a goner."

Croaky Frog: left chat range

Chris: Thanks for the RP Croaky. Sorry for the interruption

Croaky: No problem Chris, it was fun

Arjun watches the scene amused. "What was that you did with the frog? You weren't talking, just describing your actions. Can you teach me how to do that?"

Chris: "OOC again. It's called 'emoting.' Pure dialog or 'chat-boxing' limits roleplay because it conveys little context. Believe me, bro, you don't wanna be seen as a chat-boxer. I can type 'Hi, I'm glad to see you,' but how do you know whether I'm saying that in a friendly, curt, surly, or facetious way?"

Arjun: "I guess you could use animations and facial expression HUDs. There are even hand gesture HUDs now."

Chris: "Yes, animations are getting better for body movements, facial expressions, and even hand gestures, but even that is limited and requires cumbersome, costly poseballs,[5] HUDs, and other devices. Emotes are a much easier, more flexible way to qualify, contextualize, and enrich your speech."

Arjun: "I know that in theater, 'emoting' means adding emotion or feeling to whatever an actor does or says, but what does it mean in roleplay, like using emoticons or something?"

---

[5] Poseballs are an old system still in limited use in Second Life, often in the form of small colored balls such as blue for males and pink for females. 'Sitting' on them puts an avatar into a static pose or dynamic animation. They have been largely replaced by including poses and animations directly in furniture itself, in an effort to achieve greater realism.

Chris: "No, definitely not emoticons. They're frowned upon in roleplay circles. Rather, think of your speech as 'dialog,' and your emotes as 'narrative.' As in acting, emotes can describe facial expressions, tone of voice, and body language, but in roleplay they have a broader meaning that includes your appearance, actions or reactions, surroundings, and even a bit of background. They give your posts more depth and clarity than simply speaking.

Emotes can describe facial expressions, tone of voice, and body language, but also your appearance, actions, surroundings, and even a bit of background.

"For instance, if I just say, 'Hello,' how do you know whether I'm happy, excited, sad, angry, or indifferent to see you? You'd respond differently in each situation, so I need an emote to let you know. For example, I can post any of the following:

Chris: /me turns to look at the woman, his eyes taking in her gorgeous form in a slow sweep from her feet to her long wavy hair, then gazes into her lovely brown eyes and purrs "Hello"

Chris: /me smiles warmly, holds out his hand for the boy to shake and says cheerily "Hello"

Chris: /me eyes the man warily and scowls, his hand hovering over his pistol as he snarls "Hello"

Arjun: "You're still saying 'Hello,' but it means something different each time."

Chris: "Exactly, and that gives your roleplay partners much more to work with when they're writing their responses. Without emotes, there is no roleplay. You can't just use dialog or one-word emotes like '/me nods' and expect anyone to take you seriously as a roleplayer. It's good to combine all your 'dialog' with 'narrative' like that in your posts.

"Try to make your emotes at least as long as your speech. It's not a rule, but challenging yourself like that could be good practice and improve your RP. Of course, you don't have to go over-board with it either, like emoting what is already obvious. For example, I wouldn't write 'You're a damn shit!' he says angrily, because it's pretty obvious that I'm angry from what I said, but you might emote snarling it with a scowl or something."

Arjun wobbles his head in agreement, then checks his snapshot of the map to see where the Gir Ashram is and sets off, Chris following close behind. As they go, Arjun starts to practice emoting.

Arjun: picks his way through the thick vegetation and says he wishes there was a path to the Ashram.

Chris: "That's good, but instead of emoting that you are saying something, you can just say it, like this: */me picks his way through the thick vegetation 'I wish there were a path to the Ashram'*

Arjun: holds his reeds out of the water as he wades, neck deep, across the river I don't want to get these wet

> Chris: "That's better. Now try making it clear when you're emoting and when you're talking. There are many ways to do that, such as these:
>
> /me smiles 'Hello'
>
> *smiles* Hello
>
> Hello -smiles-
>
> "It's like scriptwriting in shorthand. There's no right or wrong way to do it, as long as others understand you and can tell your narrative from your dialog. Just decide on a method you feel comfortable with and use it consistently."

Arjun decides on Chris's first option and tries again:

Arjun: /me scrambles up the opposite muddy bank, water running in rivulets down his bronze body, and shakes his head to dry his long black hair "Good thing the water isn't too cold this time of year"

> Chris: "Much better. You can also use a colon (:) instead of typing '/me' each time, but first, you have to activate the option ':' as a synonym for '/me' under Preferences - Chat - Typing"

Arjun adjusts the setting, and the boys wander around the Ashram until Arjun spies a workbench with reeds and half-finished baskets lying around it. Under Chris's guidance, he sits on the bench, loads the reeds, and chooses the first basket type offered. He then picks up the tools—a punch and a knife—and starts the process. A basket-making animation starts, and a collecting basket enters his Inventory after a few minutes, which Arjun pulls out to admire.

> Chris: "Good, you have the technique down. Now let's think about how you can describe your actions. Don't let the scripts and animations roleplay for you. If I couldn't see your animations but could only read the Local Chat, how would you let me know what you're doing? For example:

Chris: /me takes one of Arjun's reeds, cuts it in half, then splits the upper half into two strips and the lower half into three strips, which he lays in a long water vat to soak. He repeats this process with the next reed

Arjun admits that he has never made baskets before IRL and isn't sure how it is done. At Chris's suggestion, he finds a short introductory video on basket-making on the web and watches it. Then he starts the next collecting basket and posts:

Don't let the scripts and animations roleplay for you.

Arjun: /me splits two large strips with the knife and, with the help of the punch, inserts two similar strips through them to form a cross. He then starts weaving the smaller split strands, now pliable from soaking, around them. Once the cross pieces are secured, he bends them out in eight directions like the spokes of a wheel and starts weaving the strands between them to form a round base.

Chris: /me watches Arjun with amazement "I thought you said you didn't know how to weave baskets" and starts splitting another reed

Arjun: /me laughs and continues his work. Once the base is almost large enough, he inserts medium-sized reeds or 'stakes' into either side of the twelve base rods, using the awl to open gaps in the weave for them, and weaves a few more rounds with the strands to secure them in place. He then bends these stakes upward, 'pricking' them at the joint with the knife, and continues weaving the strands between them to form the sides.

Chris: /me nods with appreciation at each step, smiling proudly at his friend's skill as he continues splitting and soaking more reeds

Arjun: /me glances up at Chris from time to time to see his reaction and, seeing it is positive, continues with renewed confidence. Once the sides are high enough, he turns down the 'stakes' and weaves them into each other to form the rim of his basket, inserting the last one into this weave, and trims the excess with the knife. He then adds the handles using two interwoven rods bound by strands on either side. Finally, he examines his work, clips the stray ends, and holds it up, smiling with satisfaction.

Chris: /me claps his hands and cheers "Bravo! You only have two more to do to finish this quest" and sets about splitting and soaking the last reeds in the bundle

Arjun watches two more videos to learn other basket-making techniques and makes two more collecting baskets, each time emoting a different method. Chris is pleasantly surprised at Arjun's determination to roleplay this quest as best he can and cheers him on enthusiastically. Finally, a message appears in Local Chat:

> Dharma Guide: Congratulations. You have successfully made your collecting baskets and advanced to Level 4 - Basketmaker. Please check your Karma Tag for your next quest.

Foraging Hacks

Status:	Basketmaker
Level:	4
HP:	7.8

Arjun accepts the next quest and reads:

> Dharma Guide: You have accepted the quest "Foraging." To complete it, use your collecting basket to gather 50 fruits and nuts. Good luck.

He glances at Chris, who is watching him expectantly, eyebrows raised. No, this time, he would *not* ask for help. Fruits and nuts were found by hunting for them, and that's just what Arjun would do. He looks around until something orange catches his eye, and sure enough, he sees a Nagpur orange tree with ten oranges. He tries to pick one when his cursor changes to the hand icon, but nothing happens.

Chris: "Read the quest instructions again"

Arjun scrolls back, grins bashfully, and takes out one of his collecting baskets, which sends a message to Local Chat: "You have used this collecting basket 0 of 100 times."

He tries to pick the orange again, and this time it disappears, while a number '1' appears over his basket. He passes his cursor over the next orange, but no hand icon appears.

Arjun: "Why can't I pick that one?"

Chris: "Trees usually have a lot of transparencies. You can use Ctrl-Alt-T to see the transparencies, then cam around them to get at the fruit."[6]

Arjun tries Ctrl-Alt-T, and immediately his screen lights up with the bright red of all the transparencies. Then, holding down the Alt key and the left mouse button, he carefully cams around until he has a clear view of an orange and clicks on it. This time, it goes into his basket.

Chris: "You can use another hack to make it even easier, but don't tell anyone I told you, or we'll both be in trouble."

Arjun: "Of course, please tell me"

Chris. "Right-click – More – More – Derender – Temporary"

Arjun tries it and gasps in amazement as the tree and all its leaves suddenly disappear, leaving only the oranges in plain view. He picks them quickly, laughing. "Oh wow, that's totally rad."

Chris: /me raises a warning finger to his lips and winks "Shhhhh..." then chuckles, "It will be there again next time you teleport or relog, or you can just re-render everything with World – Asset Blacklist – Clear Temporary"

When Arjun clicks on the highest orange, he gets the message, "You need to be within arm's reach to collect this," so he moves as close as he can and manages to pick it.

Arjun: /me picks the last orange and smiles. "TY buddy. UR awesome." LOL

Chris: "You're welcome, but to be taken seriously as a roleplayer, never use internet shorthand in character, except for very few things like BRB or AFK. Say 'laughs,' not 'lol,' 'thank you,' not TY, 'you,' not 'U,' and so on. The same goes for emojis such as :-) or ^^ for smiles, :P or :-P for sticks out tongue, and :-(or :(for frowns. Shorthand is okay for OOC messages in IMs, but according to roleplay convention, it's a big no-no in Local Chat.

Arjun: "Oh, yeah. Sorry, I guess it's a bad habit."

---

[6] 'Cam around' means to move the location and angle of the viewer as if you were positioning a camera. The methods to achieve this are discussed in a later section of this book.

Chris: "No problem. If you can't break the habit, you can make 'Gestures' to change them to words, putting the shorthand under 'Trigger,' the long version in 'Replace with,' and removing the default 'Steps.' There's a tutorial at https://wiki.phoenixviewer.com/gesture_preview. If your shorthand only has letters, you can also use the Auto-Replace feature, which is explained at https://wiki.phoenixviewer.com/autoreplace_settings.

Arjun: "I guess the ideal would be to break the habit and force myself to type without netspeak."

To be taken seriously as a roleplayer, never use internet shorthand or emojis in character.

Arjun looks around and sees a Nanjanagud banana plant. Coming closer, he realizes it is mesh with no transparencies, so he can pick all eight bananas without derendering the plant. He goes on to collect Vazhakulam pineapples, Malihabad Dasheri mangoes, Tezpur litchis, and Nashik grapes. As soon as the number on his basket reaches fifty, he gets a message in Local Chat:

> Dharma Guide: Congratulations. You have successfully filled your collection basket. You are now at Level 5 - Forager and can increase your HP to 15. Please eat some of the food you have collected to buff up your Health Points and check your Karma Tag for your next quest.

Arjun: "How do I eat this food?"

Chris: "Rez your collection basket next to you, open your Karma Tag, and select 'Eat,' then click on your basket and choose what you want to eat."

Arjun selects 'Eat,' and a message in Local Chat says, "You can now eat as much as you need, but if you eat more than that, it will go to waste and can even make you sick."

He clicks on the basket, and a menu appears with the contents' names and amounts. His HP is down to 7.9 now, so he chooses seven items and hears munching sounds as the basket numbers drop accordingly. He then rechecks his Karma Tag, which reads:

Status:	Forager
Level:	5
HP:	7.9

Arjun: "Why haven't I gained any health points?"

Chris: "It just takes a while to digest."

After a minute, a chime sounds, and Arjun's HP jumps to 14.9. "Wow, this is great," he says. "I can actually survive here now. How can I ever repay you, Chris?"

Chris grins, "Oh, well, actually... there IS one little thing you can do for me..." and hesitates as Arjun does the Indian head wobble and smiles expectantly. "You can write a report of how I guided you through your first five quests—leaving out the hacks, of course. I need your reports to complete my mentoring quest."

"No problem," Arjun says, quickly writing up a report and handing it to Chris.

Chris: "Thanks, and speaking of quests, check out your next one. You have a class to attend."

Arjun accepts the next quest and reads:

Dharma Guide: You have accepted the quest "Basic Emoting." To complete it, go to the Gir Ashram on Friday evening. Pay attention because you will be tested on it. Good luck.

Friday is tomorrow, so Arjun thanks Chris and takes his leave. Exhausted after a long, productive day, he mentally tells his atman he is ready and feels the jungle swirl around him as he poofs.

CHAPTER THREE

BASIC ROLEPLAYING CLASS

A crackling fire in the Ashram patio throws orange sparks into the night, spreading a golden glow on the faces of those gathered, some sitting cross-legged on woven rugs and others leaning against the mahogany tree overshadowing them. The firelight casts moving shadows on the ancient plaster walls of the two-story building, further enriching the variegated tones caused by the gradual erosion of different-colored coats of paint applied over the years. On owl hoots in a nearby tree, and leaves rustle with the comings and goings of nocturnal creatures.

Crouching near the fire and poking it with a stick, Arjun inhales the forest's earthy scents and the mouth-watering aroma of the bird turning on a spit, and smiles contentedly to himself. He had spent the day collecting more food, meeting people, and practicing his RP skills, and was ready for his next adventure.

Mentor Mahir clears his throat as the initial greetings subside, "Welcome to the Basic Roleplaying class. I'd like to introduce my mate Mamakie..." He gestures to his right, where a handsome woman with deep dark eyes sits, black hair cascading in luxurious waves to her waist and wearing a striking burgundy and gold saree. She smiles around the circle in greeting.

"...and this is our techie Chiptag," gesturing to his left where a slender youth sprawls, sporting clashing bright city attire and black horn-rimmed glasses under a tousled tuft of multi-colored hair, who waves nonchalantly at the group. "They will be helping me with the class. This is an OOC event, so feel free to talk openly about any roleplay and technical topics."

There is a general stir as an old, balding white-haired man with a long beard and a yellow robe approaches the group and unassumingly sits cross-legged on a cushion to one side.

Mahir: /me performs the Anjali mudra, bowing his head deferentially in greeting, "And we're also honored with the presence of dear Platistotle, our resident

Guru and Director of the Ashram here. If we're lucky, he will be adding more in-depth insights to our practical and technical discussions."

Platistotle: /me nods to Mahir and all, pressing palms in greeting and smiling.

Emotes versus Gestures

Mahir: "So, welcome to the Basic Roleplaying class. First a basic rule—although these classes are officially OOC events, I still want you to remain in character, in the sense that your character is attending a roleplaying class. I don't need or want you to para-roleplay—that is, write entire paragraphs of narration. Short emotes are enough to spice up your dialog, but mostly, show us your personality, okay?

"Now, to start, I want to emphasize that there are no hard and fast roleplay 'rules' as such, but rather an 'etiquette' and several 'conventions' developed over time. These are in response to the need for basic agreements to make our roleplay smoother and avoid misunderstandings."

Mahir recaps some of the basics that Chris had already explained about IC versus OOC, how to emote, use /me or a colon, and so on. Arjun starts organizing his Inventory. His attention wanders to a red fox running across the circle, then snaps back to the class as something new arises.

Mahir: "There are different styles for writing posts. Some write grammatically correct sentences like in a novel. Others prefer a script-like format, separating narrative from dialog with symbols such as dashes, asterisks or double colons. The important thing is that others understand you, no matter what style you use."

Just then, a newbie—her tag announcing her as Dorketta—interrupts.

Dorketta: raises a timid hand and pipes up in a high, nasal voice "Excuse me, Mentor Mahir, but... um... I don't like using emotes and don't even know where I would find them. Can't we just say what we think?"

All eyes turn to stare at the girl, with her clunky, outdated white prim body, yellow hair like layers of clay on her head, and pasty clothing. A twitter of derisive laughter is heard until...

Mahir: /me raises a hand to silence the group and turns to Dorketta, smiling amiably, "Thank you for asking, miss. The only bad questions are the ones nobody asks," then glares around the circle.

Several heads bow in shame while Dorketta sticks out her tongue at them.

Mahir: /me turns back to Dorketta, "I think you're confusing 'emotes' with canned 'gestures'—for instance, packages of automatic texts, sounds, and movements. They are overused and tacky, and I definitely would NOT advise using them in roleplay, especially ones with sounds and/or busy texts. True roleplaying means writing your own ideas in your own words as the story evolves. Emoting means that you're acting, not just speaking."

Dorketta: screws up her face, "But when I roleplay, I'm not acting; I'm just being myself"

Mahir: "I don't mean acting in the sense of play-acting, although there certainly is an element of that in roleplay, but rather in the sense of performing actions—that is, stroking or hitting, smiling or frowning, laughing or crying, sweating or shivering, standing straight or slumping...

Canned 'gestures' are overused and tacky. Don't use them in roleplay.

"Emotes can include your body language, facial expressions, and any of your avatar's physical features that you want to call attention to, even if they are not evident in the pixels. Your posts can also include the environment and how you perceive, are affected by, and respond to it, what you are doing, and even relevant background information on your character.

"The key is for every post to show something of your character's personality while carrying the story forward. As author Kurt Vonnegut said, 'Every sentence must do one of two things—reveal character or advance the action.'"

Dorketta: "I see... But why do we have to write 'me' before that? It's bad grammar to say, 'Me hits you.' Wouldn't it be better just to say, 'I hit you'?"

Mahir: "The '/me' is not part of your text. It's a code telling the program to put your name before the post without the colon. You don't see it in your chat post. For example, if I write '/me hits him,' what you see is '*Mahir hits him.*' This is why the convention is to write your posts in the third person, present tense, because if I write 'I hit you,' what people will see is 'Mahir: I hit you.' Most roleplayers wouldn't see that as good style and some might even confuse it with dialog, wondering whether it's a typo and I meant to say, 'I hate you' or something."

Dorketta: smirks and says "Alright then, me thanks you..." then hesitates "But I still don't understand why we should post in the third person, present tense"

Mahir: /me chuckles good-naturedly, "No, in that case, you would just say 'Thank you.' Emotes are part of your narrative. Your dialog should be separated from the narrative by quotation marks or other signs." He becomes serious, "As for the third person, we use it because it makes the final product—the story we're writing together—consistent...

"Stories written in the first person tend to be from only one perspective—usually the main character's. If every post is written in the first person, the story would have as many perspectives as characters. But if everyone writes in the third person, there is a consistency of perspective throughout.

"You also asked about the present tense. Some older roleplayers still use past tense, but in Virtual India we discourage that. We're building a story together, so present tense means the action is ongoing and others can add to it. When you post in the past tense, it's like saying, 'This has already happened; it's over, and there's nothing you can do about it.' In a future class, we'll see how historical context can be provided in the past tense, while plans and intentions can be written in the future tense. We won't go into it right now, but just to give you a little example:

> *Mahir: /me sips his coffee pensively as his eyes scan the newspaper. Things were going from bad to worse again—or rather still—but he didn't want to sour his children's day by grumbling. He would wear a happy face today and grumble on Monday. He folds his newspaper on the table, looks up with a cheery grin, and exclaims heartily, "Who wants to go to the zoo?"*

Dorketta: raises both hands high and waves them around as she jumps up and down happily, yelling "Me! Meee! Meeeeeee!"

Taking Turns

Mahir: /me chuckles, "That's the idea," then turns to the rest of the class. "Okay, let's talk about one of my pet peeves: multi-posting, also known as chain-posting, which can take two forms. The first is what some call 'machine-gun roleplay':

Mahir: This is dividing

Mahir: your dialog and narrative

Mahir: into several short posts

Mahir: instead of one complete post,

Mahir: like this,

Mahir: which is annoying

Mahir: and makes it hard to read

Mahir: and to know when you can

Mahir: get a word in edgewise.

Mahir: "The second kind of chain-posting is writing more than one complete post without waiting for the other roleplayer or players to respond. For example, let's say Nadin is fishing in the river, and Zaina approaches him. Nadin posts:

> */me looks up and smiles, 'Hi Zaina, would you like to join me?'*

"Zaina starts typing:

> */me smiles back, 'Hey, thanks. I'd love to,' then takes out her fishing rod and starts to cast her line.*

"But Zaina types slowly, and before she can finish her post, Nadin whips out a second line saying:

> */me gets out an extra fishing rod and offers it to you, 'Here, you can use this rod. I have two.'*

"Now Zaina has to go back, erase part of what she was typing and change it to:

> */me takes the rod with a smile, 'Thanks, Nadin. I left mine in my hut,' and starts to cast her line.*

"This is frustrating, especially when people make a habit of it. We can only hope Nadin didn't type yet another post before Zaina could finish this one. He should have taken the time to include everything he wanted to say in a single post:

> */me looks up and smiles, 'Hi Zaina, would you like to join me?' –he gets out an extra fishing rod and offers it to her– 'Here, use this rod. I have two.'*

"Or better yet, he could have waited to see whether she accepted his invitation to join him or said she didn't have a rod before offering her one. Take turns posting for a smoother interaction, and be patient with slow typists."

Take turns posting for a smoother interaction, and be patient with slow typists.

Mamakie: "That's the ideal, of course, but if you're in a group where everyone is posting at once and changing topics rapidly, you may have to resort to shorter, more concise narration and dialog. If you wrote a long sentence or a whole paragraph in such a situation, by the time you finished, it probably wouldn't be relevant anymore."

Mahir: "This is true. However, the roleplay convention for such cases is to establish a 'posting order.' If there are only three or four people, it can be whatever order they first posted in. Or for something like a discussion group, it can follow the seating order. Otherwise, the group or its moderator can decide on the posting order beforehand.

"But in any size group, it's essential to know and respect the posting order. If nothing else, it's common courtesy to wait until everyone has had a chance to say something before you post again. Breaking the posting order by posting out of turn is known as 'cross-posting' because you cut across the posting order, maybe to answer something someone else has said before it's your turn.

"If you tend to write a lot, start drafting your post in response to what the next person says, and add to it as others post in that round. Then, when it's your turn, you can just edit and hit 'Enter.' Contrariwise, if you don't have anything to add when your turn comes around, you can just post something like ((I pass)) so that the next person won't be left' waiting for your post."

Mamakie: "When I don't have anything to add to one of the rounds, instead of just passing, I will usually post something like this: '/me listens attentively to each of her mates, chewing on her lips reflexively but saying nothing.'"

Chiptag: "People sometimes cross-post because they think you're not writing anything. To make sure they know you're typing, turn on the 'typing indicator' by going to Preferences – Chat – Visuals and enabling the checkbox 'Show Typing Indicator in bubbles above avatars.' This will show three flashing dots or the word 'typing' in your tag. If you want, you can also activate 'Hear typing sound when people type in nearby chat' under Preferences – Chat – Typing.

"Some go even further and turn on 'Play typing animation when chatting,' but I don't like it because it interferes with other animations" –chuckles– "You don't want to be waving your hands around while you're hugging someone...

"While you're there, I suggest you check the option ':' as a synonym for '/me' so that you can save keystrokes by using a colon instead of writing '/me' every time."

Mahir: "Yes, but be aware that, for some crazy reason, when you start a post with '/me' or ':' the program takes that as a cue not to put the typing indicator in your tag. Consequently, if your post is long or you're a slow typist, some players may assume you're not typing anything because they won't see the three dots, and they may post something else to fill the vacuum.

"In this case, omit the '/me' or ':' so that they will see the typing indicator in your tag and wait for you to finish. That's why many roleplayers prefer to start their emotes with an asterisk (*) instead of '/me,' like this: *waves*."

Chiptag: "Another trick I often use for long posts is to start writing without the '/me' or ':'. Then, when I've finished writing, I go back and insert the '/me' or ':' at the beginning of the post before pressing 'Enter.' That way, others see my typing indicator while I'm writing, but the post comes out correctly in the end."

Arjun is busy adjusting his Preferences when a sweet voice falls like music on his ears: "What if we make a mistake? Is it chain-posting to correct it?" Turning to look for the source of that musical speech, Arjun jaw-drops as his eyes fall upon the most beautiful girl he has ever seen. She is about Arjun's age and size, petite but athletic, luxurious waves of long black hair framing her radiant, golden-hued, heart-shaped face, full lips and deep, dark eyes.

Urstud: -smirks and leans forward, reaching out his hand to push Arjun's jaw up and close his gaping mouth

Arjun: /me winces as his teeth snap shut on his tongue and raises his hand to cover his smarting mouth. "Owwww... Why did you do that?"

Urstud: -sits back again and laughs, "Close your mouth, dude. You'll catch flies"

Eswaria: /me sees Arjun gawking at her and lowers her gaze bashfully, blushing, two slender fingers toying with the hem of her sarong

Arjun: /me notices Eswaria's demure manner and smiles contentedly to himself, then tears his attention away from her and back to Mahir.

Mahir: /me tries to ignore this exchange. "Good question, Eswaria..."

Arjun: /me rolls her name over his aching tongue as if to taste its sweetness. "Ees... waa... riaa," and lets out a long, wavering sigh.

Mahir: "In that case, just post the correction. People often add an asterisk (*) before or after it to signal it's a correction, not a new post. For example:

/me points to the valley below "I ground a lot of corn down there"

I found*

"It's important to try to write the best you can and even re-read each post before hitting 'Enter.' You can also use the automatic spelling checker by going to Preferences - Chat - Typing - Spell Checking and activating 'Enable spell checker.'

"However, don't correct every little typo after you post. If it's reasonably understandable, just let little mistakes slide to avoid cluttering up the chat with unnecessary tweaks. I use the POGE—principle of good enough— in this regard. For example, I wouldn't do this:

/me points to the valley below "I found a lo tof corn down there"

a lot of*

Eswaria: /me take snotes, noddnig "Than kyou ver ymuch Cheif," then giggles

Again, Arjun turns to gaze fondly at the girl and finds her glancing sideways at him, but this time he thinks he sees a wisp of a smile softening the features of that lovely face before she looks bashfully away again.

Powerplay

Only write what your own character does, not how others' receive your actions or respond to them.

Mahir: "Another common mistake is powerplay, called 'powergaming' in some regions. Some also use the more general term 'godmodding,' especially when players are allowed to post other characters' actions or responses. In any case, according to common roleplay convention, you should only write what your own character does, not how other's receive your actions or respond to them. An example of powerplay would be:

/me grabs Chiptag's wrist and twists it quickly behind his back, forcing it upward and making him cry out in pain.

"Here, I'm not only TRYING to apply an armlock but also deciding that all three steps of the move—grabbing his wrist, twisting it behind his back, and forcing it upward—will be successful. Worse yet, I'm deciding that he will cry out in pain. In normal roleplay, you can't do that—it's up to Chiptag to decide how the action will affect him and how he will respond. A better post without powerplay would be (uppercase added for emphasis):

/me darts his hand out TO grab Chiptag's wrist and, IF SUCCESSFUL, WOULD twist it behind his back and TRY TO force it painfully upward.

"In this case, all I do is reach FOR his wrist without actually grabbing it, then I state the INTENTION of my move, leaving Chiptag to decide whether it will be successful. That way, I avoid powerplay. I start my part of the action, but now Chiptag is free to determine how it will affect him and how he will respond. Let's see if Chiptag can come up with a few alternatives.

Chiptag: *feels his arm forced painfully behind his back and cries out* Okay, okay, I give up

> Chiptag: *feels his right arm forced painfully behind his back and swings his free left hand down and back WITH THE INTENTION of landing a solid punch to Mahir's groin while raising his left foot and driving the heel hard toward Mahir's left foot*
>
> Chiptag: *whirls to his right, pulling his right wrist away just in time to keep Mahir from grabbing it, then raises his left elbow TO land a solid elbow-strike to his jaw*

Mahir: /me laughs, "Excellent, Chiptag. I'll be careful not to get into any fights with you." He turns to the group. "Notice that Chiptag has added WHICH wrist, arm, elbow, and foot were involved, which helps me to visualize what he has done and respond accordingly. In the last two alternatives, he not only defends himself but also initiates offensive action while leaving me to decide whether his strikes will land and how I will respond. Most sims allow only two actions per fighting post—two defensive, two offensive, or one of each."

Mamakie: /me snorts, shaking her head and rolling her eyes, "Typical of men to think of fighting first, but powerplay can take many forms, even something as simple as shaking someone's hand versus holding out your hand FOR a handshake, patting someone's back versus raising your hand TO pat their back, grabbing something from someone's hands versus holding out your hand to receive it, turning your partner over in bed versus reaching out TO take them into your arms with the INTENTION of turning them over, and so on."

Urstud: -raises his hand, "Mentor Mahir, you said 'WOULD twist' his hand behind his back, but I've heard a lot of arguments about whether and when to use 'would' in a post"

Mahir: "Yes, 'would' is often overused, especially in Gor sims, where people put it before just about any action—like 'would smile' or 'would shake his head'—where you really don't need it. 'Would' should only be used to make your actions tentative when they are taken toward or against other people so that they, in turn, can decide whether the action will be successful. When we smile or shake our head, we're not doing something directly TO another character that they have to decide on, so we shouldn't use 'would' in those cases."

Mamakie: "Powerplay can include putting thoughts, feelings, or intentions into another player's head, which is worse. For example, once a man posted, '/me reaches back and pats her butt.' The woman ignored his powerplay and wrote, '/me dodges out of the way of his pat,' but then he posted, '/me sees her make great strides to avoid his pat lest he tarnish her honor.' Now the man has imposed an intention on her: that she dodged the pat in order to preserve her honor.

"This was ludicrous because they both knew she had roleplayed sex with several men. She could have dodged the pat because she hated this character's guts, wanted to play hard to get, or for any number of other reasons. It was up to her to post the why—or not—as she preferred. Later, we will see how she could have added more context to her post about dodging his pat to show her true motives."

Mahir: "Bear in mind that you're writing a story together with others, not alone. That's what makes it so much fun. Each player takes what others have posted as their starting point and then goes a step further with their own narrative and dialog. It may take a lot of concentration at first until you get used to it, but soon, you will be doing it automatically."

EyeCandey: :raises her hand, 'A few minutes ago, you said that powerplay is also called godmodding (with two d's) in some RP sims. What's the difference between that and godmoding with one d?'

Mahir: "Different regions use different terms, so I can't give you a hard and fast definition for either word. However, the way I understand it, godmodding (with two d's) was originally short for 'god moderating,' but now it more often refers to either controlling another player's character without their consent—like powerplaying or powergaming—or playing an all-powerful, invincible character."

Mamakie: "In some regions that have game masters or moderators, godmodding can refer to a player writing something story-changing without permission from the GM or moderator."

Mahir: "On the other hand, 'god mode' originally referred to a video-game cheat that used scripts or code to gain invincibility or other powers not available to other players. But in roleplay, godmoding—with one d—is often used to mean playing as though a character has godlike powers, such as omnipresence, omnipotence, omniscience, omnicompetence, and so on."

Mamakie: "It is sometimes also used as an umbrella term that includes metagaming, godmodding (with two d's), powergaming, and powerplay."

Writing Inner Dialog

Arjun: /me raises his hand, clears his throat, and speaks in his soft, youthful voice, "Someone said I shouldn't emote my thoughts and feelings. Why is that?"

Mahir: "Good question, Arjun. Emoting thoughts is not a problem *per se*. But unless your roleplay partners are telepaths (which is very rare) or metagaming (which is not allowed), they will have nothing to work with if you don't include something to make those thoughts tangible and perceivable.

Be creative and show what your character is thinking or feeling without saying it.

"Fiction writers will often not speak of feelings directly but rather will try to EVOKE an emotion by describing how it's expressed in a character's body language, tone of voice, and so on. To 'evoke' means to bring something to the reader's mind by using descriptions that will spark shared recollections of sights, sounds, tastes, smells, or feelings.

"Following the writer's maxim 'show; don't tell,' be creative and SHOW others what your character is thinking or feeling without saying it. For example:

> /me looks at the man, thinking he looks dangerous and that she needs to be on her guard and ready to fight at an instant's notice.

"That's called a 'thought emote' or 'thought post.' If someone posted this, you wouldn't have much to work with in your response. Theoretically, you would have to carry on as though he had only written '/me looks at the man.' A more 'evocative' emote might be:

> /me eyes the man warily and frowns, her fingers moving slowly toward the grip of her pistol.

"This way, you give the man tangible signs of your distrust, something he can work with when writing his response. If you post thoughts and feelings, some people will even respond with a friendly OOC post such as ((I can't read your mind. Please rewrite that post)).

Mamakie: /me breaks in with a soft, conciliatory tone of voice, "An OOC post like that could be seen as offensive, and it's important to be courteous and respectful in your OOC messages, even if your character is a nasty brute. So, you might want to use that recourse with caution. I've seen people deal with this kind of thing by emoting something like:

> /me sees a flicker of suspicion and wariness crossing the man's face and his body tensing ever-so-slightly and grins nervously, raising open palms, 'Hey, take it easy, dude. I'm not gonna attack you. I just wanna talk.'"

Mahir: /me turns to Mamakie and strokes his chin thoughtfully. "Yes... that might be a half-way solution if you don't know the other player and are afraid of offending them... But it wouldn't be perfect RP form either, because the man didn't actually emote the suspicion and wariness in his face or the tenseness in his body, so you'd be assuming he doesn't have the nerve of a poker player."

Mahir: /me turns back to the class, "Okay, let's look at some examples of emoting inner dialogue. Think about how you could change them to EVOKE the thought or feeling and give your RP partners something perceivable to work with:

> /me smiles and continues to eat before saying, 'Hello,' knowing I can't talk with my mouth full.

EyeCandey: :nods and smiles but continues to chew her food, holding her hand in front of her mouth diffidently before swallowing and saying, 'Hello'

Mahir: /me claps his hands. "Good. Covering your mouth with your hand EVOKES a memory we all share of not wanting to speak with our mouths full and trying to convey that to someone. Let's try another:

> /me feels the rain shower hitting her face, hoping it doesn't last too long but only enough to give the plants a good drink.

Eswaria: /me smiles up at the rain as it hits her face, lifting her open hands to the heavens, opening her mouth and sticking out her tongue to catch a few of the sweet drops, then turns to her friends and laughs, "I hope it doesn't last too long... just enough to water the plants."

Mahir: "Okay, great. You've evoked how it feels when the rain hits your face, but then you've turned the thought into spoken text. Excellent. Here's another:

> /me looks at the girl, thinking that she's the most beautiful creature he has ever laid eyes on and that he would love to hold her in his arms and kiss her.

Arjun: /me smiles and winks at Eswa, then holds his hands to his chest, biting his lower lip with an expression of admiration and longing.

Mahir: /me chuckles and shakes his head. "I wouldn't expect anything less of you, you rascal."

Eswaria: /me blushes and looks away with a demure smile.

Mahir: /me's eyes flit from one to the other, then clears her throat to break the awkward silence. "Another way to convey emotion is through what you DON'T say. As they say, 'Silence is golden.' Here are some examples:

> */me mumbles something inaudible under his breath.*
>
> */me opens his mouth as if to say something, then closes it again and holds his tongue.*
>
> */me gets a sinking feeling in his stomach. What does she really think? Will she understand how he feels? He decides to keep quiet for now and wait to see what she says."*

Mamakie: "Good point... Now I wanted to add one thing before this class ends. Although some of you are quite new to roleplay, please don't be shy to engage with more experienced players. Be courageous. We all started as beginners. Most people here are tolerant of new players and eager to help you learn and improve. If you make mistakes, they might correct you, but welcome their suggestions and try again. You won't be ejected for poor roleplay—unless you just refuse to learn, that is. Rule number one is that we're all here to have fun, so go for it."

"Time for the test," Mahir announces, handing out a notecard. Arjun opens it and grins to himself as he reads the instructions: "Summarize in a few short sentences what you learned about emoting." He bites his tongue at the corner of his mouth and starts to write:

- When in Local Chat, put short OOC messages like 'BRB' or 'AFK' in ((double parentheses)). Put longer OOC messages in a group chat or in personal IMs.
- Never discuss RL or RP-related topics in Local Chat.
- Emoting means posting anything aside from dialog, mostly tangible things that can be perceived using our senses.

- Use quotation marks, dashes, asterisks, double-colons, and so on to clearly differentiate between emoting or narrative, on the one hand, and speech or dialog, on the other.
- Never use internet slang, shortcuts, smileys, or gestures in character.
- Avoid chain-posting or cross-posting, which means writing more than one post before others have had their turn.
- Avoid powerplay, which means deciding how your actions will affect someone else.
- Avoid emoting things that others cannot perceive without being mind-readers.

Arjun saves the notecard and returns it to Mahir, sitting back and sighing with satisfaction, when the following IM exchange takes place.

Mamakie: I have a personal quest for you, Arjun. Will you accept it?

Arjun: I don't know. Tell me what it is first and what I get when I finish it :P

Mamakie: I want you to figure out why you're here. Don't tell me yet. Just think about it and let me know when you're sure, okay? Oh, and what you get out of it will depend on what you put into it :-)

Arjun: /me raises an eyebrow but says nothing and just nods slowly, chewing on his lip

After a few minutes, a message pops up on Arjun's screen:

Dharma Guide: Congratulations. You have passed the "Basic Roleplaying Class" and advanced to Level 6 - Emoter. You now have access to a Region Map HUD in your Karma Tag. While there, please check for your next quest.

Munching on some fruit from his basket to buff up, Arjun opens his Karma Tag and, sure enough, sees a new 'Region Map' button in the menu. He clicks it, and a map HUD appears on the right of his screen, with several green dots showing places to find food. Arjun then clicks on 'Quests' and reads, "You have a new quest available: Exploring." He clicks 'Accept,' and a message appears in Local Chat:

Dharma Guide: You have accepted the quest "Exploring." To complete it, reconnoiter the 12 sims of the Virtual India region and make your own map showing all the food sites and what kinds of food are found there, then show it to your mentor. Bon voyage.

Arjun smiles and then yawns, "I'll start on that tomorrow, then..." as he relays his weariness to his atman. Closing his eyes to keep the swirling jungle from making him dizzier than he already feels, he poofs for the evening.

CHAPTER FOUR

LEARNING TO MAKE A LIVING

Status:	Emoter
Level:	6
HP:	12.6

The next morning, Arjun logs in at the Landing just as the first rays of sunlight are striking the treetops, bathing the jungle in a golden glow. He checks his messages and finds one that interests him titled, "Are you a slow typist?" followed by, "If you think you type too slowly, here are some ideas to help you." Opening the attached notecard, Arjun reads:

- Have you ever roleplayed with someone and had to wait several minutes watching the three dots go on and off in their tags, only to receive a short post? That's good for developing patience and tolerance, but not for much else. If you're the slow typist, here are some ideas to help you speed up your roleplay:

- Take a typing course: There are several online programs available to help you learn to type with all 12 fingers (wait, did I just say 12?) and improve your speed and accuracy.

- Don't be a perfectionist: Do you make lots of mistakes? Don't sweat it. If your roleplay companion can decipher your meaning, that's all that matters. You don't even have to apologize. Nobody really cares that much. Well, I care, but who am I? If someone doesn't understand you, they can pole ray that fact: /me scoffs, "What the f*ck is a 'pole ray'?"

- Build up your Autocorrect list: If you find yourself repeatedly misspelling the same words, put them in the Autocorrect and save yourself and your partner(s) a headache or three. For example, if your "sighs" often come out as "signs" and you hardly ever talk about signs, make an autocorrect for that. Go to Preferences – Chat – Typing – Auto-Replace – Spelling Corrections, click on 'Add' and putt 'signs' as the Keyword. Then put 'sighs' as the replacement and click on 'Save Entry.' (For more information, see *wiki.phoenixviewer.com/autoreplace_settings.)*

- Create gestures: Is there a longish phrase you repeat often? Put it into a gesture and give it a keyword you can easily remember. For example, if you often introduce yourself saying, "I'm FIRSTNAME LASTNAME, but my friends just call me SHORTY," you can make a gesture that will replace a prompt such as 'myname' with the full text.

- To do that, right-click on the 'Gestures' folder in your Inventory and select 'New Gesture.' In the pop-up window, write 'myname' as the 'Trigger' and 'I'm FIRSTNAME LASTNAME, but my friends just call me SHORTY' in 'Replace with.' Remove any default 'Steps,' then Save, Rename, and make sure it's activated. The complete text will then be inserted into your posts wherever you type 'myname,' even if you have other text before or after it. (See *wiki.phoenixviewer.com/gesture_preview for further information.)*

- Use speech recognition software: Finally, for the worst cases, try using a speech-to-text function that will write your posts for you. More and more popular programs include text-to-speech functions, but so far, Second Life doesn't have one. Until then, one solution is to speak your text into a program that does, edit the results, and then cut and paste it into Local Chat. Cumbersome? Maybe a little, but much faster than two-finger hunt-and-peck for sure.

Exploring the Region

"Hey, mate, want some company while you explore?" comes a familiar voice near Arjun.

He turns to see Chris's friendly grin and returns the smile, pleased to see that Chris now considers him a friend and not just a chore. "Sure... Actually, I was hoping you'd be my tour guide." They take a small motorboat up the Western River.

> Arjun: "Ever since Mentor Mahir and I first talked at the Landing, I've been thinking about what character to choose but still haven't decided."

Chris: "That's okay, take your time. But don't confuse your CHARACTER with the ROLES your character will play. Whether your role is a farmer, tradesperson, merchant, healer, warrior, or commissioner, your character can be kind or cruel, prudish or promiscuous, happy or angry, courteous or rude, reliable or fickle, honest or deceitful, and so on. It's up to you. Even an animal role can have different characters, such as peaceful and timid or fierce and savage."

> Whether your role is a farmer, healer, or warrior, your character can be kind or cruel, prudish or promiscuous, reliable or fickle.

They arrive at a large lagoon where the Western and Eastern rivers are fed by a magnificent waterfall that tumbles down from the mighty Himalayas. Turning westward, they hike through the snowy heights of Hemis, pick their way through Hemis Village, and see the golden-domed Buddhist monastery in the distance. They then turn back to descend into the lush meadowlands of the Gangotri valley and village—home of musicians, artists, and the nine-sided Baha'i Lotus Temple, with its graceful white petals. Continuing eastward, they cross the bridge to the highland steppes of Khangchendzonga, with its blue-tiled Moslem mosque and tall minarets from which a muezzin chants out the call to prayer, then on to the pine forests of Namdapha, with its grungy mining town and ancient stone Christian church. As they go, Arjun thinks about what Chris said.

Arjun: "Should I make my character like my atman or completely different?"

Chris: "Your character will probably reflect certain parts of your atman's personality, but if you want your roleplay to be more challenging, try to add differences. If you need ideas, think of a movie character that's close to what you're looking for, an ancient mythology character, or maybe even someone you know."

They turn south to visit the middle sims, trekking through the scorched wastelands of Sundarbans, where they skirt around the looming black Raider Castle. They enter the temperate forests and farming country of Simlipal, pick their way through the steamy jungle of Sanjay Gandhi—home of the Temple of Knowledge—and cross the desert dunes of Rajasthan, where they admire the gold-crowned Sikh temple, with its severe architecture.

Arjun: "Do you know any methods that could help me design my character?"

Chris: "Sure. People usually write up a background story or 'backstory' that describes their character. It can include things like where and how you grew up, events that shaped who you are now, how you ended up in this region, and what you're trying to achieve... things like that."

Turning south again, they visit the southern-most sims, starting with the lowlands of Gir, where they had already been to the Ashram and the Swamp, on to

Indravati, with its tangled mangroves and elaborate Love Temple, and Betla, with its bamboo thickets and Hindu mandir, rich in carved stone sculptures.

Arjun: /me spies a large round beehive hanging from a tree branch and, curious, moves closer to inspect it.

Chris: /me calls out to him, "Careful not to disturb the hive, or the bees might sting you"

Arjun: /me lights a fire to smoke the bees out and cuts down the hive.

Just then, two swarms of angry bees attack Arjun and Chris, and their HPs start dropping rapidly.

Chris: /me starts swatting at the stinging bees and shouting, "Get in the water. It's the only way to stop them"

The two boys run to submerge themselves in the river, and the attack stops as suddenly as it began. They climb out, soaked and smarting all over from the stings. Their HP is in the critical range, but at least they have harvested a large jar of honey.

Finally, the boys end up in Papikonda Town, with its vibrant urban life and busy beaches, and spend some time roaming its streets and looking into the various establishments. Shops sell Indian wares—from clothing and accessories to buildings and furnishings—and they see a restaurant, bar, theater, night club, and hotel, all apparently active. During a break in Chris's explanation of what they are seeing, Arjun IMs him:

> Arjun: "Once I write out my backstory, does it have to stay that way, or can I change it if I want?"
>
> Chris: "Even for highly experienced players, new characters often go through a period of 'character puberty,' trying to figure out who they are and what their character will be like. It's a creative process, so don't worry if your backstory is incomplete or unclear to you from the start. Keeping it general at the beginning can give your character room to grow organically. Over time, you can tweak and complete it as you grow into your character, which can also change and evolve, just as people change and mature in RL. But having a basic backstory from the start will help you develop your character and be consistent in your roleplay."
>
> Arjun: "But one region I applied to said I had to submit a complete character profile before they would invite me to their group. They didn't like what I wrote, so I didn't get in. What would you do in that case?"
>
> Chris: "Right, yes, well, at one extreme are the regions with long and involved centralized processes that include lots of back and forth with the admins to adjust your backstory, profile, and avatar design. Some even try to ensure that players are well-versed in the region's lore before accepting them. Other regions ask that your character adopt a particular role within the region's lore and dress accordingly but are more lenient about letting it grow and develop into that role. Both types of regions often keep character bios in a centralized database, sometimes available to all players. In these cases, my best advice

would be to keep it as general as they will let you at first, or you might find your character evolving naturally in directions that run contrary to its initial profile.

"Then there are the regions that only ask you to include a Pick in your profile showing how your character fits into one of several very general roles. Think native versus foreign, cowboy versus Indian, pirate versus navy, and so on. This leaves a lot of leeway to develop your character and revise your profile accordingly. All three region types will often ask you to provide a sample of your roleplay skill, either as part of your written application or 'on the ground' through interaction with evaluators. Then there is Virtual India, which accompanies players through a mentoring process designed to help them discover and develop their characters while they perfect their roleplaying skills."

Throughout this excursion, Arjun uses his Region Map HUD to find the food sites and picks all the fruits and nuts he can, sometimes doubling back to harvest more than once since they re-rez every twenty to thirty minutes. He adds Kashmiri apples, coconuts, Indian kiwifruit, and watermelons to his list of fruit from his first day. Meanwhile, he draws his own map using the photo from the Temple of Knowledge as a template. By the end, his basket is full of hundreds of items, and his map is complete. (See Arjun's map at the beginning of this book).

They rest at a tropical-themed spa on the southern edge of town, where Chris buys some tall glasses of fruit juice to replenish the HP they used during their long day of exploring. As they sip their juice, the two talk excitedly about the wildlife they have seen while exploring: a snow leopard, Asiatic lion, and Bengal tiger; wolves and foxes; black bears and sloths; antelopes and musk deer, bison and buffaloes; macaque and langur monkeys; otters and mongooses; and even a small herd of Indian elephants. They have watched the flight of eagles and vultures, hornbills and partridges, run from alligators and crocodiles, and Arjun has even been bitten by a king cobra that clouded his sight and paralyzed him for a while.

As they chat, Arjun's atman takes a photo of his map and uploads it to his Inventory.[7] He then checks its permissions and shares it with Mentor Mahir. Soon, a message pops up on his screen:

Dharma Guide: Congratulations. You have completed the Exploring Quest and advanced to Level 7 - Explorer. You have also received a coin purse and the key to the Virtual India Trading Kiosks, which can now be seen on your Region Map HUD. Remember that 10 coppers equal one silver, and 10 silvers equal one gold coin. Please check your Karma Tag for your next quest.

Arjun opens his Quest, "You have a new quest available: Trading," accepts it and reads the message:

---

[7] To know how he did this, see wiki.firestormviewer.org/fs_upload.

Dharma Guide: You have accepted the quest "Trading." To complete it, sell at least one item at each of the six Trading Kiosks scattered around the Virtual India region. Happy trading.

Glancing at his Region Map HUD, Arjun sees six green squares now show where the Trading Kiosks are located. He remembers seeing a few of them during his Exploring quest and chuckles to himself, "Good thing I gathered so much food today." He types out a brief report and poofs for the night, thinking,

Why are you here, Arjun?

To explore this beautiful region, for now.

Trading at the Kiosks

Status:	Explorer
Level:	7
HP:	14.9

Chris is not there yet when Arjun logs in the next morning, so he runs over to the nearest Trading Kiosk—at the Nomad Camp—where a middle-aged woman with a yellow tag identifying her as Suhana Anand sells some goods. She wears traditional clothing with tan salwar trousers, a light blue kameez top, and a grey dupatta covering her head, shoulders, and bosom.

The kiosk has several crates labeled with each of the meats and crops grown in the region, plus cooked foods and other resources. Arjun watches the woman and finally works up the courage to speak to her.

Arjun: /me watches over the woman's shoulder, then says hesitantly, "Excuse me, ma'am... could you please explain what you're doing?"

Suhana: /me turns to the boy, reaching up to adjust her veil over her mouth and nose, and looks him up and down, measuring him up, "Hello, young man. Don't you know it's rude to look over people's shoulders while they work?"

Arjun: /me hangs his head, squirming under her critical gaze, and says in a small voice, "Sorry, ma'am... I... I just got the Trading quest yesterday and have never sold anything before..." then smiles bashfully up at her, pressing his palms together at his chest, "I'm Arjun, by the way... Could... um... could you teach me?"

Suhana: /me softens her expression and sighs reluctantly, bobbling her head in agreement, "I guess I could a take little time from my chores, Arjun... I'm Suhana. Come closer, and I'll show you how it's done."

Suhana IMs Arjun to rez his collecting basket near the kiosk and click on the crate with the type of item he wants to sell. He does so, and when a menu appears with the options 'Buy' and 'Sell,' he clicks on 'Sell,' and a message tells him to rez the items he wants to sell. Suhana explains that the basket rezzes the oldest items first since raw food goes bad after a week, so it's important for him to collect new food and sell the old items at least once a week.

Arjun then clicks on his basket and selects 'Oranges.' Another menu allows him to choose 1, 5, 10, 20, or All. He clicks on 1—just to try it out—and the basket rezzes an orange. The Trading Kiosk takes it, and he reads the messages that have appeared in Local Chat:

> Virtual India Trading Kiosk: Make sure you have rezzed an item - checking...
>
> Virtual India Trading Kiosk: You are not wearing your coin purse. You will receive no coins in exchange for your goods. Thank you for your contribution.

Arjun: /me growls in annoyance at himself, "Darn, I forgot about the coin purse."

Suhana: /me laughs remorsefully, "Oh, I should have reminded you. I also forget sometimes. I've lost a lot of earnings that way."

Arjun 'Adds' his coin purse, which appears at his waist. He then repeats the process and reads the messages:

> Virtual India Trading Kiosk: Make sure you have rezzed an item - checking...
>
> Virtual India Trading Kiosk: Normal trading day. Standard rate.
>
> Second Life: An object named [Virtual India Trading Post] gave you this object: 'Copper coin.'

Arjun: /me wags his head from side to side happily, laughing with relief, "That's better. Thank you very much, Suhana," and sells a few more items.

> In real life, there are subtle non-verbal clues that don't exist in virtual worlds, so your Profile should fill that void.

Meanwhile, Suhana has been reviewing Arjun's profile, and she IMs him: "You're welcome, Arjun. Glad I could help. By the way, I always read people's profiles to know what makes them 'tick' before I roleplay with them, but I see yours is almost empty. Have you written a background story for your character? You should add a Pick summarizing it."

> Arjun: "Oh, yeah, I'm still working on my backstory. I'll summarize it in my profile as soon as I finish writing it. Any other advice to improve my profile?"
>
> Suhana: "Well... anyone who reads it should come away with a basic idea of your character before roleplaying with you. In real life, you can tell a lot about people from subtle non-verbal clues in their body language, facial expression,

tone of voice, scent, and so on. This isn't possible yet in virtual worlds, so your Profile should fill that void."

Arjun: "Wow, I didn't realize it was so important."

Suhana: "Oh yes, very much so. There are many people to roleplay with, and if your profile isn't complete and interesting, they are likely to move on to look for someone else. The more effort you put into it, the better the chances people will want to roleplay with you. I even recheck profiles when roleplaying again with the same people in case I forget or they change something important."

Arjun: "What are the most urgent parts to complete?"

Suhana: "I would say the first and fourth tabs. The 'About' space under the '2nd Life' tab is the first impression people get from your profile, so you should really make it count. Right now, you just have 'I don't know what to write here, so if you want to know about me, just ask.' When I see things like that, I usually just move on. You could replace that with what your character is like, how you roleplay, and what you expect of others and what they can expect from you. But leave any RL info for the '1st Life' section.

"The 'Picks' tab is where you can summarize your backstory. If you roleplay more than one character or in more than one region, you should have a backstory Pick for each. Serious roleplayers don't clutter it up with the kinds of Picks you have of stores, clubs, and music venues unless they're the owners. Most people see that as distracting and tacky. Sorry if I'm being too blunt."

Arjun: "No, that's fine. Thanks for the advice. I'm working on those as we speak. Any advice for other parts of my profile?"

Suhana: "The profile picture under the '2nd Life' tab can tell a lot about you. Why not change your mug shot for a more evocative photo? I'm sending you a folder of full-perm static poseballs you can choose from to put your avatar into an action stance. The photo's backdrop should also reflect something about who your character is. Several good tutorials about SL photography are on the web, or you can search for an experienced SL photographer if you want the best quality photo."

Arjun: "Great idea, thanks. I'd like to put a picture of me running through the forest with my foraging gear."

Suhana: "That would work. Also, many don't realize the importance of the 'Groups' section of the '2nd Life' tab. The groups you make visible to others should say something about your character: the region or regions you roleplay in, events you frequent, and other groups that share your character's main interests. I can usually tell a lot about people just by looking at the groups they choose to show in their profiles...

"Less is more, so don't show any groups that don't convey who you are. For example, I recommend hiding all the commercial groups that don't really add to your character, but the ranch shows you're into horses and the Classic Rock club shows your taste in music. You can show or hide groups by going to your 'Groups' list, opening the group profile, and clicking or unclicking the option 'Show in my profile' in the lower-left of the 'General' tab under 'My Group Settings.' Don't forget to click 'Save' afterward."

Arjun: "Good point. I'm changing it right now. Anything else?"

Suhana: "The 'Interests' tab can also provide valuable information about you or your character. What are you looking for? What are your skills in SL? What languages do you speak? Some people have their characters speak a different language as part of their backstory, even if they know English.

Arjun opens the 'Interests' tab. Under 'I Want To,' he clicks on 'Meet and Explore,' and in the space below, he adds, 'Make friends and learn new things.' Under 'Skills,' he puts 'Foraging and trading' for now, and under Languages, he writes, 'English, Typonese, and Kindness.'

Suhana: "The 'Web' tab is where you can add a link to a representative webpage and post photos and comments on major events in your roleplay, to give people an idea of key stages in your character's development. You can do that when you take a photo by clicking 'Selection' in the snapshot window, choosing 'Share to Profile Feed,' and adding an interesting caption. Again, less is more, so delete those posts about changing your name and profile picture.

Arjun quickly revises those sections and thanks Suhana effusively. Back at the Landing, he finds Chris chatting with EyeCandey and tells them about his talk with Suhana.

Chris opens a group IM with the three: "The 'Real Life' tab can also be useful. Some people post a real-life photo and summarize their real-life situation, such as "forty-something housewife from Mumbai." Others leave it blank or only put their time zone (mine says SLT +9). SLT means Second Life Time, by the way. Or they say something to the effect that they either won't share their real life or will do so only with their closest friends."

Arjun opens his First Life tag, inserts a photo of some Indian boys, and writes, "No, that's not me—just some friends who were an inspiration for Arjun. Yes, I'm an adult in both worlds. No, I don't do voice, cam, or share my RL. Yes, I log all chats."

There's a certain magic in relating to others as they present themselves in character. Talking about our 'real lives' breaks that mystique.

EyeCandey: "For me, there's a certain magic in being able to relate to others exactly as they present themselves in character. Talking about our 'real lives' breaks that mystique, so I just put my eye—the window of my soul—as my real-life photo and wrote:

> EyeCandey has heard about that horrible place people call Ar-El, but she has never been and doesn't want to go there. If she's asked about it, she either won't reply or will just make something up not to seem rude. Please don't tell her about your RL either."

Chris: "That's a good approach. Some people even go as far as building a fictional RL backstory to satisfy people's curiosity. Some may see that as devious, but I see it as a way to support who your character is. I mean, a fictional RL backstory can reflect important aspects of your character, such as age, sex, ethnicity, and so on."

Arjun: "That's what I do. I tell people I'm a young man working in India as a consultant for international organizations. I've found it makes my character more credible and keeps me from having to talk about my REAL real life."

Chris: /me looks at Arjun aghast, "You mean to say that all that talk about your real-life adventures in India were just made up?"

Arjun: /me grins mischievously, "You'll never know..." and chuckles

EyeCandey takes her leave, and Chris and Arjun set off to visit the other Trading Kiosks. There is one on every other district, and Arjun sells several items at each while adding the locations to his personalized map. He also collects more food along the way and is pleased to see how much money adds up. At the fifth kiosk, Arjun is surprised when the message changes to:

Virtual India Trading Kiosk: Make sure you have rezzed an item - checking...

Virtual India Trading Kiosk: Slow trading day. Bonus rate.

Second Life: An object named [Virtual India Trading Post] gave you this object: 'Copper coin.'

Second Life: An object named [Virtual India Trading Post] gave you this object: 'Copper coin.'

Arjun: /me kicks himself and exclaims, "Darn, I should've saved more of my stuff to sell here."

Chris: /me laughs, chagrined, "Oh, sorry, I thought you knew about that. There's a different bonus kiosk every day. People usually go around selling only one item in each one until they find the bonus kiosk before selling all their stuff. Then the word gets around until everyone who's in the loop knows."

Arjun unloads all but a few items to sell at the last kiosk while keeping enough to eat for a couple of days. Shortly after his sale at the last kiosk, a message pops up on his screen:

Dharma Guide: Congratulations. You have completed the "Trading" Quest and advanced to Level 8 - Trader. You have also received a key to the Papikonda Bank, and a new "Account" button has been added to your Karma Tag. Please check for your next quest.

Opening a Bank Account

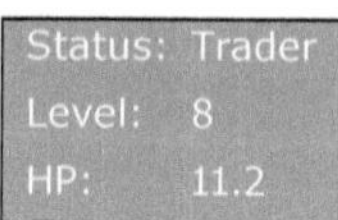

Since the boys end the Trading Quest at the Kiosk near Papikonda Beach, they go to the spa again for a break. This time Arjun pays for the juice, happy to have enough money to do so. While ogling some pretty girls strolling, sunbathing, swimming, and playing on the beach in colorful swimsuits, they talk about their scant experience with the—to Arjun—enigmatic female gender.

Meanwhile, Arjun opens his Karma Tag, clicks on the new 'Account' button, and sees a menu with 'Balance: 0' and buttons for 'Deposit,' 'Withdraw,' and 'Cancel.' He cancels that menu, then clicks on 'Quest,' accepting the prompt "You have a new quest available: Banking" and reading:

> Dharma Guide: You have accepted the quest "Banking." To complete it, go to the Papikonda Bank and open an account. Happy banking.

Arjun: /me scrunches up his face with uncertainty. "Okay, so the bank is in Papikonda Town, but… why do I need to open a banking account if I already have my money in my coin purse?"

Chris: /me grins deviously, slips two fingers into Arjun's coin purse, extracts a copper, and drops it into his own, then laughs, "That's why"

> Virtual India Coin Purse: Christopher Eric has stolen 1 copper from your coin purse.

Arjun: /me gasps, seeing what his friend has done "Hey, give me my copper back!"

Chris: /me laughs again, slapping his coin purse "Why don't you just take it back?"

Arjun clicks on Chris's coin purse and a menu with the options 'Pay,' 'Request,' 'Pick,' and 'Cancel' appears. He chooses 'Pick' and sees another menu with the options 'Copper,' 'Silver,' 'Gold,' and 'Cancel.' He clicks on 'Copper,' and a message appears in his Chat:

> Virtual India Coin Purse: You have stolen 1 copper from the coin purse of Christopher Eric.

Arjun: /me reaches out and recovers his copper from Chris's coin purse, dropping it back into his own, then laughs, "Wow, I guess it DOES make sense to have a bank account."

They finish their juice, and Arjun follows Chris across the town, this time paying more attention to its tightly-packed townhouses, including a few rickety old bare-plank structures, several elaborate colonial styles, and here and there a modern minimalistic building.

Arriving at the Papikonda Bank, of Roman design with its imposing white marble columned façade, Arjun clicks on the ATM and sees a menu with 'Exchange,' 'Deposit,' 'Withdraw,' 'Open Account,' 'Rob,' and 'Cancel.'

Arjun: /me furrows his brow. “Can people actually rob the bank?”

Chris: /me laughs and nods. “Oh yes, but they trip an alarm that calls in all twelve guards to arrest them, and the thief has to stay within arm’s length of the ATM for ten minutes to get a maximum of 50,000 gold. Only the warrior class can rob a bank, and it takes many warriors to defeat the guards, so it usually fails, in which case the warriors involved are taken to court and spend a week in jail.”

Arjun clicks on ‘Open Account’ and receives a message, “Deposit 500 coppers to open your account. You have 2 minutes.”

Arjun: /me sighs and wipes his brow in relief. “Good thing I sold so much today; otherwise, I’d have to go back to foraging and trading to earn that much. So... how do I do this?”

Chris: /me grins. “Wear your coin purse and click on it, then select ‘Pay’”

Arjun does so, and a box opens saying, “Select the person or object you wish to pay,” followed by a menu listing ‘Christopher Eric’ and ‘Papikonda Bank ATM.’ He chooses the latter and reads, “Type in the amount of coin you wish to pay.” He types in 500 and accepts. The ATM takes his money to the sound of falling coins, and a message pops up on his screen:

> Dharma Guide: Congratulations. You have successfully opened your bank account and advanced to Level 9 - Banker. Please check your Karma Tag for your next quest.

Opening the menu, Arjun clicks on ‘Account,’ and it now says ‘Balance: 500.’ Of course, his coin purse is almost empty, so he will have to forage and sell some more to fill it. He opens his Quest menu, accepts the prompt, and reads:

> Dharma Guide: You have accepted the quest "IC/OOC." To complete it, take the class at the Papikonda Theatre on Mondays at 2:00 pm SLT. Pay attention because you will be tested on it. Good luck.

Monday is tomorrow, and his atman needs some family time this afternoon, so Arjun quickly writes up his report on Chris’s mentoring and takes his leave as the jungle swirls around him, and he poofs, thinking,

Why are you here, Arjun?

Um... to do the quests?

CHAPTER FIVE

IN AND OUT OF CHARACTER

Status: Banker
Level: 9
HP: 14.4

Arjun is the first to arrive at the IC/OOC class, eager to start his next lesson. He has spent the morning foraging and selling goods to recover the balance in his coin purse, depleted when he transferred 500 coins to his new bank account.

Standing at the podium on stage, Mahir starts by introducing the meanings of IC and OOC and how they are used. Arjun's attention strays to the theater's elaborate design, with its plush seats, intricately carved wood paneling, burgundy velvet curtains, and large crystal chandeliers when something snaps his thoughts back to the class.

Mahir: "If someone sends you an object, that's also OOC until they say in Local Chat that they're giving it to you, so don't thank them until then, except maybe in an IM. Even that's not necessary unless the exchange is not part of a roleplay scene. For example, if someone gives you some food, you should wait until they say something like, '/me passes you a bowl of steaming hot soup' before you RP taking it and thanking them.

Being aware of what happens behind walls, closed doors, or drawn curtains is metagaming.

"Also, being aware of what happens behind closed doors and drawn curtains is metagaming. Even if you do cam into a home and see a couple having sex (which is creepy, so please don't), you CANNOT refer to it later in your roleplay because what you saw was OOC, and roleplaying as if you knew about it would be metagaming. You would actually have to hear them moaning and groaning, peek through an opening in the curtains, or barge in and catch them in the act to include it in your roleplay, although this could have some very unpleasant consequences later on, of course."

-laughter around the circle-

"Similarly, you're not supposed to be able to know what's being said inside a building you're not in, or through any walls or closed doors for that matter, even if you're within local chat range to 'hear' it—unless it's shouted, of course. You wouldn't walk down the sidewalk, hear the neighbors talking at home, and spread the news with your roleplay partners. One exception to this would be if the scene involved you listening at the keyhole and overhearing what was said, all of which would have to be appropriately narrated in one or more posts."

OOC Information Given IC

Mahir: "Now, we all need to sleep, eat, or use the toilet in real life, right? Why not merge this into your roleplay? Don't simply poof in front of other players, which is unrealistic in IC terms besides being lazy roleplay. Please don't turn into an AFK zombie either, especially if you're wearing a yellow tag in a place where you might be vulnerable to attack.

"If it's your bedtime, say you're sleepy and need to take a nap, then go home, lie down, and poof. When you come back inworld, you can return to your last position to 'wake up' and start a new day. If it's your dinner time, say you're hungry and need to find some food, then go out of sight before logging out. If you have to pee, you can roleplay going to a bathroom—or, if you're camping, run to the bushes and come back to throw wet leaves on the fire.

"How about things like lagging, crashing, the Karma Tag color, health points, IMs, photos, and even telling someone about your alts... do they HAVE to be OOC? Not necessarily. Lagging can be roleplayed as feeling dizzy or slow, crashing might be getting spirited away by the gods, getting an IM can be receiving a sparrow, photos can be paintings or drawings, and health points can be calories:

> */me gingerly passes him a steaming bowl of fish stew and smiles, "This'll warm yer innards 'n give ya eight hundred calories ((8 HP))."*

Arjun: "So many people have asked why I insist on keeping my Karma Tag green that I finally developed a whole spiel about 'following the tao of the green karma.' Oh, and I talk IC about 'alts' like this:

> Arjun: /me eyes the newcomer dubiously. "This isn't your first incarnation in this world, is it?"
>
> Nadin: /me shakes his head and smiles. "No, I've reincarnated several times, even as a wolf once."

Mahir: "Good example... And speaking of incarnations, please don't try to second-guess people. If you're wondering whether the sexy broad coming on to you is the alt of the fearsome 2.5-meter warrior who spilled your guts with one swish of his sword just yesterday, or that her atman is actually a 75-year-old man with three-day stubble, smelly breath, and still in his tattered pajamas, please don't try to find out.

"Are you wondering whether that newbie who approaches you all 'excuse-me-sir-can-you-help-me' is actually your best friend from another region? Who cares? We're here to roleplay, not to second-guess each other's RL identities. I'd rather NOT know. My personal approach is to deal with each character exactly as they present themselves to me. Nothing more, nothing less."

Treat each character exactly as they present themselves. Nothing more, nothing less.

Mamakie: "While we're on the subject, if you're worried a player may be underage IRL, you're only legally liable if they tell you so or if you hear a child's voice over mic. In that case, the TOS (Terms of Service) are unequivocal: No adult-rated content or interactions with children. This is another good reason for keeping transcripts of all your Local Chats and IMs as a backup."

Chiptag: "In Firestorm, you can easily save transcripts of all local chats and individual or group IMs by going to Preferences – Privacy – Logs & Transcripts and selecting the option you want under 'Save.' You can also decide where the files should go for easy access by going to Preferences – Network & Files – Directories – Conversation Logs and Transcripts Location, then clicking on 'Set' and choosing the directory you want to save them to."

Avatars and Alts

Just then, Dorketta blurts out, "I have an alt. Wanna see?" She immediately changes into a huge red dragon that flaps its wings, roars, and spits fire.

Mamakie: "That's nice, Dorketta, but your dragon is a different avatar, not an alt. An avatar is the pixels you see on the screen, but an 'alt'—short for alternate account—is a completely different login with a different username, password, and everything. Some people have a separate account for each character they play, and others play various characters using the same account, just changing the look of the avatar. It's a matter of preference. Most experienced players I know combine the two, having various accounts and playing more than one character on each."

Mahir: "Just remember, if you play more than one character with the same account, be sure to clarify what character you're playing at any given moment. The obvious way is to design a different avatar for each character, as Mamakie mentioned. In addition, you can wear a 'character tag' with a floating text indicating your name and other useful information, as we will see in the class on Character Definition. You should also have a separate Pick in your profile describing each character you play."

Mamakie: "Speaking of which, be very careful if you play the same character in more than one region, known as cross-region roleplaying. For example, a group of characters might go from Virtual India to a dark urban region on a shady job, a vanilla suburban region as exchange students, or a jungle region on vacation.

Cross-region roleplay can introduce a new twist in the storyline but can also cause confusion.

"Using cross-region roleplay, players can introduce a new twist in their storyline by taking their characters to roleplay in another region. But unless all players involved are aware of what you're doing, it can also cause a lot of confusion—'Wait, weren't you the head of the Wizengamot?'—so take the time to clarify it with everyone first."

Mahir: "Right, and if you opt for cross-region roleplay, be very respectful of what is going on in the new region you're entering. Don't just barge in with your own agenda, ignoring the ongoing storylines already in place. Start slow, keep your eyes and ears open, and look for ways for your story to fit into what's happening in the region."

Joining an Ongoing Scene

Mahir: "This is a good place to talk about how to enter an ongoing scene. As I said before, roleplay doesn't have 'rules' per se, but rather an etiquette and a set of conventions to help make our interactions smoother and fun for everyone. This includes how we join and leave ongoing scenes without disturbing the other players.

"Briefly, we should avoid interrupting other people's roleplay unless we're invited. For starters, if someone offers to teleport you to their location, ask where they are first to avoid materializing suddenly in the middle of an ongoing roleplay.

"When approaching a roleplay group on foot, the convention is to stay back but within chat distance, watching and listening (known as 'lurking'). This is especially true when you don't know the people well. Even if you're close friends, if you see them roleplaying, wait to be invited before barging in.

"While you wait to be acknowledged, you can signal your interest in joining the roleplay by writing one or more posts about what you're doing there and responding to what is happening around you. However, wait at least one full round before you do so, and then respect the posting order. Your posts don't need to be long, just enough to show that you are willing to roleplay and in sync with what is going on.

"Then wait until one or more of the other characters actually includes you in the roleplay by speaking to you or calling you over to join them. Be aware that merely acknowledging your presence with something like 'glances over at the person nearby' or even 'nods at you' or 'waves distractedly' may be simple courtesy and not an invitation to join in.

"When in doubt, you can always IM one or more members of the group. Then, instead of simply asking if you can join in, consider suggesting what role you could contribute to the scene. If one of them is injured, you could play a healer or distraught friend. If they're sitting at a café, you could be the waiter or waitress, or even play the violin. And if they're having sex, well... three's company, right?"

-laughter around the group-

Mamakie: "If for any reason they don't invite you, please don't take it personally. Sometimes there's simply not an opening for your character in a particular scene. In that case, either stay and watch (lurking) or go do something else and come back later. Oh, and if you're just watching as an OOC observer, you should wear the 'OOC' tag provided in your Karma HUD to avoid confusion."

Mahir: "By the way, 'lurking' is usually not seen as a bad thing in roleplay. Most players appreciate having an 'audience,' and it's also a good way to learn from others and find out what's happening. BUT... most players will assume that if you were only lurking and not involved in the roleplay in any way, you were not really there for IC purposes. According to this view, if you don't post into a scene, you're not in it IC, you don't obtain any information IC, and you can't use it IC afterward without meta-gaming."

Most players appreciate having an 'audience,' a good way to learn from others and find out what's happening.

Mamakie: "If you ARE invited, then having 'lurked' for a while will ensure your involvement is in keeping with the scene. You might IM them to ask for the posting order and where you can fit in. Don't impose your own agenda or do anything that might clash with the prevailing mood, at least not at first. If someone is writhing on the ground in agony, you wouldn't just saunter up, all smiles, and say, 'Hey, how's it going?' ...unless you're roleplaying a totally clueless dork, that is" -laughs-

Mahir: "Also, don't assume that everyone has read your backstory and knows who they are dealing with. If any characters are present who don't know you, it's good practice to use an 'opener' or 'starter,' which is an initial post with a brief appositive phrase describing your character, like this:

Mahir: /me, a middle-aged Indian man dressed in a commissioner's fine silk robes, takes measured steps into the yard, pressing his palms together at chest level, and booms out in a sonorous baritone, "Namaste, friends. May I steal a moment of your time to share a friendly invitation?"

Mamakie: /me swoons at the sight of him

Leaving an Ongoing Scene

Mahir: "As for leaving an ongoing roleplay, the most common reasons are crashing, RL interruptions, and when someone oversteps your RP limits. Everyone crashes sometimes, even with the best computers and internet connections. If you're the one crashing, simply log back in using the 'Last location' option and type ((crashed)) in Local Chat.

"If someone else crashes, wait patiently to see if they return before giving up and leaving the scene. If and when they do come back and say ((crashed)), common courtesy dictates that you say ((wb)) and that they answer ((ty)). However, if several people are involved in the scene, it's enough for one of them to say ((wb)) to avoid cluttering up Local Chat. Some roleplayers say that any such OOC exchange is understood and therefore unnecessary, but that's up to you."

Mamakie: "Crashing isn't usually immediate—it can take a minute or two before you even realize you're crashing and your avatar disappears from the other players' view. During that process, they or you may have posted something the others didn't see, so it's a good idea for each party to repeat their last post to make sure you're all at the same place before continuing the roleplay."

Chiptag: "You can easily repeat your last post by simply pressing 'Ctrl-Up Arrow' to find the one you want, followed by 'Enter.' Oh, and while I have the floor, in a fight situation, it's against the rules to use your opponent's crashing as an excuse to leave the area. You must stay there for a reasonable length of time, waiting for them to log back in."

Mahir: "Yes, and when they do come back, don't be a dickhead. Wait for them to recover fully, and ask them to let you know when they're ready to continue the fight. It's cowardly and discourteous to take advantage of their vulnerability when just logging back in."

Mamakie: "As for RL interruptions, they happen to us all. If your absence from the keyboard will be brief and your character is not at risk, you can just say ((BRB)) and leave your avatar there. But if it's likely to be more than a minute or two, or if your character might be in danger, it's better to log out or go to a safe zone like the Landing after posting something like ((GTG - RL)) in Local Chat—or, if necessary, a more detailed explanation in an IM.

"If you expect to be gone longer than you can reasonably expect your RP partners to wait, you might offer to pick up the scene at another time. And as we've discussed before, it's poor style to just poof in front of everybody. It only takes a few seconds to walk out of chat range or around the corner before logging out.

"Then there's the issue of your 'RP limits.' If you really feel uncomfortable with where a particular scene is going, open a friendly IM with your RP partners and say so *politely*. Even the nastiest character usually has a kind, caring, understanding person behind the keyboard, who will most likely be glad to change direction.

"However, if they refuse to accept your request, even after *courteously* explaining your reasons, then you're justified in excusing yourself from the roleplay. But try to talk it out first, even to the extent of calmly letting them know that you'll log out if they don't respect your wishes."

If you feel uncomfortable with where a scene is going, open an IM with your RP partner(s) and say so *politely*.

Mahir: "It shouldn't be necessary to say this, but we would be remiss if we didn't. Do NOT log out just to escape capture. Everyone is victorious and vanquished at some point, and your roleplay wouldn't be fair or even as rich as it could be if that were not the case. So accept defeat honorably and just roleplay the hell out of it.

"Finally, if you expect to be away from the roleplay for a significant period, it's important to announce your hiatus to your roleplay partners. You can even build it into the story by roleplaying that you will be taking a trip or going away for school.

"If you plan to drop out of a region, RP group, or storyline entirely, it would be a slight to your partners, would disrupt the storyline, and you would discredit yourself if you just 'ghosted' or disappeared without a word. Roleplay your way out of it properly by moving to another town, dying, or whatever else fits in with the story, and let the other characters play out their reaction to your disappearance."

Insults and Rudeness

Mahir: "We've been emphasizing courtesy because this is an area that confuses many people. Not all RP characters are kind, gentle, and polite. Some are grumpy, rude, foul-mouthed, or even violent. But that's their CHARACTER, not necessarily the person behind the keyboard, so don't take it personally. For example, if I post:

> */me scowls at Chiptag and snarls, 'Shut up, you damned bastard. You don't know what the f*ck you're talking about. You're just a spoiled, arrogant, entitled city shit.'*

"What's going on here? Is the person behind my screen insulting the person behind his screen? NO, my CHARACTER is insulting his CHARACTER in roleplay, in the hopes of eliciting an IC response from that character. It's an act. If I were to say those things in ((double brackets)) or in an IM, then we would have a problem."

> Chiptag: *is about to snap back at Mahir but catches himself and hangs his head, biting his lips and wobbling his head submissively* I'm sorry, Mentor Mahir. I was out of line. I won't do it again.

Mahir: /me chuckles and turns to the class, "You see? Just like in RL, your character can choose to ignore rude people, confront them, or submit to them like Chiptag has shown—as long as you remember that it's their CHARACTER doing it and not the RL person. Otherwise, their rudeness, PLUS your misunderstanding of it as being their RL character, could cause issues.

"Of course, we all put some of ourselves into our characters and our roleplay. Maybe deep down, we have always wanted to express our inner frustrations by lashing out at someone, but social norms have kept us from doing so. We don't do it to offend others. If we did, we'd be trolls or bullies, not true roleplayers. Rather, we do it to explore another facet of life. Roleplay gives us the chance to do so safely.

"The Linden Lab Terms of Service forbid 'derogatory or demeaning language,' 'actions that marginalize, belittle, or defame users,' 'communicating or behaving in a manner that is offensively coarse, intimidating, threatening, or causes annoyance or alarm,' and any act of violence toward a user's avatar, including intimidation or bullying. However, all these things can occur in roleplay, as long as it remains IN CHARACTER.

> In-character actions can have in-character consequences that we will have to live with in character.

"The key is not to take it OOC or let it affect our real lives. If I thought the person behind Chiptag's screen would be offended IRL, I wouldn't insult him like that. Also, I'm fully aware that his character might choose to get angry, lash back, and even attack my character. We all have to live with the IC consequences of our IC actions. Let me repeat that: IC actions can have IC consequences that we will have to live with IC."

Mamakie: "Don't expect a scene to go exactly as you have planned. If you do, you can become frustrated and angry. Roleplay is fluid and unpredictable. Different roleplayers will react to the same situations differently. You need to be willing to go with the flow and respond to whatever happens without getting upset. You never know how it will evolve, which is one of the beauties of roleplay.

"And don't forget to thank your roleplay partners afterward, especially if a scene involved a fight or a highly emotional interaction. A friendly IM, even if it just says, 'Thanks for the RP,' can go a long way toward calming the waters. It's the courteous thing to do and reminds both them and you that it was roleplay and you are still friends OOC."

Roleplaying as Yourself

Dorketta: raises a timid hand and speaks in her high-pitched, nasal voice "Why can't my character just be myself?"

Mahir: "Well, it can, of course, and that's called a 'self-insert.' But in my experience, when people roleplay as themselves, they tend to identify too much with their characters and take things too personally. So, like we just explained, when someone else's character insults theirs, they feel personally offended instead of realizing that it's one character insulting another character and not someone insulting them."

Mamakie: "One of our most basic human needs is to feel that we have a positive identity, so roleplaying as yourself can work against giving your character certain flaws. You may be tempted to take your character too seriously and make it too perfect—known as a 'Mary Sue' or 'Gary Stu'—a character with no flaws or weaknesses and without all the interesting nuances that make for a well-rounded personality."

Mahir: "Added to that, your survival instinct may tempt you always to want to come out on top of any situation, be it a simple argument or an all-out fight. If you see your avatar as a character you're managing and not a virtual personification of yourself, it will be much easier to accept that sometimes your character won't, can't, and even shouldn't win. Does that answer your question?"

Dorketta: "Yes, but I'm me. How can I be someone else? Although I see your point about this being just roleplay..."

Mamakie: "Well, the way I see it, I already roleplay being myself in the real world 24/7, and to tell you the truth, it can get a little boring sometimes. I roleplay as Mamakie to add a little fantasy to my life and to explore other possibilities. If I roleplayed as myself, I'd be wasting a great opportunity to make it as interesting and challenging as I possibly can."

Arjun: "Personally, I find that roleplaying a completely different personality from my own is much easier, less stressful, and more fun than playing myself."

Eswaria: "I see roleplay as both an art form and a journey of self-discovery. My characters may inevitably reflect certain facets of myself, but not my entire RL personality. Anyway, if I just wanted to be myself, I certainly would not do it in an RP region."

Mahir: "Yes, a roleplay region is not a social media hangout. If you want to just be yourself in your current account—which is perfectly alright—then maybe you should consider creating an alternate account or 'alt' and giving it a distinct character for your roleplay. Of course, any character you develop will have certain traits of your own, which can be an easy starting point, but with time, you can gradually exaggerate, distort, or change them however you like to develop a unique, distinctive, and memorable character."

Mamakie: "Here's a technique you can use to help your characters 'find their voice' and separate them from yourself. Sit down and have a 'talk' with your character. Write down what both of you say and how you say it, like posts with lots of emotes. Repeat the exercise until your character has found its own voice, which should be different from yours, and until you're comfortable seeing it as distinct from you."

Mahir: "In any case, remember that others have no reason to suspect that the character you're playing is YOU. They will assume you're playing a CHARACTER, just as they are, and will feel free to insult or even attack you without hurting your RL feelings. That's because, according to convention, everything that happens in Local Chat is roleplay."

Platistotle: /me suddenly breaks his silence as though coming out of a trance. "If I might add something, I'd like to mention for those new to the subject that a lot of what has just been said is part of an ongoing debate between augmentationists and immersionists, originally posed by Henrik Bennetsen.

"Briefly, augmentationists see virtual worlds as extensions of their RL, as tools to achieve their ends... whether as a sort of social media on steroids (aka Facebookers or FBers), a website for developing an online business, an alternative channel for promoting their pet ideas, a virtual venue for distance education, and so on. They tend to have no qualms about using voice chat and video, sharing their real life, and even meeting with others outside of the virtual world.

> Augmentationists use virtual worlds to promoting real-life concerns. Immersionists treat them as places totally separate and different from real life.

"Immersionists, on the other hand, view a virtual world as an actual 'place' different and separate from their first life, complete in and of itself, entirely divorced from the 'real' world. They tend to avoid using voice chat and sharing RL information about themselves but rather concentrate on living their virtual life to the fullest, which is the essence of roleplay. They are also known as 'life stylers.'

"I personally don't see this as an 'either-or' or 'us versus them' debate. Rather, I see augmentation and immersion as distinct types of activities that any one of us can engage in. At times, you may want to use a virtual world as a tool or extension of your real life, while at other times, you will want to put RL away and fully immerse yourself in a roleplay situation. And yes, you would do well to have different accounts for these two activity types.

"While I have the floor, I'd like to question the common assumption that what we are doing is 'just' roleplay. That's like telling musicians that they are 'just' playing, telling serious athletes that it's 'just' a game, or telling a novelist that it's 'just' fiction.

"Actually, everything we do, even in real life, is roleplay, and we act like a different person in each role. We behave one way with our boss and another with our subordinates, one way with our spouse and another with our children, one way with our siblings or friends and another with our enemies. But we never say that it's 'just' roleplay; we call it real life.

"As William Shakespeare famously said, 'All the world's a stage, and all the men and women merely players. They have their exits and their entrances, and one man in his time plays many parts.' He then describes several of the 'roles' each of us plays during our lifetime. Similarly, mystical masters speak of 'multiple selves,' and social psychologists hypothesize the existence of 'sub-selves.'

"Gary Gygax, the father of modern RPGs, reflects on the same idea when he says, 'As children, we all, in all cultures and societies, learn behavior from observation, imitation, and encouragement of various kinds. So we all pretend most of the time.'[8] Think of the 'persona' you present on a first date compared to the 'persona' you let show after being married to that person for several years. Would you be the same person if you had been born in a different country, ethnic milieu, or with a different socioeconomic status if your life had been very different from the one you've had?

"To conclude, let's all try to rise above such false dichotomies as roleplay versus real life and approach our art more seriously. If we do, I think we will find it much more satisfying and fulfilling."

Identifying with your Character

Arjun: /me grins sheepishly, "When I cry, my typist tears up, and when I laugh, my atman chuckles. My atman feels everything I feel. I've become so real, taken on a life of my own, so to speak, that I often tell my atman what to write. And vice-versa—when my atman is sad, I'm sad, and when my atman is happy, I'm happy."

It can be hard NOT to identify with your character because virtual worlds can feel very real."

Mahir: /me looks down at Arjun condescendingly. "You'll get over that eventually. It's just because you're new to roleplay. At the start, it can be hard for some people not to identify with their character because things in virtual worlds can feel very real."

Arjun: /me raises his hands, palms up at shoulder level, and shrugs. "I'm trying to separate the two, but it's not easy. It's like when you laugh, cry, or get frightened reading a novel or watching a movie. It can be cathartic."

---

[8] Gary Gygax, www.brainyquote.com/quotes/gary_gygax_413229.

Mahir: /me frowns. "Maybe you're not trying hard enough to be objective. Have you considered that maybe you enjoy feeling those emotions and don't want to let go?"

Mamakie: /me sighs, shooting a critical glance at Mahir. "OR... maybe it's the other way around. Maybe those who CAN'T empathize with their characters aren't quite there yet. Or maybe they've been roleplaying for so long with different characters that they've lost some of the mystique that comes from immersing themselves more deeply in their roles and stories."

Platistotle: /me waggles his head gravely at Arjun and Mamakie. "I agree. Studies show that people tend to design their avatars and develop their characters to express and explore certain facets of their inner selves that social pressure has obliged them to suppress, and that many come to identify with their virtual characters.

"This seems similar to how we tend to identify with our physical bodies, how we dress and adorn them to reflect the ways we perceive—or want to perceive—ourselves, and how we feel and act differently depending on whether our flesh-and-blood avatars are clean or dirty, informally or formally dressed, skinny or well-rounded, in ugly or beautiful surroundings, and so on.

"When people use alternate accounts or 'alts,' they often find that their personality changes to match whatever avatar they're using or character they're playing at the time. Some thinkers have even suggested that the emotional link between our two avatars—the one of flesh and blood, and the other of pixels and code—may be due to our human capacity to empathize with others, to put ourselves in their shoes."

Mahir: /me wobbles his head reluctantly. "Okay, point taken. I guess Mahir has some of me, plus some things I'm learning from him, such as a liking for Indian food. I guess there's always something of ourselves in each avatar. But... and this is a big BUT, he is also very different from me. He's my CHARACTER. I'm not Mahir, and Mahir is not me. I created him, and I make him live. It's important to recognize that difference to avoid OOC issues."

Arjun: "Yeah, I guess I could have a grumpy character, which is also how I feel sometimes." He glances up at Mahir and quickly down again, grinning mischievously.

Mamakie: /me laughs. "I started with only one account, then changed roleplay regions and opened another. I've had several alts but I only roleplay in one region with each character. Otherwise, switching gears all the time would be too confusing, and I couldn't keep them straight. It's hard enough not to take Mamakie's character into real life."

Mahir: "Speaking of which, to emphasize the separation between IC and OOC, it's a roleplay convention to speak of your characters in the third person when writing OOC, not in the first or second person. This ensures other players that you're talking about your character, not your RL persona.

"For example, in an OOC chat between the players behind two characters John and Sally, they would not write, 'I will rescue you,' but rather 'John will rescue Sally'; not 'I am feeling frustrated' but rather 'John is feeling frustrated'; not 'I'm falling for you' but rather 'Sally is falling for John.'

"Especially in emotionally-charged scenes, this will help everyone distance themselves more from emotional involvement and look at the story more objectively, with more detachment, as the writers of the story and not as the characters themselves."

Chiptag: *pipes up, speaking in his characteristic matter-of-fact, know-it-all voice* "Even in table-top RPGs such as Dungeons and Dragons, people often come to identify with their characters, even though they exist primarily in written profiles. So it's not surprising that in a setting as immersive as a virtual world, you would find it hard NOT to identify with your avatar and character."

Mahir: /me clears his throat. "Okay, that will be enough for today. Time for the test..." and hands out the notecard.

Arjun reads the instructions: "Summarize in a few short sentences what you learned from the IC/OOC class." He bites his tongue at the corner of his mouth and starts to write:

- Be creative and try to find ways to turn RL issues into IC events.
- Don't worry about who the players are behind the characters.
- Wait to be invited before joining an ongoing roleplay.
- If someone gives you an inventory item, wait for them to mention it IC before thanking them.
- If you see or hear anything through walls, mentioning or acting on it would be metagaming.
- If you crash, log back in at the 'Last location' to continue your roleplay.
- Don't assume that a rude character means the player behind it is rude.
- Try to work emotions into your roleplay and enjoy the feelings they awaken in you.
- Be careful about identifying with your character to avoid OOC problems with others.

Arjun saves the notecard and returns it to Mahir, sitting back and fidgeting nervously. After a few minutes, a message pops up on his screen:

> Dharma Guide: Congratulations. You have successfully passed the IC/OOC Class and advanced to Level 10 – Roleplayer. Please check your Karma Tag for your next quest.

Arjun lets out a sigh of relief and does a little victory dance. He is curious about the next quest but, feeling exhausted after a long, productive day, he decides to leave it for tomorrow and poofs for the night, with Mamakie's whisper ringing in his ears:

Why are you here, Arjun?

Um, to learn how to roleplay, I guess...

CHAPTER SIX

FISHING AND HUNTING

Status:	Roleplayer
Level:	10
HP:	14.9

When Arjun logs in the next morning, Chris, already waiting for him, grins and claps him on the back, "Hey mate, cheers on levelling up to 10. You're making quick progress. What's your next quest?"

Dharma Guide: You have accepted the quest "Fishing." To complete it, make a fishing rod and catch 10 fish. Happy fishing.

Arjun: /me takes a crumpled piece of paper from his pocket and squints at it. "It says here that I'm supposed to make a fishing rod, but I have no idea how to do that."

Chris: /me nods slowly, eyeing the crumpled paper disapprovingly, then shrugs. "Well, let's see... what material would you use to make a fishing rod?"

Learning to Fish

Arjun: /me thinks for a while, screwing up his face, looking up and to the right while tapping his chin with his forefinger, then his expression brightens, "Oh, I know... bamboo."

Chris: /me rolls his eyes, "Well, duh," then grins. "And where would you look for bamboo?"

Arjun doesn't answer but turns and runs south toward the bamboo thickets they had seen on either side of the Southern River at Betla, a chuckling Chris trotting after him. Arriving at the thicket, he passes his cursor over it until it changes to a hand icon. He clicks on a thin, strong stem and receives it into his Inventory.

Chris: /me watches him with an approving twinkle in his eyes. "Good job, mate. Now you might want to take that stick to the tackle shop to turn it into a fishing rod and buy some bait."

They walk over to Betla Village and ring the bell of a small shop with a fish-shaped sign advertising fishing gear. While waiting for the shop keeper, they look around curiously at the hodge-podge of items for sale—fishing nets draped from the ceiling, rolls of nylon line hanging from hooks on the front wall, various types and sizes of fishing poles leaning against the back wall, barrels of foul-smelling bait on the floor, and various types of flies and other lures on display in the glass counter, behind which are several photos of people posing with enormous catches.

Soon, a small man bustles in, dressed in a strange combination of slippers, white pajama pants, a blue dress shirt under a brown sporting vest, and a khaki cloth fisherman's hat bristling with hooks and flies. The boys greet him with brief posts, but he just stands there in silence for several minutes. Thinking the man is waiting for them to say more, Arjun starts to write another post when Chris sees his typing indicator and IMs him: "Don't chain post. Wait for him to say something first."

Amit: /me sips his customary mid-morning tea as he reads the daily news under his favorite parasol in the village park, grumbling to himself about the state of the world. Spying two handsome young men entering his shop, he folds the newspaper neatly, flips two coppers onto the table, and thanks the lovely waitress with a wink and a smile as she comes to clear the table. He then staggers painfully onto his gouty feet and walks as fast as his raggedy old slippers will carry him, skirting the stinking piles of rubbish and dog poop with a frown and looking both ways before crossing the street to enter his humble shop. Opening his arms in a welcoming gesture, he bows his head slightly and smiles wide, eagerly exclaiming in a wavering, high-pitched voice, "Good morning, gentlemen. My name is Amit Shukla. Welcome to my shop. What can I do for you today?"

Arjun: /me smiles and presses his palms together at chest level. "Pleased to meet you, Mr. Amit. I'm Arjun, and this is my friend and guide, Chris. I'm on the fishing quest and need to complete my rod and buy some bait." He holds out his bamboo rod to the man.

Amit: /me nods at Chris with a warm smile of recognition. "Yes, Chris has frequented my shop and brought new customers regularly, for which I am most grateful." He then takes the rod respectfully with both hands, palms upward, head bowed, and inspects it carefully, nodding in appreciation. "Good choice, Arjun. It's light but strong, firm but supple, and just the right length. Very good indeed." He hobbles over to the display and hesitates before selecting the right reel and three 'eyes,' then goes to his bench and skillfully fastens the reel and eyes to the rod. Finally, he threads the nylon line through the eyes and squints as he slowly ties the hook to the end of the line, fumbling a little with his old, gnarled fingers. Handing the finished rod back to Arjun with a nod, he smiles, "This service costs only one gold, and the rod will last for about 100 fish. With the bait costing one silver per 100 worms, it's quite a good deal considering that you get two coppers per whitefish and three per yellowfish."

Arjun: /me takes the rod, holds it up to admire Amit's handiwork, and smiles, "Excellent craftmanship, Mr. Amit. Thank you. I'll take a package of 100 worms," and hands him one silver and one gold.

Arjun clicks on the bait barrel, passes the silver from his coin purse at the prompt, and receives a package of 100 worms into his Inventory.

Amit: /me waggles his head, smiling contentedly at the compliment, and holds out his hand, palm up, to receive Arjun's coins, which he raises to his forehead in thanks to the gods and slips into his coin purse. He then hobbles over to the bait barrel and counts out 100 of the best worms, dropping them into a white plastic container and snapping on the perforated top. Handing it to Arjun with both hands, palms up, and a respectful nod, he smiles and coos pleasantly, "It's a pleasure to serve you, my young friends. When you have any fresh fish to sell, I'd be glad to take them off your hands. Many people come to my shop for fish, too. Happy fishing, and namaste to you both."

As they leave the shop, Arjun asks Chris where they should fish, which turns out to be near any of the eight bridge/dock combos around the region with shallows where they can stand without drowning. They walk to Betla Bridge, find the shallow area, and wade out into the shallows. Wearing their fishing rods, they rez their bait to load it and click their fishing HUDs to start.

As they cast their lines toward the deepest part, Arjun is delighted to see what excellent fishing animations and sounds the rods have as they draw them back, cast their lines, and reel them in with smooth motions. However, he is startled to see that he has been slipping slowly down the muddy bank and is starting to drown.

Chris laughs as Arjun clambers back up, slipping and spluttering, and suggests that he use 'Movelock' (Ctrl-Alt-P) to avoid that. He explains that Movelock is also useful to avoid getting pushed off a cliff or carried off by a bird when captured. "I started using Movelock when some scoundrel pushed me away from the rock that I was AFK mining in another region and made me lose several hours of earnings," Chris admits with chagrin.

Roleplaying Styles

Arjun: /me gazes out over the water pensively, then turns to Chris, a questioning look on his face. "Why did Mr. Amit write such long posts?"

Chris: "We should talk about this in IMs because roleplay is an OOC topic."

Arjun: "Oh yes, I forgot."

Chris: "No problem. To answer your question, some people write long, descriptive paragraphs like Amit, which is called paragraph roleplay or para-RP for short. Others use single sentences, known as one-line roleplay, but most of us fall somewhere in between, known as semi-para RP."

Arjun: "So Amit was para-RPing? Wow, I've never seen that done before."

Chris: "Yeah, I've mostly played at fantasy RP sims, where the RP is like writing a novel. Some even define themselves as multi-para roleplayers. I couldn't be arsed. Sometimes a single post can max out the post allowance and flow automatically into a second post, taking ten or fifteen minutes to write, especially when people are slow typists.

"That's too slow for me. I like the momentum of one-line and semi-para RP better, which some call 'relaxed RP.' After all, roleplay is about interaction. To me, maintaining all players' interests and involvement is more important than giving lots of detail. A few well-chosen words can mean more than a long, fluffy paragraph."

> A few well-chosen words can mean more than a long, fluffy paragraph. Quantity is not necessarily quality.

Arjun: "So you're saying it's better not to para-roleplay?"

Chris: "No, I wouldn't say that one style is better or worse than another. They're all valid ways of roleplaying, although some claim that their way is the best or only way. Strict para-RPers will tell you that anything less than a paragraph is not true roleplay but more like a series of tweets because it lacks the depth to really convey your character. Others will say, 'If you para-RP, bring me a bottle of vodka to while away the time. I didn't come here to read a novel.'

"Of course, there's no need to go overboard and explain how an elevator works just to say you stepped into the lift. Quantity is not necessarily quality. For me, a short paragraph is plenty, one full sentence is most common, and a word or two is sometimes enough. Jumping freely from one style to another, depending on what's appropriate for each situation, is known as freestyle roleplay. A good rule of thumb is to adopt the style used by your RP partner or by the region in general."

Arjun: "Yeah, that makes sense. When in Rome and all... but I WOULD like to learn how to para-roleplay in case I come across someone who does that."

Chris: "Well, if you want to try your hand at para-RPing, in addition to some quality dialog, try to build an atmosphere using all six senses—sometimes called a mood post—describing your appearance and surroundings, how they affect you, and how you respond to them, like brushing back the hair whipping around your face in the breeze, dabbing at the sweat forming on your forehead under the hot sun, blinking tears from your eyes burning with smoke, scratching at the sand that irritates your skin under your clothing, swatting at the insects buzzing around your head... the possibilities are endless.

"If you want to start a post with a possessive, write '/me apostrophe s' (/me's) then the emote. For example, to say 'Arjun's eyes shine in the firelight...' you would write, '/me's eye's shine in the firelight...' If you've set your Preferences to use a colon (:) instead of '/me,' don't use the colon for the possessive (:'s), because that would come out 'Arjun: :'s eyes shone in the firelight...'

"The same goes for when you want a comma after your name. For example, to say 'Arjun, unsure of what to say next, remains silent,' you would type '/me, unsure of what to say next...'. Again, always use /me for that; using a colon won't work.

"You can also provide context and background information, motives and conflict in your posts, and include something about the past, present, and future. For example, 'He had never liked this kind of thing but was determined not to let his disgust show on his face,' or 'He hesitates before speaking. What could he say? He doesn't want to offend her but knows that if he doesn't tell her the truth, he will regret it sooner or later.'

"Just remember that when someone narrates historical context and inner reflections without actually saying it as part of their dialog, you can't use that information in your roleplay without metagaming unless your character is already aware of it. I once dated a girl roleplaying a virgin who wrote this steamy post when I kissed her:

> */me whimpers softly as his kiss stirs something deep inside her. She had kissed boys before, but never anyone this handsome, mature, and self-confident. So this was why girls fell over the edge and surrendered to men. She can feel the edge of the cliff near—warm, wet, and slippery—but is determined to make him wait. She is worth it and will not give herself to him that easily. 'Make him work for it,' her mother would say. She inhales deeply, steels her nerves, and raises her hands to place them firmly on his chest, pulling her head back from the kiss, knitting her brows, a pleading look in her eyes, murmuring plaintively, "Oh Chris... don't..."*

Chris: /me takes a hankie from his back pocket and wipes his sweaty brow with a flustered grin, then regains his composure, clears his throat, and stashes the handkerchief. "Think of it like writing one or more paragraphs of a novel, with all the descriptions, background, and actions you would expect from a good story. Just be sure that what you write isn't mere fluff, what some call 'purple prose.' Everything you write should either move the roleplay forward, further define your character, or create the necessary ambiance—preferably all three at once."

Arjun: "I can see how that could take some time. What do you do while you're waiting for others to finish typing their paragraphs?"

Chris: "Sometimes I take a bathroom break, make myself a cup of coffee, or surf the web, but you can also use the time to compose your own descriptions for when it's your turn to post, if and when they fit into the scene. But keep it simple—not everyone is a brilliant roleplayer, and some have limited English, so avoid colloquial and idiomatic expressions as much as possible. Hell, even the difference between British and American English can cause confusion. For example, 'what's up' means 'what's wrong' to Brits and 'how are you' to Americans."

The two boys continue discussing the pros and cons of the different roleplay styles, rezzing bait and clicking their fishing HUDs each time they catch a fish. Chris explains that in some regions, people can just leave their avatars fishing while they do other things in real life, which he calls 'AFK fishing.' Having to rebait and click after each catch means that people actually have to remain present ingame while fishing, which makes it more realistic and promotes more and better roleplay.

After some time, Arjun has caught seven whitefish and three yellowfish, and a message appears in Local Chat:

Dharma Guide: Congratulations. You have completed the Fishing Quest and advanced to Level 11 - Fisher. You have been granted a license to carry a hunting weapon, and a new category has been added to your Region Map HUD: Prey. Please check your Karma Tag for your next quest.

From Hunter to Hunted

Chris: /me squints up at the sky as he reels in his line, "It will be midday soon. Let's fish some more until it's time for lunch, and we can do your next quest this afternoon. We'll need to be strong for that one."

Arjun does his head bobble thing, casts his line again, then accepts his next quest and reads:

Dharma Guide: You have accepted the quest "Hunting." To complete it, arm yourself where warriors dwell and catch at least one of each of the following, in this order: a Rhesus macaque monkey, a chicken, and a mountain goat. Happy hunting.

Arjun: /me reels in another fish, pries the hook out of its mouth, and drops it into his basket. He then checks his region map HUD, which now has several red dots indicating prey. He looks over at Chris, a doubtful expression on his face. "I can see hunting chickens and mountain goats, but monkeys?"

Chris: /me shrugs, watching a large fish swim warily around his baited hook. "I've heard that the monkey population has grown so much they're becoming a plague, so we've been asked to help control their numbers."

Arjun: /me casts his line again and sighs in resignation, "Alright..." –then looks worried– "Hmmm... 'arm yourself where warriors dwell'? Apparently, I'm supposed to go to the Raider Castle to make a weapon."

Chris: /me gets tired of waiting for the wise old fish to take the bait and reels in his line to cast it out in a different direction, "True, mate... into the lion's den we go. But you get a break this time; no need to collect materials for this quest. You can just buy the weapon of your choice at the Weaponsmith's Shop."

After catching another dozen or so fish, the boys climb up to sit on the bank and have lunch. Then they pack up their fishing gear and head northeast toward the Raider Castle, where they find the Weaponsmith's Shop in a room built into the lower southwestern wall. Arjun sighs with relief at not having to go into the castle proper.

On one side of the shop are melee weapons such as knives and daggers, swords and spears, axes and clubs. On the other side are range weapons and ammunition, such as bows and crossbows with arrows, pistols and guns with bullets, and even exotic items like boomerangs and blowguns. The Weaponsmith doesn't show up, but each item group has an automatic vendor, so Arjun selects a finely-crafted bow, buys a quiver full of arrows, slings them onto his back, and grins. "I feel like a real warrior now."

Chris: /me looks at him and smiles broadly "Looks good..." –then, more seriously– "Although you won't be able to do any PVP damage as long as your Karma Tag is green or yellow"

In response to Arjun's question, Chris explains that PVP means player-versus-player. Only red-tagged warriors can down and capture yellows and other reds using the scripted weapons system. Players with yellow tags can take damage from, but not inflict damage on, warriors, as their weapons only work against animals, although they can roleplay text-based fights with reds. Reds cannot attack greens, even in text-based roleplay, but greens can have text-based fights with other greens or yellows. Arjun comments on Chris's yellow tag, and Chris explains that he and many others just want that added element of realism in their roleplay.

Armed and ready, they head southwest and wade across the Eastern River into Betla, where they find a troop of Rhesus macaque monkeys foraging peaceably on tender shoots among the trees just south of the Hindu Temple. Chris teaches Arjun how to draw his bow and load the arrows, then how to go into 'mouselook' by typing 'M' or rolling his mouse wheel forward,[9] and how to aim and shoot.

Arjun catches on quickly and slowly approaches the troop of monkeys. As soon as he comes within about twenty meters from the closest one, it starts to scream and run around frantically. Arjun draws his bow and starts to shoot, but can't hit it. Luckily, he finds that he uses no arrows when he misses.

---

[9] See wiki.phoenixviewer.com/fs_mouselook for further information on mouselook.

Chris: "Aim just a little ahead of it to compensate for distance and delay ((lag))"

Arjun does so, and soon, a number above the monkey's head starts counting down its health. When it reaches zero, the monkey breaks into pieces of meat, and a thrilled Arjun picks them up by going within arm's reach and clicking on them.

Aim just a little ahead of a moving target to compensate for distance and lag.

"Good job, mate," Chris shouts. "Now for the chickens."

They head north through the bamboo thicket, across Betla Bridge, past the Communal Garden, across Simlipal Bridge, and turn right to find a brood of chickens just south of Simlipal Village. This time, when Arjun approaches them, they start squawking, flapping their wings and running in all directions at once, faster than the monkey had run, making it even harder to hit them. Arjun starts shooting at anything that passes his crosshairs, but none of them lose more than one HP, and they recover quickly.

"Pick one chicken and concentrate only on that one. Otherwise, it'll regain health while you shoot at the others," Chris calls out.

Arjun tries to follow only one chicken with his eyes, but as they crisscross in front of each other, he loses track of it and has to start over. Straining every nerve to focus, he finally gets one to fall and runs up to collect it with a triumphant whoop.

"Bloody awesome," Chris cheers, and the two dance a little jig in their excitement. "Come on, let's go find you a mountain goat."

Just then, they hear a terrifying roar as a Bengal tiger charges out of the forest toward the boys. Chris is sent tumbling with a swat of its powerful paw, while Arjun jumps aside just in time. Aiming his bow, Arjun starts peppering the enormous cat with arrows, but none of his shots do any damage. The snarling beast lunges at Arjun again and again, each time taking chunks from his health points, which plummet to dangerously low levels.

Suddenly, a quick series of shots ring out, and the tiger falls dead at Arjun's feet. Looking up, he sees Chris standing there, rifle raised and smoking, aiming at the cat.

Chris: /me runs forward to help Arjun, panting "Are you alright???"

Arjun: /me stands frozen in place, trembling with fear, and gasps, "Gods, that tiger scared the sh*t out of me. It almost finished me off. Why couldn't I kill it but you could?"

Chris: /me presses sterile bandages to Arjun's wounds, trying to stanch the flow of blood. "Until you complete the hunting quest, you won't have the power to hurt savage beasts and will need the help of a protector who can, like me." He gets up to slice eight large slabs of meat from the tiger

Arjun: /me winces as Chris tends his wounds, his knees wobbling as he struggles to remain standing. "We have to hunt that mountain goat right away then. Where..." he starts, then shakes his head. "...Oh yeah, in the mountains, of course," and turns to stumble northward.

Chris: /me reaches out to grab Arjun's arm "Wait. First, we need to eat to regain our strength, and then we'll take a boat. It'll be faster"

Prim Jumping

Chris and Arjun quickly eat enough to buff up their HP, then run to the dock by the bridge. Boarding a fast canoe, they paddle upriver as quickly as their sore limbs allow and disembark at the northernmost dock. It takes them a while to spot a lone mountain goat nibbling on some sparse vegetation half-way up a steep slope. But as soon as they come within range, it bounds up the slope and disappears behind a rocky outcropping.

Arjun starts to climb up after it but keeps sliding back down, as the slope is too steep for him. Then he tries jumping but can only advance one meter before sliding back down. Chris watches his clumsy efforts with a smug expression on his face, then leaps up the slope in a few quick jumps and stands at the top, grinning down. Gawking at his agility, Arjun calls out, "Hey, Chris, how did you do that?"

Chris IMs him to explain that no-flight regions such as these have 'gravity,' which he can use for 'prim jumping' by holding down the jump key (normally E or PgUp) and going against an object. This leverage will make him leap several meters into the air, even while jumping in place. Arjun tries it and soon finds himself practically flying up the slope to land next to Chris with a panting laugh. Chris then shows him how to go into 'always run' mode by clicking on the running icon in the 'Walk/run/fly' window or simply pressing 'Ctrl-R.'

Armed with these new abilities, Arjun runs in the direction the mountain goat has gone, taking great leaps and bounds from one rock to the next. The goat's agility is no longer a match for this new, improved hunter, but Arjun soon discovers that aiming while running and jumping is much harder than while standing still. The few shots that find their mark are wasted as the animal springs back and forth away from him, regaining its health.

Chris calls Arjun back for an OOC huddle and teaches him how to toggle between the A and D keys (or left and right arrows) to go from side to side while running. "Mirror its back-and-forth movements with yours, so that you only have to tweak your aim a little whenever it changes direction," Chris advises him.

Arjun tries it, holding down the W key to run after the goat while toggling right and left with the A and D keys to mirror the animal's changes in direction. The difference is amazing. In only a few minutes, he is standing over his fallen prey, raising a victory cry, and Chris is running up, cheering his friend ecstatically while a message appears in Arjun's Local Chat:

> Dharma Guide: Congratulations. You have successfully learned to hunt and have advanced to Level 12 - Hunter. Please check your Karma Tag for your next quest.

As their celebration dies down, Arjun starts to feel exhausted from all the excitement of this day, so he quickly writes up his report for Chris and logs off, reflecting on his special quest for Mamakie:

Why are you here, Arjun?

To learn all the neat tips and tricks
you can use in Second Life.

CHAPTER SEVEN

CHARACTER DEFINITION

Status: Hunter
Level: 12
HP: 13.8

Dharma Guide: You have accepted the quest "Character." To complete it, attend the Character Definition class at the Buddhist Monastery on Wednesday at 2:00 pm SLT. You will be tested, so pay attention. Good luck.

Arjun spends the next morning practicing his new hunting skills on the monkeys and mountain goats. He stays clear of the chicken area, though, not wanting to risk another run-in with the tiger with no Protector around. By lunchtime, he has become quite proficient and has his basket full of meat.

Just before 2:00 PM, Arjun picks his way through Hemis Village's narrow streets and climbs the steep slope to the Buddhist Monastery. A few students are already milling around the stone patio flanked by one-story structures built like long halls with areas for resting, taking tea, and purchasing incense holders, wall-hangings, wind chimes, and the like. Low box planters filled with sand sit on the floors, each holding a statuette of the Buddha, two or three jade rocks, a flower, and some incense sticks, the slender plumes of sweet smoke twisting skyward.

Beyond them is an extensive green lawn where cherry trees sway in the breeze, their pink blossoms gently falling like pink flurries. Here and there, chiming bells hang like large, upside-down wine glasses, decorated with what look like Hindu and Japanese writings, some with colorful streamers fluttering from their clappers and a couple so large they have their own wooden structure and roof.

Once everyone is gathered, the Hemis Commissioner leads them across a wooden walk over a shallow pond populated with water lilies, cattails, koi fish, and mandarin ducks. Climbing a steep flight of stairs, they arrive in front of the Temple, a square, white marble structure on top of which is a large, spike-topped golden dome with four smaller ones around it. Japanese-looking wooden structures on either side of the entrance hold large cylindrical prayer wheels that turn solemnly on their axes to reveal the writings around them.

Stepping inside, Arjun sees a large golden meditating Buddha on a raised dais dominating the interior, with a few red notables' cushions at the foot of the statue where the Commissioner and teachers sit and blue lotus-patterned cushions in a large semicircle around that for the students. The back is open, affording a magnificent view of the Hemis Valley and Western River below.

Mahir clears his throat and looks around at the students. Mamakie sits at one side of him and to the other side sits—or rather slouches—Chiptag. "So far, most of you have been thinking about the *roles* you want to play, but today, we will be helping you think about building your *character*—what kind of person you will be, how you will think and act, your attitudes and beliefs, what you will seek to achieve, and how you will relate to others. The Monastery has offered to host this class, since Buddhism emphasizes self-awareness, and Commissioner Ananda Ramaputra would like to say a few words before we start."

Physical Bodies as Avatars

Ananda Ramaputra: /me presses his palms together with a little bow to his colleagues, next to the students, and then speaks in a soft but high-pitched voice that carries easily to every corner of the temple. "There has been much discussion lately about whether we should identify with our avatars. As some of you will know, 'avatar' comes from the Sanskrit अवतार or avatāra, literally 'descent,' meaning incarnation or manifestation of the 'atman'—spirit or soul—in a body.

Our physical bodies are only avatars or outer vehicles of the atman.

"According to a Buddhist worldview, our physical bodies are not our 'real selves' but only avatars or outer vehicles of the atman. In this sense, Teilhard de Chardin was correct in saying that we are not physical beings having a spiritual experience, but rather spiritual beings having a physical experience—or, in our case, a digital experience.

"Tom Boellstorff, who studied embodiment and place-making in VR, says, 'In the physical world you get to know people from the outside in, but in [a virtual world] it's from the inside out.'[10] One century ago, Oscar Wilde said, 'Man is least himself when he talks in his own person. Give him a mask [avatar], and he will tell you the truth.' In The Reality of the Virtual, Slavoj Žižek says, 'When I deal

[10] Our Digital Selves: My Avatar is Me [full feature film]: youtu.be/GQw02-me0W4.

with you, I'm basically not dealing with the 'real' you; I'm dealing with a virtual image of you, and this image... structures the way I deal with you.'

"All this suggests that identifying with our flesh-and-blood avatars is no less of an illusion than identifying with those of pixels and code. The atman—our true reality—uses both these physical and virtual bodies to experience the material and virtual worlds *vicariously*. When we see and hear, it is the atman that sees and hears; when we think and feel, it is the atman that thinks and feels; when we speak or act, it is the atman that speaks and acts, much like the person behind the computer managing a virtual avatar.

"Just as we are not 'inside' our virtual avatars but relate to them electronically, our atman is not 'inside' our physical body but relates to it like a reflection in a mirror. The same light source can reflect in more than one mirror. So, too, the atman can manifest itself in more than one avatar in more than one world—in our case, a physical and a virtual world—at the same time. This is one of the beauties of virtual worlds: they teach us this important lesson while still in this life.

"So my advice, dear students, is this: it is alright to identify with your flesh-and-blood avatars or your pixel-and-code avatars as long as you remember *why* you are experiencing these worlds: to develop your atman and approach Nirvana."

Arjun's attention had started to wander but snaps back at those last words, and he quickly writes them down before he forgets: "You are experiencing these worlds to develop your atman and approach Nirvana." He then sits back, nibbling on his pencil eraser and reflecting on this statement while Mahir starts the class.

Defining a Character

Mahir: "One tool that fiction writers use extensively is 'character definition.' In roleplay, we can learn from novelists to make our characters come alive for us. And the better your character definition, the richer your roleplay will tend to be.

The better your character definition, the richer your roleplay will tend to be.

"For this class, we will assume that you will not be using a 'canon character' (i.e., a character from a novel, movie, comic, and so on) but rather designing an 'original character' from scratch. To define your character, it's useful to write its profile or bio, which should include its background story or 'backstory,' physical attributes, and personality traits.

"The backstory is important because people behave differently according to their past experiences, and so should your character, which should stand out—not in the sense of being 'better' than the rest, but of being *different* from all others, unique, unforgettable, with distinctive features, mannerisms, speech, and so on. Its profile can be simple at first, but the more your character grows and develops, the more nuanced and interesting it will become.

"If you're having a hard time defining your character, one trick I've used is to choose a similar character from a movie or novel as a starting place and work from there. Another is to choose from among the Myers-Briggs or Enneagram personality types. Some even use the 'Johari Window' technique of defining for their character: what I know that I know about myself, what I know that I don't know about myself, what I don't know that I know about myself, and what I don't know that I don't know about myself.

"There are many websites on character definition. Some offer character sheets you might want to try. Here are a few initial questions you can ask yourself to start." Mahir passes out a notecard with points for the students to consider:

CHARACTER DEFINITION QUESTIONNAIRE

- Basic personal data: name, age, place of birth, nationality, current location, education, occupation, economic status, social class, favorite sports, affiliations, sexual orientation, etc.
- Your character's life history, even from before birth, its parents or family as a whole. What kind of childhood did it have? Who were its role models, and what were they like?
- What does your character look like? Be detailed. How did it grow into that appearance, and what does it do to maintain it? How does it wish it looked?
- What are your character's prejudices, biases, assumptions, beliefs, values, principles, or worldview? How attached is it to them, enough to try to impose them on others?
- What are your character's main skills or abilities, and how did it acquire them? Don't try to make it omnicompetent; give it just a few main ones so characters with other skills and abilities can contribute their share to the mix.
- Is your character street-smart or book-smart, optimist or pessimist, selfish or generous, courteous or rude, introverted or extroverted, sense-driven or intuition-driven, more logical or more emotional, structured or flexible?
- What primary and secondary goals drive your character, and why? Have they changed over time? As Kurt Vonnegut said, "Every character should want something, even if it is only a glass of water." Make the goals realistic, reasonable, and achievable, even if only in the long term, with the help of others and/or through great sacrifice.

- Is your character's current life the one it wants? What outcomes would it see as living 'happily ever after'? What plans does it have to change its life and achieve its goals? What skills/resources does it have and need to achieve those goals? What would it be willing to risk or sacrifice to be successful?
- What internal and external conflicts could keep your character from achieving its purpose? Self-doubt? Guilt? Fear? An addiction? Opposition? A nemesis? Others?
- What are your character's greatest strengths and weaknesses? All characters must have a healthy balance of both to avoid godmodding. Even Superman has his kryptonite weakness. Maybe it has a physical, mental, or emotional disability. They need not be extreme; most strengths and weaknesses are moderate or relative.
- What are your character's flaws? If it has none, that's the definition of a 'Mary Sue' or 'Gary Stu,' which is not something you want to be. Most roleplayers don't like Mary Sues and Gary Stus; they like believable characters that are just as vulnerable, flawed, and imperfect as theirs are.
- Nobody is all good or all bad; we are all a mix of good and bad. To achieve this balance, make a two-sided list with the format 'Perfection... but... flaw,' like this: friendly but manipulative, handsome but uncoordinated, smart but forgetful, courageous but impulsive, loyal but clingy, etc.
- Does your character have a dark side or skeletons in its closet? What is the deepest darkest secret it is afraid others might discover? What would happen if others found out? What does it hate/fear? What is its worst nightmare?
- What are some of your character's happiest/saddest memories? Are any memories so terrible that they have been suppressed? From what traumas or phobias is it escaping, or to what idyllic past would it like to return?
- Can your character form deep personal connections with others? What does it seek in a romantic relationship, and what would its ideal partner be like? Does it separate sex and love? Was/is there a significant someone on or off stage?
- How has your character changed and evolved so far, and how might it change and evolve in the future? The second part of this question might only be answered over time as you get to know your character better. Or will your character be static, never changing, like a stone pillar in a chaotic world?

Mahir: "It's a good idea to write this out and make it as complete as you can, if only to clarify it for yourself. You can then summarize it in your profile, including something about your character's strengths and weaknesses. Be careful not to reveal too much at once; let people discover your character little by little. You should keep a much more complete version for your own use. Then, as you roleplay, look for ways to reveal a little bit more in each scene.

"In addition to Profile Picks, some people also use 'titlers,' also known as character tags, which are hovertexts that offer vital character information and an immediate impression of your character. They can include metainformation such as name, rank or title, and current mood, but also perceivable things such as accent, voice, scent, mannerisms, and appearance like scars, injuries, sickly skin, and so on, which would be apparent to your character but are not built into your avatar. They may even be used to inform other players that your character is in disguise and therefore not easily recognizable. These titlers are actually required in some roleplay regions."

Mamakie: "The better you define your character, the more it will become, in effect, an independent entity with a life of its own, separate from but 'married' to your RL self. As other characters see, hear, and interact with your character, it will have a magical, almost psychosomatic effect on them, and they will have that same effect on your character, making both evolve and develop further in an ongoing, retroactive, cyclical process.

"So, don't think you're just playing with an inanimate, lifeless doll or puppet; you're actually creating a new being—one that has parts of you and yet is not you. Perhaps it would be useful to think of your character as the person you might have been had you been born into the world your character was born into."

Eswaria: /me raises her hand. "When I come inworld, I disappear and become my avi's character. I take on Eswaria's way of thinking, feeling, acting, her strengths and weaknesses, and she almost 'forces my hand' to say and do what she wants to. My RL character has no place here, except as it informs my SL character...

"My RL character is only one facet of my life, and not necessarily the best facet."

"The same happens when I roleplay using an alt with a completely different character. It's like flipping an on/off switch. It almost feels like those different characters live in different parts of my brain and come to the fore as needed. My RL character is only one facet of my life... and not necessarily the best facet," she chuckles self-deprecatingly.

Personal Quirks

Mamakie: "Yes, that's what actors often refer to as 'getting into character.' It makes for much more immersive roleplay. And that brings us to another important aspect of character definition, which is to decide on a set of personal trademarks, such as mannerisms, obsessions, and ways of speaking. Mannerisms are what your body language typically says when you're happy, sad, nervous, doubtful, angry, afraid, excited, or lying.

"You can bite your fingernails or pick your nose, scratch your head or stroke your beard, wipe sweaty palms on your pants or wring your hands, toss your head or grit your teeth, clench your fists or crack your knuckles, jump from one foot to the other or shuffle your feet.

"You can play with the hem of your skirt or put your hands in your pockets, wink with a lop-sided grin or flick birdies, wave by raising your hand and wiggling your fingers, scratch your left ear or chew on the inside of your cheek or lips, push up your glasses or spit on the ground, and so on.

"With regard to obsessions, what kinds of food do you love and hate? What turns you on? What drives you crazy? What is your 'kink'? Are you a clean freak? A slob? Do you tend to correct other people's speech? Do you usually cry after an adrenaline rush? Or do you get the hiccups after something surprises you?

"Are you often drunk or stoned? Do you sometimes hum a tune related to whatever is happening? Do you like to give people funny nicknames? Do you try to make puns or sentences that rhyme? What allergies do you have? Are you a hypochondriac? Do you try to mother everyone around you? Or do you analyze everything in scientific terms?

"As for your speech, will it be eloquent and refined? Crass and unschooled? Will you watch your tongue or pepper your language with obscenities? Do you speak formally with your superiors and more informally with your mates or underlings? You might develop a list of trademark words and phrases, such as exclamations, catchphrases, refrains, sayings, and the like.

"Will you laugh with a giggle, a chuckle, a belly-laugh, a snort, or a sneer? Will you have an accent and pronounce certain words differently? For example, instead of 'I've been waiting for you,' someone from southern USA might say, '*Ah bin waitin' fo' ya.*' But be careful with your accent and don't make it so thick that it's hard to read, especially for non-native English speakers."

Chiptag: "If I might insert something here, you can also speak a foreign language through a translator HUD, even if you're fluent in English. There are also translators that will automatically change regular speech to a different style, such as Baby Babble, Bork Bork, Cockney, Elmer Fudd, Jive, L33t Sp34k, Nerd, Pirate, Redneck, Robotic, Wizard, and many more."

Mahir: "Yes, but as Mamakie said, be very careful about using thick accents. They can be hard to read and don't necessarily add much value to the roleplay, especially if the accent bleeds over from your speech into your narration, and more especially if you're just making up words and accents to sound distinctive. That's known as wolfspeak and is not much appreciated in the roleplay community. It's far better to state your accent in your character tag (e.g., 'Speaks with a French accent') and leave it at that.

"Quirks can make your character unique, but unless they somehow relate to the storyline or your backstory, they are rarely useful. Instead of filling your character with unnecessary quirks, try to find just a few trademark characteristics that highlight aspects important to the plot. For example, every scar or limp has its story, which in some way has made your character who and what it is."

Flat and Round Characters

Arjun: /me raises his hand "My character is usually easy-going, friendly, and courteous, but the other day he lost his patience with a bully and threw a temper tantrum. The other players said I had acted out of character. So my question is, do I always have to act the same way, or can I change my behavior sometimes?"

Mahir: /me chuckles. "Someone I knew wrote in their profile, 'Don't confuse my personality with my attitude. My personality is who I am. My attitude depends on who you are.' Actually, adding nuances to your character is not only allowed but even encouraged.

"It's known as having a 'round' character, while 'flat' characters are two-dimensional, uncomplicated, predictable, and static, never changing. That doesn't mean flat characters aren't interesting, mind you. Sherlock Holmes is fascinating, but he's a 'flat' character in that he never changes his main personality traits of logic, objectivity, and emotional detachment.

"In contrast, a 'round' character is dynamic, evolves and changes, is more complex, may have inner conflicts or contradictions, and can respond to situations in unexpected ways. Ebenezer Scrooge went from flat to round because he became a changed man. This is known as 'character development.' Over time, you may need to revise or extend your character profile because of these changes.

"A 'bad guy' doesn't have to be angry and vicious all the time—that would make him a flat, far less interesting character. He could round out by also being a loving family member, a loyal friend, or a staunch defender of underdogs. He could even surprise his captives by feeding them, tending to their wounds, befriending them, congratulating them on putting up a good fight, and inviting them to join his gang.

"Some differentiate between a character's 'nature' and its 'demeanor.' Your nature is how you really are inside but often hide, while your demeanor is how you act in public, the face or front you show others. We often have very different or even contrasting 'natures' and 'demeanors.' Classical examples are people with low self-esteem who act with exaggerated bravado around others or people with high self-esteem who act humbly toward others.

"If you find your character has gotten into a rut, change it. If it is too shy, cautious, 'normal' or a goody-two-shoes, give it a traumatic experience that pushes it over the edge and makes it more daring, outgoing, or multi-faceted. If it has become too twisted, dark, and violent, give it some life-changing therapy. Character development is vital to keeping roleplay fresh, interesting and exciting."

Mamakie: "Speaking of multi-faceted characters, some RPGs have included 'evil races' such as D&D's orcs and dark elves. Lately, however, this has been heavily questioned because it reflects actual real-life racist attitudes that differentially attribute 'essential natures' to people with certain physical characteristics.

"These RPGs are now being revised to ensure that characters of all races can have a balanced mix of good and bad characteristics. This is much closer to reality since every individual combines a complex combination of positive and negative traits. Please be aware of this issue in designing your character, and avoid defining particular races as completely good or totally evil.[11]

"Be creative and explore other potential facets of your character. That doesn't mean you can get away with being a devil one day and an angel the next—unless you can somehow justify it within the roleplay, like in The Strange Case of Dr. Jekyll and Mr. Hyde, or maybe you've been patient with a difficult situation for so long that you finally snap. You need to be consistent, even if that means having a consistently inconsistent character."

Whatever you do can have IC consequences that your character will have to live with.

Mahir: "You can also play different roles and have a distinct character for each one. For example, Platistotle is the Director of the Ashram, but he is also a Guru and teaches students. In each role, he has a different character: severe and exacting in one, patient and tolerant in the other."

Eswaria: "Can you play the same role with more than one person? I've roleplayed finding my first love and losing my virginity with a few guys. My relationship with each one wasn't cheating like it would be in the real world because they were completely different storylines."

Arjun: /me blinks at Eswaria incredulously, his mouth gaping in astonishment.

Eswaria: /me smirks at Arjun, flutters her eyelids and smiles innocently.

---

[11] See, for example: www.npr.org/sections/live-updates-protests-for-racial-justice/2020/06/29/884824236/dungeons-dragons-tries-to-banish-racist-stereotypes.

Mamakie: /me laughs at the two. "That's known as a multiple-storyline character, which is entirely legitimate. As long as everyone agrees to keep the two storylines separate, no problem. But if one of your lovers decides he wants those lines to cross, then sparks could fly."

–laughter among the group–

Mahir: "Especially if he decides to roleplay the jealous boyfriend. Remember that whatever you do in roleplay can have IC consequences that your character will have to live with."

Designing your Avatar

Mahir: "I hope you've realized by now that the quality of your roleplay is far more important than your avatar's looks. You can even roleplay with no avatar at all through IMs, like in table-top or chat-based games. But in a virtual world, you can also make your avatar reflect your role and character, so why not take full advantage of this and develop a truly distinctive avatar? This can include the kinds of clothes you wear, your body size and shape, your skin color and muscle definition, your makeup and hair... It can even include the stands, walks, and sits you choose to include in your animation overdrive (AO).

"For example, if you're a flirt, you'll want to dress provocatively; if not, your outfit will be more modest—unless, of course, you're roleplaying a naïve young girl who doesn't realize how provocative her skimpy outfit really is. Commissioners might dress with a regal flair, while their lackeys might dress more simply and may even have dirty skin. If you're a warrior, you might want a hardened, severe look with lots of weapons, while a peaceful hunter-gatherer, farmer, or trader might carry the tools of the trade and prefer a gentler, kinder look."

Mamakie: "The advice to start with a general backstory and develop the details as you grow into your character also applies to designing your avatar. Take your time, reflect on your profile, and design your avatar accordingly. Also, think about what props or accessories your character should wear, such as weapons, the tools of your trade, glasses, a cane or pipe, jewelry, and the like.

"Try to convey as much as you can about your character through your avatar's appearance so that people will know as much as possible about you even before you interact with them. For example, a stewardess who narrowly escaped death in a plane crash might have a torn uniform, bruises, cuts, and burns."

Chiptag: "When you're shopping for these things, it's helpful to use the search functions on the SL Marketplace (marketplace.secondlife.com). You can also use a 'What is she wearing' HUD to get lists of others' outfits. A web search for 'SL Outfit blog' will give you other ideas with complete shopping lists.

"Just remember that the more complex or 'heavy' your avatar is, the less likely it will be to rez fully for others, the more lag it will cause, and the more it will affect your Frames Per Second (FPS). So keep your attachments to the bare minimum needed to represent your character as best you can. You can see your complexity by clicking on the last option in the 'Advanced' menu. It's best to keep your complexity under 100.

"Oh, and try to avoid wearing the old 'sculpts' or 'sculpties,' which are laggy. You can see them full of numbers on your avatar by clicking on Developer – Render Metadata – Sculpt. Open the 'Developer' menu with Ctrl-Alt-Q, but use it with caution because you can really mess things up with some of its functions."

Mamakie: "If you want to mix things up a bit, you might even like your physical appearance to contrast with your character to challenge social stereotypes and keep people on their toes. For example, a dashing beauty can be shy and chaste; a strong, angry-looking man can be peaceful and gentle; a humble, simple person can be a village commissioner, and so on."

Mahir: /me thinks for a moment, then waggles his head slowly from side to side. "Yes... that's certainly a possibility. The point is to be creative and imaginative and to make your avatar as unique, distinctive, and memorable as you can."

Mamakie: "I've found that changing my look helps my roleplay. It helps me to really FEEL the situation and empathize with my character by creating an illusion of reality, which sparks my imagination to the point that I just KNOW how to respond. For example, I add teary eyes to my face when I cry. When I see that, my heart goes out to my character, and I can feel her pain as my own. This immerses me more deeply in the scene and makes my roleplay come more alive.

"But don't limit your roleplay to what is in the pixels. Paint your own picture in your mind, then describe it in your posts. If your avatar can't show an emotion or make a movement, don't let that stop you from emoting it. You can write anything into existence, within reason. The only limits are the boundaries of your imagination, so let it fly."

> Changing my looks helps me feel the situation and empathize with my character.

Mahir: "I'd like to finish by quoting Madame Thespian Underhill, the Director of the virtual troupe Artist Repertory Theatre in Second Life. She says that the ability to make our avatars look like anything we want '...levels the playing field when we interact with each other... You're being judged by what you say. By what you say! – the pure essence of who you are.'"[12]

[12] The Drax Files: World Makers [Episode 24: Madame Thespian Underhill]: youtu.be/jkm9mQlejCw.

Arjun Takes the Exam

"Okay, time for your test," Mahir says, handing out a notecard. Arjun opens it and reads the instructions:

> CHARACTER DEFINITION TEST
>
> Part 1: Summarize what you have learned in this class.
>
> Part 2: Complete the following:
>
> a) Summarize your character traits under the Second Life tab of your profile.
>
> b) Summarize your character's backstory in a Pick in your profile.
>
> c) Make sure your avatar design reflects your character as much as possible.
>
> d) Present yourself in character for inspection and emote some of your character's quirks.

Under Part 1, Arjun writes:

> - Write your character's backstory and goals, making them as detailed as you like. Only a summary of it will go into your profile.
> - Define your character's physical appearance, mental models, strengths and weaknesses, personality traits, mannerisms, and way of speaking, making them as unique as you can while related to your backstory and the overall plot.
> - Return to the backstory and explain how your character got that way and how it might change in the future.
> - Don't divulge too much of this in your profile. Instead, find ways to reveal it little by little through interaction with others.
> - Flat characters are predictable, never changing. Round characters are dynamic, evolve, have nuances, and may unexpected things.
> - Your character should not be entirely good or entirely bad but a unique combination of the two.
> - Carefully design your avatar's appearance to reflect its defined character but without making it too complex.

For Part 2 a), Arjun puts the following under the Second Life tab in his profile:

> Arjun is an 18-year-old boy struggling to become a man but not sure he wants to. He is usually happy and carefree but can be shy around strangers and authorities, and rebellious when he feels something is unfair. His mischievous streak often gets him in trouble, but he's sensitive, caring, generous, and a loyal friend. He enjoys cuddles and is quite a flirt but is sexually awkward.

For Part 2 b), Arjun goes to the 'Pick' tab in his profile and adds a Pick titled 'Virtual India.' He leaves the default photo for the time being and writes:

> Arjun was raised in a small rural village. His father was an absentee, and his mother homeschooled him but died when he was 15, leaving him to fend for himself. Since then, he has been wandering from region to region, learning to survive and getting himself into trouble.

Going on to Part 2 c), Arjun takes a long, hard look at himself and decides his outfit is a little too refined for his character. He goes on the SL Marketplace and purchases a dirt layer for his skin, a set of crooked teeth, a grungier loincloth to replace the fine silk he had been wearing, and a tousle of longer, more disheveled hair. Wearing and adjusting them, he gives himself another once over and wobbles his head from side to side in satisfaction.

Once ready for inspection, Arjun waits for the girl ahead of him to finish flirting her way through her exam, then goes up to Mahir and starts roleplaying:

Arjun: /me approaches Mahir, performs the Anjali mudra with a broad smile, then clears his throat and speaks in his soft, youthful voice, "Excuse me, Mentor Mahir, Sir... I... I've finished the test..."

Mahir: /me looks up testily from his work, scowls at the boy, and thunders, "I'll be the one to decide whether you've completed it, young man. Come closer and let me take a good look at you."

Arjun: /me takes a faltering step closer, cringing under Mahir's glare and looking down at his feet, his shoulders slumped, wringing his hands at groin level, and stammers in a barely audible squeak, "Um... I... I hope you're satisfied... with my work, Mr. Mentor... sir."

Mahir: /me looks him over slowly from head to toe, frowning, and growls, "Stand straight and speak up, boy. And for heaven's sake, stop fidgeting. What kind of a man are you, anyway?"

Arjun: /me raises his head slightly and glances nervously up at the mentor, scratching his head with one hand while wiping the sweaty palm of the other on his grungy loincloth, shifting restlessly from one foot to the other, and hesitantly says in a scarcely louder voice, "Um... a *young* man... like you correctly said, Mr. Mentor, sir... I... um... it's just that... I was homeschooled by a single mother in a small rural village and... well... I'm not used to being examined like this... It's... um... making me a little nervous, I guess."

Mahir: /me lets out an annoyed 'humph,' trying to hide his amusement, and continues to inspect the timid youngster, then booms out, in a slightly kinder voice, "Well, I see you've made SOME progress in your self-knowledge... Yes... hmmm... seems like you've been doing a little soul-searching... I see... yes indeed... a LITTLE better... although I dare say it couldn't have gotten much worse either..."

Arjun: /me starts to sweat profusely as the minutes tick by and clamps one hand firmly under his bare, wet armpit while pressing his other hand against his stomach to stop the butterflies from dancing, wobbling his head while trying to smile, and mumbles in an almost pleading voice, "Yes, sir... I mean... I did the best I could, sir... Honest, I did. But... well... if you'd tell me how to improve... I'd... um... be glad to try harder, sir."

Mahir: /me lets out a hearty laugh, unable to contain his mirth, "You did fine, son. Just one thing... Do us all a favor and take a bath, will you? You're sweating like a pig, and you look like you've been wallowing in the mud with one, too."

Arjun: /me waggles his head compliantly, wiping beads of sweat from his face with one hand, which only smears the grime around more, and running the fingers of his other hand through his tousled hair, wincing as they catch on a tight knot. "I'll do that right away, sir. Thank you, sir. Will that be all, sir?"

Mahir: /me writes something in his ledger, closes it with a thump, and relaxes back in his chair with a sigh as he waves the boy away with the back of his hand. "That'll be all, Arjun. See you in the next class."

Arjun backs away respectfully, bowing and pressing his palms together at chest level. Then, grinning with satisfaction at his performance, he turns and scuttles away to where Chris is waiting for him, just as a message pops up on his screen:

> Dharma Guide: Congratulations. You have passed the Character Definition class and advanced to Level 13 - Character. You now have a capacity for up to 20 HP and the option to change your tag to yellow. Please check your Karma Tag for your next quest.

Arjun: /me shouts, "WOOHOO, I can eat more now."

Chris: /me laughs "You'll need it for your next quest, grungy boy"

Munching happily on some fruit to buff up to 20 HP, Arjun saves his new outfit, says his goodbyes, and signs off for the evening, a sense of elation filling his chest.

CHAPTER EIGHT

FIGHTING SAVAGE BEASTS

Status:	Character
Level:	13
HP:	19.8

Arjun gulps painfully, a look of worried shock on his face. "I have to kill a croc and a big cat... in WHAAAT???" After logging into the Landing and meeting up with Chris, Arjun had accepted his next Quest prompt:

> Dharma Guide: You have accepted the quest "Protecting." To complete it, change your Karma Tag to yellow and kill a crocodile and a big cat in melee. Good luck.

Arjun: /me rereads the instructions and frowns "That can't be good... It says 'Good luck' instead of 'Happy hunting' this time."

Chris: /me laughs at the expression on Arjun's face "You read it right, mate. Melee means within arm's reach, which is actually nought to three metres. Anything from three to 96 metres is 'range' in the raycast system Virtual India uses"

Arjun: /me gets a sinking feeling in his stomach. "You mean I have to kill them with my BARE HANDS???"

Chris: /me chuckles "Well, you COULD melee with only kicks and punches, but a melee weapon will do twice as much damage per hit, so I suggest we visit the Weaponsmith's shop again. We can hike over to the Eastern River and take a boat from there"

Arjun: /me shudders as he turns silently eastward to start the trek. After a while, he turns to Chris, worry on his face. "So... that means hand-to-hand combat with not one but TWO bloodthirsty beasts? I almost got killed when that tiger attacked us... Not sure I want to go through THAT again."

Kiting Crocs

Arjun holds his tongue as they paddle downriver, but Chris sees him biting his nails and shuddering involuntarily from time to time. He still says nothing as they dock the canoe, climb out, and walk slowly back to the Castle. Arjun's silence is partly due to his worry about the quest but also because it's hard to steer and type at the same time, especially at sim crossings where lag makes them do crazy things. He IMs Chris about it:

> Arjun: "Sorry, I was concentrating on navigating, so couldn't type anything. What do you do when you have to steer a vehicle and post at the same time?"
>
> Chris: "When the setting for a scene is a boat, a car or a plane with complicated controls that you're in charge of handling, you can simply excuse yourself from posting during the travel, maybe with an initial post saying that you turn all your attention to driving or navigating and ignore those around you...
>
> "That isn't the best solution, of course. Another approach could be to park the vehicle and roleplay traveling in it without actually having to drive it, and then teleport OOC to wherever you were supposed to be going. After all, the vehicle is only a prop to inspire roleplay, so don't let it interfere with your participation in the scene. You can still post about handling the controls, seeing how the scenery changes, and so on."
>
> Arjun: "Great tips. Thanks."

Arriving back at the weaponsmith's shop, Arjun stands facing the row of melee weapons and tries to imagine himself fighting crocodiles and tigers in hand-to-hand combat with each weapon. Just as he is wondering whether to go with the long scimitar or an enormous axe, Chris IMs him that in Virtual India, regardless of what the pixels looked like, all melee weapons do the same amount of damage from the same distance. Arjun finally decides on a large hunting knife, rezzes the required gold coin onto the vendor, and slips the blade into his belt.

Chris: /me looks Arjun over and chuckles "You look like you've borrowed your father's knife"

Arjun: /me frowns and looks down at his feet. "I... um... I never... met my father, so... I wouldn't know..." then sighs and looks up. "But something tells me I'll be meeting him soon enough in the next world."

Chris: /me gulps, mortified. "Oh... sorry, mate... I... I didn't know..." then grins and aims a punch at Arjun's shoulder to cheer him up "Well, let's just say it looks like Indiana Jones' knife then... exactly what you need for your little romp with the beasties"

Arjun: /me staggers a little at the punch and looks down at his new knife, patting it proudly, then grins up sheepishly at Chris. "Yeah, that's right. It's my Indiana Jones knife. Watch out, beasties... here I come."

Chris: /me says with a classic Jones' growl, "You wanna talk to God? Let's go see him together. I've got nothing better to do"

Arjun: /me frowns, growling, "Die? Maybe..." –then shakes his head and sets his jaw– "...but not today."

Chris: /me gasps again, wringing his hands, and squeals "What're you gonna do, Jones?"

Arjun: /me turns to leave, sighing in resignation, "I don't know..." –then looks back and mumbles– "I'm making this up as I go."

The two friends succumb to fits of laughter as they clap each other on the back and run out of the shop, their arms around each other's shoulders, to continue the quest. They dash back to the canoe, take the Southern River to the swamp, then run southward to the beach.

Arjun: /me looks out over the swamp through the drizzle to where the crocodiles are resting on the little island with the tumble-down shack, eying the beasts nervously. "Um... Chris... you wanna give me a little demonstration first?"

Chris: /me unsheathes his knife nonchalantly "Sure, mate. Just stay right here and watch a pro in action"

Chris slowly approaches the group of crocodiles until he aggroes the nearest one. It turns to lumber after him, snapping its vicious jaws. Arjun gasps as he sees Chris wait until the beast is barely within two meters of him before turning and *walking* ahead of it toward the beach. Perplexed, Arjun mumbles to himself, "Why has he turned his back on it? Wasn't he going to fight it?" But then he sees that the crocodile is rapidly losing health, and soon it disintegrates into several chunks of meat on the beach.

Chris goes to collect the meat, and Arjun runs up to ask how he did it. Chris patiently explains the concept of pulling and kiting. He has let the croc get close enough to hit it in melee and then has held the down arrow (or S key in Arjun's case) while clicking on it in mouselook. That made his avatar seem to turn its back on the creature when he was actually facing it in mouselook and walking backward, just close and long enough to kill it. Chris repeats the process as Arjun watches until he grasps the idea.

"Don't forget to change your tag first," Chris reminds him. "You can't kill savage beasts as a green." Arjun clicks on his Karma Tag and sees a new option labeled 'Color.' He clicks it and sees a menu saying 'Green,' 'Yellow,' and 'Cancel' as a message scrolls out in Local Chat summarizing the features of each tag color. He reluctantly makes the change, and his tag turns to a bright yellow color.

Taking a deep breath, Arjun wipes the raindrops from his face with his palms, draws his knife, and steps hesitantly toward the crocodiles. The nearest one breaks away from the group. Arjun nervously waits for it to come close, but gets flustered and presses D instead of S, making him sidestep the croc. The beast swats him with its long tail, taking 2 HP, while Arjun rains ineffectual blows on its back.

In the time it takes Arjun to realize what he has done and switch to the S key, the crocodile has gnashed him with its teeth, taking another 2 HP. Now Arjun starts kiting it and shooting, still without doing any damage AND without realizing that he is backing straight into the cluster of crocodiles, which start swarming toward him.

From the corner of his eye, Arjun sees Chris leap into the swamp, gun drawn. He is taunting the beasts to aggro them toward him and pulling them away from Arjun. Chris leaps nimbly around them with 'prim jumping' in 'always run' mode, staying just out of reach of the gnashing jaws as he downs them one by one, including the one that Arjun had aggroed and but hadn't been able to kill. "Quick, help me collect the meat before more crocs rez," Chris calls out to Arjun, who is just standing there, trembling from head to toe.

"It's under the water," Arjun calls back. "I can't see it."

"Shift-Ctrl-Alt-7," Chris shouts as he scrambles to collect as much meat as he can. Arjun quickly presses that combination, and the water disappears, leaving the meat in plain sight. They collect almost all of it before the crocodiles start to rez again, and the two boys high-tail it back to the beach out of aggro range.

"Well, if at first, you fricassee, fry, fry a hen," Chris cackles after Arjun regains his HP and explains what went wrong. "I'd wager you won't make THAT mistake again. And besides, we got a LOT of meat from it. Just 'keep calm and carry on,'" he chuckles.

"I was hacking away at the croc, but its health wasn't going down," Arjun complains. "What was I doing wrong?"

"Weren't you aiming at its hitbox?" Chris asks. When Arjun admits he doesn't know what a hitbox is, Chris shows him how to activate them by opening the Developer menu – Metadata – Avatar Hitboxes. Following his instructions, Arjun sees a box appear around Chris's avatar and cubical ones at each crocodile's snout. "If you don't aim at their hitboxes," Chris explains, "you're just hacking away at inert pixels."

"NOW you tell me," Arjun humphs.

"Hey, I keep forgetting how much of a NOOB you are," Chris chuckles, giving him a friendly poke in the stomach.

With a feigned smirk and a friendly punch on Chris's arm, Arjun sighs resignedly, "Okay, here goes nothing..." He squares his shoulders, wipes back his rain-drenched hair, then takes a deep breath and approaches the crocodiles again, step by hesitant step. This time when a croc comes close, he presses the S key while aiming at its hitbox, downs his prey quickly, and collects the meat, then runs back proudly to be congratulated by Chris.

They spend the rest of the morning killing crocs and collecting meat until Arjun feels completely comfortable with his new skill.

Tiger Tango

"Ready for the next challenge?" Chris asks as they finally stop to rest and have a quick lunch to buff up their HP. Arjun bobbles his head in the affirmative, not without some trepidation. "Alright," Chris says, "but this time, you'll need to use everything you've learned so far to avoid getting bitten. The tiger won't follow you in a straight line, and he's faster than the crocs, so just running backward will not work. It will pounce at you quickly one way then the other, so besides staying in 'always run' mode, you'll need to use all four WASD keys and prim-jump when necessary. Stay within melee distance as much as you can, but don't sweat it if you lose contact and it regains health. Just keep at it until it falls."

"Or until I fall," Arjun shudders. "I've never fought in melee like that before."

"Oh, right, I keep forgetting you're a total noob," Chris chuckles. "Okay, let's practice here on the beach first so you can get used to the WASD keys." He makes Arjun practice running in tight circles, clockwise with WDSA and counter-clockwise with WASD, until he is doing it smoothly. Then they spar in melee for a while, with no weapons to minimize the damage. Chris hits Arjun easily the first few times, dodging and circling behind him with ease until Arjun gets the hang of it and starts dodging and landing his own blows.

"Good job, mate," Chris cheers. "You learn fast. I think you're ready for that tiger now." They re-buff from the sparring hits, then run eastward along the beach to where the tiger first attacked them. "Remember, the tiger will take 2 HP from you with each hit, but it only has 5 HP, so five good hits in a row, and it's down."

Arjun: /me does a quick mental calculation and grumbles, "So ten hits on me versus five on the tiger? That's only a two-to-one ratio."

Chris: /me shakes his head, smirking "Actually, mate, it's less than that 'cause once you drop below 5 HP, you're downed. Plus, it can recover HP quickly if you let it, but you can't"

Sighing, Arjun draws his hunting knife and steps into the clearing. Ignoring the chickens squawking and flapping around him, he scans the forest warily for any signs of the tiger. Sure enough, after a few minutes, the beast emerges with a terrible roar and charges straight at him.

With a sinking feeling in his stomach, Arjun sees that the hitbox is on its hindquarters. He sidesteps with D, slashing one HP from the beast, and it turns with a snarl to lunge at him again. This time, it mauls two HP from Arjun before he can think to dodge, but Arjun hits it again, taking it down to three before kiting himself free. The next time the beast jumps at him for another two HP, Arjun misses his aim while prim jumping against it and goes flying ten meters into the air. Confused, the tiger just stands there looking around as Arjun, still holding down the W key, lands several meters away from it. He turns to see that the cat's HP has buffed back up to four.

"This is gonna be tough," Arjun mumbles to himself through gritted teeth as he prepares for the next attack. He hadn't remembered it being so huge and so *fast.*

"Try to stay behind it," Chris calls out, just as the tiger charges Arjun again with another hair-raising roar.

Arjun sidesteps it again, landing another blow, but this time he starts dodging back and forth with the A and D keys to circle behind the cat as it turns this way and that, trying to face him. From time to time, Arjun taps his S or W key to stay just out of its reach but within melee distance. Hacking its HP down another notch, he realizes that although the beast can attack him, it can't back up or dodge. All Arjun has to do is stay behind it and keep it from touching him, and he will be fine… at least, that's what he hopes.

The two furious fighters dance a frenetic tango around each other, the tiger snarling and trying to turn on its foe and Arjun kiting and circling to stay behind it. Finally, when Arjun has less than 8 HP left, and the tiger is down to 1 HP, the beast manages to face him and charges. Arjun prim jumps against the tiger as it clips another 2 HP from him, but this time he stops running by releasing the W key, turns in mid-air, and manages to land two meters behind the beast, dealing the fatal blow with a resounding THWAP and watching it fall to pieces at his feet.

Standing over his prey, face and fists raised skyward, Arjun lets out an ecstatic victory cry as Chris runs up to hug him, cheering wildly and dancing around him. Soon the hard-earned message appears in Local Chat, celebrating his achievement:

> Dharma Guide: Congratulations. You have successfully learned to kill savage beasts and advanced to Level 14 – Protector. You have also earned an invitation to the Advanced Emoting class. Please check your Karma Tag for your next quest.

"Wow, that was CLOSE," Arjun exclaims as he looks at his yellow Karma Tag, which now reads:

Status:	Protector
Level:	14
HP:	5.8

A Surprise Attack

Suddenly, Arjun startles out of his self-congratulation as a shot rings out. He turns to see what Chris is shooting at but feels his legs give way under him and collapses to the ground. Three red-tagged warriors are stepping out of the forest and firing at Chris, who is just drawing his gun and only manages to fire two ineffectual shots before he also falls next to Arjun. The warriors wear baggy trousers of brightly colored silk, tucked into black leather boots, and open black vests over bare, hairy chests.

"Well, well, WELL," booms a tall, black-bearded warrior as he kicks the boys' weapons out of reach. "What have we here? Why, it's two yellowbellies, Akbar."

"They killed our poor little kitty-cat, Farid Khan," snivels a shorter, chubby man with a short goatee as he bends down to handcuff the boys' wrists in front, then turns to the third warrior, a wicked grin spreading across his pudgy face. "Whatcha think we should do with them, Rajendra?"

"Mayhap we should tie 'em up 'ere an' call da tiger back ta play wid 'em fer a while," growls a bald, muscle-bound giant with a black patch over his left eye, yanking their heads back by their hair to get a better look at them and ripping off Chris's shirt. "Tho' it'd be a cryin' shame ta spoil such perty boy meat."

Chris: /me writhes on the ground, groaning in pain, and snarls "Leave us alone, damned Raiders. I was just helping my friend Arjun finish his Protector Quest"

Farid Khan: /me sneers, bending down to fasten a chain to the boys' handcuffs and drag them to their feet. "That means you probly just finished the Hunting Quest and have lots of fresh meat in your baskets, huh?"

Akbar: /me cries out in a high-pitched voice, "No wonder there was no game left in the region, boss." He thrusts his hands into the boys' brimming collecting baskets and starts emptying them. "So THAT's why I couldn't fill my cooking quota for today."

Rajendra: /me weighs their coin purses with an enormous paw and pulls a gold coin from each, growling, "Help ya-selves to theys purses, fellas. I say we pleasure us-selves wid 'em 'til they BEG us ta take da rest o' theys cash."

Virtual India Coin Purse: Rajendra Chola has stolen 1 gold from your coin purse.

Virtual India Coin Purse: Farid Khan has stolen 1 gold from your coin purse.

Virtual India Coin Purse: Akbar Moghal has stolen 1 gold from your coin purse.

Arjun: /me moans, staggering to keep his balance as his head spins. "You sick bastards. You leave my buddy Chris out of this. I'm the one who killed your tiger. He was just mentoring me."

-A tall leashing pole appears next to them out of thin air.-

Farid Khan: /me fastens the boys' chains to the top of the pole, heaving the boys up to dangle from it helplessly, their arms stretched painfully upward, and booms out, "OH-ho-HO. Hear THAT, men? He wants us all to himself."

The three warriors strip off Chris's jeans and Arjun's loincloth, jeering and taunting them as they lasciviously eye and fondle their youthful flesh, licking their sneering lips hungrily. Chris spits vituperations as Arjun whimpers and cries out. The two boys writhe this way and that, trying to evade the men's groping hands.

Arjun: /me musters his waning strength and cries out, "HELP! PLEASE, SOMEBODY, HELP US!!!"

Chandra: Are you boys alright, or would you like to be rescued?

Chris: Sure, a rescue RP would be fine

Samudra: We don't want to interfere if you're okay with where the roleplay is going.

Arjun: Yes, please save us from these bullies.

Just then, two guards step into the clearing, rifles drawn. "What's going on here?" they demand with the authority of their rank. "Are you Raiders at it again???"

Startled, the three warriors raise their hands high and start backing away, feigning smiles, aware that the guards have far more HP and damage power than they do.

"We were just having a little fun, is all," says Farid Khan.

"No harm done, honorable guards," whines Akbar.

"Yeah, akchuly, we wuz jest leavin', officers," growls Rajendra, as they turn to high-tail it back to Sundarbans Castle.

Chris: /me calls mockingly after them "That's right, run back to your mummies, coward bullies"

Farid Khan: /me calls back over his shoulder, "We've got you pegged, yellowbellies. You'll be hearing from us again soon."

Farid Khan: Thanks for the RP, guys :)

Chris: NP fellas. It was fun, wasn't it, Arjun? :D

Arjun: Um... sure... if you say so

Rajendra: Hehehe, sorry if we were a little too rough on you :P

Arjun: That's okay - I still have a lot to learn about roleplay

The guards, who introduce themselves as Chandra of Betla and Samudra of Simlipal, carefully unchain Chris and Arjun. The boys slump to the ground in a daze from the loss of blood and emotional shock. The guards proceed to untie the boys' wrists and tend to their injuries as best they can.

Chris: /me grimaces as Chandra tends his wounds "Thanks for rescuing us from those damned Raiders. Good thing you got here when you did—who knows what they might have done next"

Chandra: /me applies pressure to staunch an open wound in Chris's side, "You boys had a close scrape, but that's what the Raiders do. Being the closest to their castle, Simlipal is attacked at least once a week, and they're not too picky about gender, either."

Samudra: /me gently spreads some antiseptic ointment on Arjun's gash and binds it with gauze. "I see you've just recently joined the people of the yellow karma, son. If you plan to stay on that path, I suggest you get used to keeping one eye out for ruffians at all times."

Arjun: /me winces and gasps through gritted teeth as Samudra's disinfectant burns. "No THANK you. When I accepted the savage BEAST quest, I never thought it would include savage HUMANS."

Arjun changes his Karma Tag color back to green.

Chris: /me chuckles, then shakes his head in remorse "I was careless... should have been on the lookout, but I was so thrilled watching Arjun kill his first tiger that I forgot"

With a bobble of the head and a smart salute, the guards take their leave and march back toward the Simlipal Bridge, and Arjun IMs Chris:

> Arjun: "I was wondering... Wasn't it powerplay when the Raiders posted tearing your shirt off, dragging us to our feet, hanging us from the pole, and fondling our bodies?"
>
> Chris: "Well, once you've been downed, your captor does have a certain amount of power over you—within reason, of course. If they had ordered me to take my shirt off or get on the pole, I could have refused, and they couldn't have simply written that I obeyed—that WOULD have been powerplay. But yes, they CAN narrate doing things forcibly to *you once you're their captive...*
>
> "What they CAN'T do is say whether you shout in anger, tremble in fear, or become sexually aroused at what they do. Each of us gets to choose our own actions and reactions. One acts, and the other reacts. Only you can control your character's response to what they do—that is, unless you've explicitly given them the power to control your behaviour beforehand, like in roleplay with jabs or hypnosis, but even that has its limits."

Once you're downed, your captor has a certain amount of power over you—within reason, of course.

> Eswaria: "Mind if I join you guys?"
>
> Chris: "No problem, Eswa, we just finished a roleplay scene"

Roleplay Limits

Eswaria: /me strolls into the clearing, waving and smiling at the guards as they pass, then sees her friends lying naked and injured on the ground and runs up to them, gasping. "Gods! What happened to you two? Are you boys alright?"

Arjun: /me startles to see Eswa approaching and quickly reaches for his loincloth to slip it on, blushing deeply and stammering "Eswa... What... what are YOU doing here?"

Chris: /me looks up at Eswa and tries to sit as his attempt to smile turns into a painful grimace "Hey girl. We just had a little... erm... run-in with some Raider bullies"

Eswaria: /me smirks, seeing Arjun's embarrassment "Don't worry, Arjun. You don't have anything I haven't seen before... in fact, not even as *much* as I've seen before." She sits behind Chris to hold his head in her lap and reaches down to stroke his bangs away from his forehead with her fingertips, comforting him and murmuring, "Don't try to sit up, Chris... just relax and rest... Do you need anything? Food, maybe?"

Arjun: /me scowls at Eswa's slight to his manhood, her tender loving care of Chris, and the latter's apparent lack of concern for his open nakedness. He hangs his head and picks at the grass with unsteady fingers, grumbling, "They downed us, chained us to a pole, and stole all our food and most of our money."

Chris: /me relaxes his head onto Eswa's lap and gazes up at her as she strokes his hair "They stripped us and were about rape us when those guards showed up" ((and neither of us has anything against rape in our RP limits)) "If you have any extra food, we sure could use some"

Eswaria: /me lowers her hand to caress Chris's cheek gently, murmuring, "You poor dears," then reaches into her basket with the other hand to pull out two stews for each of her friends. "Here, eat this to get your strength back." ((Is that because you're okay with rape, or did you just forget to include it in your RP limits?))

Virtual India Collecting Basket: Eswaria has given you 1 fishstew.

Virtual India Collecting Basket: Eswaria has given you 1 meatstew.

Arjun eats the stew and opens a group IM with Chris and Eswaria to avoid long OOC messages in Local Chat:

Arjun: "Pardon my ignorance, but what are RP limits?"

Chris: "If there's anything that you find upsetting or repulsive, or that makes you really feel uncomfortable IRL, you should put it in a 'Roleplay Limits' Pick in your profile, especially for capture and erotic RP situations, since some people don't like violence and others are opposed to certain forms of sex."

Eswaria: "Once a roleplay starts, it's no fun to receive IMs saying you've overstepped someone's bounds, so it's better to add a 'Roleplay Limits' Pick to let people know beforehand. Some 'meanies' will take the lack of that Pick as implicit consent for whatever they want to do to you. Consent is the opposite of limits."

Arjun: "What kinds of limits do people usually have?"

Chris: "I have read other people's limits to get an idea of what to include, and they often say things like no violent or deviant sexual acts, no potty play, no torture, no injections, nothing permanent, capture without RP no longer than 15 minutes, release after capture to be done safely, other RP to be discussed and agreed upon, and so on. Some add 'no childplay' but since that's already in the Terms of Service, it's not really necessary to restate it. The Pick should be as short and simple as possible if you expect people to read it."

Eswaria: "The reasons for a limit can range from simple preferences to moral qualms to previous traumatic experiences IRL. For example, an RL rape victim would most likely want to avoid RP situations that might evoke the same feelings. Not respecting RP limits could trigger painful memories they're trying to forget and even unravel years of therapy...

"What you can't do is use your RP limits to avoid the IC consequences of IC actions. For example, if you're a warrior, you obviously can't have 'No form of violence against my avi' in your limits. IC actions have IC consequences. People who don't like violence should keep their tag green or choose a more vanilla region to roleplay in. Of course, the stricter your RP limits are, the less likely it is that some people will want to roleplay with you."

> You can't use your RP limits to avoid the IC consequences of IC actions.

Arjun: "Interesting... Do people actually read and respect RP limits?"

Chris: "Unfortunately, many people won't look at your RP limits before roleplaying with you, so you need to let them know in IMs as needed. But once you do, if they don't respect your limits, they can't expect you to continue roleplaying with them, and you will have every right to excuse yourself from the roleplay.

"Also, it's bad style to do something to others that's against your own limits—that's just common sense and good etiquette. One of the Raiders had "no rape" in his limits but roleplayed raping others, so I just put 'Nothing beyond your own limits' in my Pick to emphasize this."

Eswaria: "You can't foresee every possible situation, so feel free to open a friendly IM at any time and let people know if you don't feel comfortable with the direction a scene is going in. If you receive such a request, you should respect it and be flexible and accepting of people's different preferences. Remember that your IC enemies can and should be your OOC friends, so keep it nice."

Arjun: "I'm looking at your RP limits, and I see Eswa just has a list of likes and dislikes. Is that the same thing?"

Eswaria: "Yes. Instead of a dreary list of 'not this' and 'not that,' many of us feel it's more positive and creative to list your preferences—what turns you on and off. I have one list of 'likes' and 'dislikes' for capture RP and another for erotic RP. That's especially important if you wear the yellow or red tag."

Arjun: "This was my first capture, and it was pretty upsetting, so I think I'll just stay green for a while until I can process this experience and see how I feel about it."

Chris: "Luckily, your next quests will be much tamer than the last two."

Arjun accepts his next quest and reads:

Dharma Guide: You have accepted the quest "Advanced Emoting." To complete it, take the Advanced Emoting Class at the Gangotri Arts Centre on Friday at 2:00 pm SLT. You will be tested, so pay attention. Good luck.

Feeling the exhaustion of a long, grueling day, Arjun quickly writes out his report for Chris, says goodnight to him and Eswaria, and turns his weary mind to his atman, who promptly logs him out for a well-deserved rest.

Part II:

Arjun Digs Deeper

CHAPTER NINE

ADVANCED EMOTING CLASS

Arjun deeply breathes in the cool, fragrant breeze blowing through the Art Center's fluted Doric colonnade and smiles. The white marble Parthenon-like building faces the central square, its green-tiled gable roof finished at each end with triangular pediments sporting carved stone figures representing the different arts. Arjun knows it is used for art exhibits, poetry readings, streamed live music, choreographed dances, and even dramatic theater productions. Now it is empty, save for a few easels sporting event posters among the large potted plants, and a circle of chairs in the center for the class.

Chris and Arjun had spent the morning foraging, fishing, and hunting. While looking for mountain goats at Hemis, they had seen a snow leopard sunning itself on a rock, which Chris had been able to get with his rifle without aggroing it. By the time they had headed for the bonus Trading Kiosk—at Papikonda this time—they had recovered far more supplies than the Raiders had stolen, and Arjun was feeling better about his hunting abilities and life in general.

After lunch, Arjun had canoed up the Eastern River to Gangotri Village. On his way, he had stopped to rest among the graceful white petals of the Lotus Temple and enjoy the choral music. There he had jotted down some of the inspiring words as he heard them. Now, relaxing in the austere elegance of the Art Center, he opens his notes to read them again, reflecting on how closely they describe how he sees his world:

The world is but a show, vain and empty,
A mere nothing, bearing the semblance of reality.
The world is like the vapor in a desert,
Which the thirsty dreameth to be water
And striveth after it with all his might,
Until when he cometh unto it,
He findeth it to be mere illusion...
Know that the Kingdom is the real world,
and this nether place its shadow stretching out.

A shadow hath no life of its own.
It is mere fantasy, nothing more,
like images reflected on the water,
seeming as pictures to the eye.

Mahir: /me clears his throat to call the class to order and stands. "It looks like everyone is here, so let's start. I would like to introduce Janus, the Director of the Gangotri Arts Centre, whom I believe some of you have already met. He has kindly allowed us to hold this class here and has offered to say a few words first."

Mahir gestures for Janus to take the floor and returns to his seat. The Director, an elderly man with receding silver hair and a kindly, age-worn face, is wearing a western-style black suit.

Roleplay as an Art Form

Janus: /me stands and nods respectfully to Mahir, then to the class. "Thank you, Mentor Mahir, and welcome, dear students. The Gangotri Arts Centre is pleased to host this Advanced Emoting Class because it promotes two principles we uphold: that roleplay is an art form and should be cultivated as such, and that we should strive for excellence in all we do. Thanks to Mahir and Mamakie for promoting these two principles in their mentoring work.

Roleplay in virtual worlds is a new art form on a par with—and encompassing—the other seven arts.

"The word 'play' in 'roleplay' has led many to believe it is 'just a game.' By that logic, it would also be 'just a game' when musicians 'play' their instruments, when a theatre company spends weeks and months preparing to stage a 'play,' or when an athlete undergoes years of hard training to 'play' a good 'game.' In other languages, 'roleplay' translates as something more akin to acting a part, as in a theater performance: *desempeñar un papel* in Spanish, *svolgere un ruolo* in Italian, and so forth.

"I am among those who believe that roleplay in virtual worlds can and should be recognized as a new art form in its own right, on a par with—and even encompassing—the other seven arts described by Ricciotto Canudo. It's set on the stage of a roleplay region, of course, but includes the plastic arts in its use of 3D modeling; the graphic arts in photography, 'textures' and more; style and fashion design in the outfits; architectural arts in the interior, exterior, and landscaping design; auditory arts to create immersive soundscapes using music, natural sounds and others; and even choreography in the animations and poses that move our avatars. In a virtual world such as Second Life, all these elements are created by the users themselves.

"To all this background, we as roleplayers add the literary element through the narrative and dialog we post, plus an improvisational dramatic or theatrical aspect as we move and interact like actors in an ongoing improvisational play. All these art forms come together in an *opus magnum* involving thousands of artists from all around the globe, ranging from professionals to wannabees—ourselves included—in an immersive, collaborative *mise-en-scène* that evolves in real time before our eyes. In his contribution to the campaign "What Second Life Means to Me," virtual worlds polymath Loki Elliot said:

> 'I... studied art, then left college conflicted. I wanted to do it all, not have to specialize... When I stumbled upon the Second Life platform, I didn't realize it straight away, but here was a place where all my creative interests—illustration, story-telling, gaming, 3D modeling, music—it all merged together, and with an audience to boot!'[13]

"Some question whether virtual art is real, to which Croatian artist Eshi Otawara answers, 'It's not a non-existing universe. It's there. It exists. If you just free yourself from that prejudice toward what's virtual—that it's not real—it will make you happy... Virtual artwork, just like physical artwork, stimulates the brain, so how much more *real* does it have to be?'[14] Zander Greene, a co-organizer of Fantasy Faire, adds, 'The medium isn't what makes it real; the experience it creates within me is what makes it real.'[15] And Second Life film-maker and documenter Draxtor Despres says:

> 'Second Life to me is, simply put, like walking into the creative minds of other people... Many people assume that Second Life is a videogame and that the avatars are non-player characters, but they're not. They are digital extensions of the people who inhabit this world... Second Life... is proof that if you learn how to derive happiness from expressing yourself creatively, you will be happier in the long run, and that obviously reverberates back into the so-called 'real world.' Second Life empowers people who have never been told, 'Hey, you're a great artist, keep on going.' People like that can now be at the table... The only thing that matters is what you contribute to this community, and that's a beautiful thing.'[16]

"Granted, much of our art is impermanent, blown away by the winds of time like the brightly-colored sand mandalas fashioned by Tibetan Buddhist monks. It will only be experienced by its creators, and there's nothing wrong with that. The greatest value of art resides in the process of creating and performing it, not in a finished product put on display. Nevertheless, our art has also transcended the virtual world and been made available to the broader public in more permanent forms such as machinima[17] and the LitRPG or RPG GameLit genres.

---

[13] Draxtor presents: Loki Eliot "What Second Life Means To Me:" youtu.be/TEiYrfROm2g.
[14] The Drax Files: World Makers [Episode 3: Eshi Otawara]: youtu.be/hNtup7U6A24.
[15] The Drax Files: World Makers [Episode 4: Fantasy Faire/RFL]: youtu.be/yjzG9g8PNFs.
[16] What Second Life means to me - Draxtor Despres: youtu.be/0QcFhbAwMVc.
[17] See a documentary on machinima at youtube.com/watch?v=JWx1KVG7hAo.

"We hope you will seek excellence in this art form—an excellence defined not as a final destination to which you can eventually arrive but as a process of continual improvement and ongoing perfecting of your craft. You have the backing of some of the most cutting-edge technologies this world has to offer and the support of many dedicated leaders in this and other regions. We look forward to hearing that you are taking full advantage of these resources as you move forward in your studies and efforts. So again, welcome, and thank you."

Mahir: "Thank you, Director Janus. I must say that I have seen three types of roleplayers. Some just fool around, pick fights, and make sleazy sexual remarks. Others treat the region as a social media, discuss RL in Local Chat, and show little interest in roleplaying. The third type is serious about roleplaying, developing their characters and storylines, and making their roleplay as rich, realistic, and satisfying as possible. We hope you will all decide to belong to the third type."

Mahir stops to gaze at each of the students in turn. They look away and glance at each other nervously, no-one wanting to be put in the first or second group. Meanwhile, Mamakie frowns at Mahir disapprovingly but holds her tongue.

Layers of Complexity

Mahir: /me clears his throat. "Okay, then. This Advanced Emoting Class is about enriching your posts to make them more interesting for you and the other players. Nobody has to be a literary genius to roleplay—all you need is an eagerness to learn and do the best you can. We all started as beginners, and most roleplay community members are committed to helping each other improve.

> You don't have to be a literary genius to roleplay, just an eagerness to learn and do the best you can.

"To do this, use your imagination and try to immerse yourself in the scene as if you were there physically. When someone does something with or to your character, stop and think, 'How would I (or my character) experience and respond to this if it happened in real life?'

"As you write your post, think about how to emote and speak in a way that will not only show your own reaction but also elicit a response in your roleplay partners. It's good form to acknowledge their posts first by saying something about them before adding your own actions and dialog. To give you a very simple example, watch how each of the following posts takes an essential part of the previous post and then builds on it to move the action forward:

Mahir: /me looks at her and winks.

Mamakie: /me sees him winking at her and blushes.

Mahir: /me notices her cheeks turning red and grins.

"What about the complexity of your posts? Seek a good balance between too much and too little, between boring your roleplay partners to tears and leaving them wondering what is going on, between filling your posts with fluff and saying just enough to deepen your character and move the story forward.

"It's common to describe roleplayers as having different literacy levels, often categorized as illiterate, semi-literate, literate, and advanced or super-literate. For reasons that I'll explain in a moment, we don't use this system in Virtual India, but I'll tell you what each one means so you'll know when you hear them.

"Illiterate: Most often found among beginners, these players write one-liners—single sentences or phrases—usually limited to dialog (chat boxing) with few actions and fewer descriptions, and frequent chain-posting. They use limited vocabulary, poor spelling and grammar, write with no capitals or quotation marks, and use netspeak, emoticons, and canned gestures. They mix IC and OOC and don't separate their RL identities from their characters', often resulting in Mary Sues, Gary Stus, and drama. They rarely develop storylines and tend to metagame, powerplay, and godmod unwittingly.

"Semiliterate: Often seen among roleplay students, these tend to be semi-paragraph (semi-para) players. They write two or three sentences, combining dialog with action and some description, and have started to think of characters and storylines. They have better vocabulary and spelling/grammar, and avoid using netspeak, emoticons, and canned gestures. They tend to use a scriptwriting style with dashes, asterisks and other means to distinguish dialog from narrative.

"Literate: Seen among the more experienced players, these are usually para-RPrs with posts of at least four to five sentences and often more, who tend to write in third-person present, add much richer descriptions to their posts, and take character and storyline development seriously. Their writing style reads more like a novel, with richly nuanced vocabulary, complex grammatical structures, correct spelling, and complete punctuation, and many edit their posts before sending, although a few may tend to post fluff or purple prose.

"Advanced or super-literate: These players write posts like pages from a well-written novel and usually use multi-para RP, also known as novella RP—several paragraphs long. This category is associated with professional-level writers and tends to cluster into groups of like-minded roleplayers.

"BUT… this talk of roleplay levels has given way to heated arguments and hurt feelings. The golden rule of roleplay is to have fun, no matter how advanced we are in our writing and roleplaying abilities. It's no fun to be stigmatized as illiterate, to suffer backlashes to your 'literate' roleplay, or to be criticized for struggling with English, whether it's your native language or a foreign tongue.

"Some folks argue that these levels describe posts and not people. Your *post* may be semiliterate, but that doesn't mean *you* are semiliterate. However, once we start categorizing posts, it's far too easy to slip from there into categorizing those who tend to produce each kind of post. So that excuse does not really solve the basic issue: that pigeon-holing does not encourage people to grow.

"So here at Virtual India, instead of categorizing players or posts, we prefer to help everyone to learn and grow as roleplayers. All it takes is the right guidance, a real desire to learn and make an effort, and the discipline to stick to it.

"Anyone can learn to avoid netspeak, emoticons, canned gestures, metagaming, powerplaying, and godmodding. Anyone can improve their vocabulary, spelling, grammar, character definition, and story-telling. Anyone can learn simple ways to distinguish dialog from narrative and then start writing with full punctuation. Anyone can increase their ability to add richer descriptions to their posts.

"Personally, I would rather see a great story with short, simple posts than a boring plot with long, elaborate posts. You don't have to use big fancy words and complex grammar to get your point across and move the roleplay along. In fact, a maxim for good writing is, 'Don't just write to be understood; write so you cannot possibly be misunderstood.'

"But unfortunately, much of what people call 'literate' roleplay is hard to understand, even for those who would call themselves as such. And much of what people call literate roleplay is actually full of 'post stuffing,' 'fluffing,' or 'purple prose.'

"In addition, regardless of their skill level, some people simply prefer longer or shorter posts—so slower or faster roleplay. Instead of literacy skill levels, in Virtual India, we have decided to refer to a post's 'layers,' which, like an onion, you can add to or subtract from as best suits your scene, region, and partners.

"Some of these layers, at least the ones we will discuss for now, include dialog, body language, action, physical appearance, environment, and context. Each new layer adds further depth to your posts as it reveals more about your character while advancing the story.

"For the *dialog layer,* most people start with little more than speech, which is a good beginning. However, it's important not to use netspeak, emoticons, and canned gestures. Write out your dialog as best you can, and remember that one purpose for dialog is to invite a response from the other characters.

Mahir: "Hey, John, pleasant weather, eh? I assume you're here for the same as me."

"With the *body language layer*, it's not just WHAT you say, but HOW you say it. This can include posture like slumping or standing tall, gestures like waving or flicking a birdie, facial expressions like smiling or frowning, tone of voice like murmuring or growling, and so forth. Most roleplay students start by adding this layer to their dialog, which is like a 'tell' in poker, where your character can give away its inner feelings.

/me grins mirthlessly through chattering teeth as he growls, "..."

"Without saying a lot about nothing, the *appearance layer* is where you describe your appearance as it relates to the scene, especially if it's not apparent in the pixels. If you have already established your more permanent physical features, such as hair, face, size, and body type, here you would describe how your appearance has varied. You may be sweating or shivering, energetic or exhausted, clean or dirty, dressed differently, wounded, scarred, and so on.

> */me wears a long woolen overcoat, freezing vapor blowing from between his chapped lips.*

"The *environment layer* is where you use all your senses to describe your environment, such as what you see, hear, smell, taste, and feel, as well as how that environment affects you and how you respond to it. Is your robe flapping around your legs in the wind, or are you wiping sweaty hair from your face in the heat?

> */me turns his back to the biting wind and huddles closer to the burn barrel, despite the acrid smoke irritating his eyes and throat, then hears a crunching in the snow.*

"The *action layer* describes not only what your character does in response to your partner's post, but also what you were doing before that, and even what you intend to do afterward. This way, you merge past, present, and future actions smoothly. Sometimes character actions will not be directed at other characters but rather occur in parallel, so to speak, such as a nervous tick or some chore they are carrying out while they talk.

> */me stomps frozen feet in snow-covered black rubber boots, shaking his head miserably, and pulls a cold hand from his pocket where he had been fingering his old .45 Colt M1911 while contemplating what he had brought it for. He looks up through the falling flakes to see his friend approaching and waves.*

"*The internal layers*: The layers I have mentioned so far can be called 'external' because they are tangible—observable by the other characters. There are also *internal layers* that can include context, background, mood, and thought posts.

"For instance, *context posts* include your character's perception of its past, present, and future, as it relates to the story. Why are you there? What else has been going on off-stage? What past events have led you to act this way? What do you know that you're not saying? What do you hope/expect will happen? Here is where you can reveal your character's secrets and imperfections—doubts, fears, regrets—to the 'audience.' For example:

> *What madness had made him leave his warm, cozy cottage to venture out into this weather? What did he hope to achieve? Did he really think that he—old and feeble as he was—could do anything to change the inevitable? His wife had begged him not to go, but his stubbornness had prevailed yet again. Well, at least he wasn't the only idiot on this fool's errand.*

"Context posts can also include flashbacks to your character's formative years, how current events relate to past ones, interpretations of or attitudes toward them, and even hopes and fears for the future. This is especially useful when you roleplay with someone who is unfamiliar with the history so far.

"However, be aware that some roleplayers reject the use of internal layers. *Thought posts*, for example, don't provide anything tangible to respond to—unless other characters are already aware of the background and can interpret your body language or dialog as somehow relating to it. This is a matter of roleplay style, and we should be tolerant of each other's preferred styles.

"Seeing your character's actions through *background posts*, which provides a historical framework—past, present, and future—does add a lot of depth to the story, though, especially if your actions would otherwise seem incongruent. The important thing is to make sure each level of your post faithfully reflects your character's personality and backstory.

"Other layers may be possible, but we'll leave it there for now and put together everything we have so far. As you will see, we now have a multi-para post. You will note that the first paragraph is what some call a 'mood' post.

> *Mahir: /me turns his back to the biting wind and huddles closer to the burn barrel despite the acrid smoke irritating his eyes and throat. He stomps frozen feet in his snow-covered black rubber boots and shakes his head miserably. What madness had made him leave his warm, cozy cottage to venture out into this weather? What did he hope to achieve? Did he really think that he—old and feeble as he was—could do anything to change the inevitable? His wife had begged him not to go, but his stubbornness had prevailed yet again.*
>
> *He hears a crunching in the snow and looks up through the falling flakes to see his friend approaching. Well, at least he wasn't the only idiot on this fool's errand. Pulling a cold hand from the pocket of his long woolen overcoat, where he had been fingering his old .45 Colt M1911, contemplating what he had brought it for, he waves and grins mirthlessly through chattering teeth, freezing vapor blowing from between his chapped lips as he growls, "Hey, John, pleasant weather, eh? I assume you're here for the same as me."*

Useful Emoting Words

Mahir: "Some who seem to feel daunted by all the reading and writing will say things like, 'I'm more a movie person, not so much a book person.' They seem to assume that gaming in virtual worlds is a matter of EITHER visuals OR text. Sure, visuals are nice, but they are not enough. You can achieve MUCH more with detailed emotes than the available animations and other scripting technologies, no matter how much money you spend on expensive gadgets and accessories.

"My answer to the 'movie person' would be... Don't be lazy about reading and writing posts—long OR short. I've said it before, and I'll say it again: Without emotes, there is no roleplay. And the better your emotes, the better your roleplay—that simple.

"So to start, in addition to your dialog, at the very least describe your body language, facial expressions, tone of voice, and so on. It's a good idea to build up your own collection of useful emoting words by reading fiction, observing other roleplayers, checking a thesaurus, and so on.

Without emotes, there is no roleplay. The better your emotes, the better the roleplay'. That simple.

"For example, when approaching someone, you could simply walk up to them, but you could also skip or mince happily, slouch or shuffle lazily, stroll, amble, mosey or saunter confidently, run frantically, tiptoe or pad quietly, limp or drag yourself painfully, waltz, slink or glide sexily, stagger, teeter or totter on trembling legs, take faltering, lurching or hesitant steps, creep warily fighting your fear, lumber or waddle clumsily, clomp angrily, sneak or creep surreptitiously, drag your feet, stumble or hobble unsteadily, stride or march with determination, stroll or mosey without a care in the world, trudge, plod, or traipse doggishly, sashay easily, scuffle noisily, skulk with your head down, strut or swagger proudly, slog through mud, or even waddle like a duck.

"Instead of just running, you could jog, hurtle, lope, scamper, scramble, scuttle, skitter, sprint, trot, or zip, and your jumps could be bounces, bounds, caprioles, hops, jumps, leaps, ricochets, skips, springs, or vaults. When you stand still, are you straight as an arrow, slumping dejectedly, leaning forward, or to one side? Do you just sit or lie down, or do you crouch, hunker down, kneel, lounge, perch, rest, roost, sit cross-legged, squat, recline with your hands behind your head, bask in the sun, nestle in someone's arms, prostrate yourself, repose, rest, sprawl, or stretch out?

"Looking at something or someone can also take the form of watching, glancing, glaring, staring, peeping, peeking, spying, observing, examining, considering, studying, narrowing your eyes, eying intently, flashing a look, gazing lovingly, blinking in surprise or indignantly, looking up with interest, doing a double-take, lowering your eyes demurely, watching ants crawling, looking at someone with amusement, dreamily, sideways, coldly or tensely, with eyes flicking or jumping from one person to the other with sparkling, shining or misty eyes, or with a glazed look.

"As for facial expressions, you can beam or your face can light up, you can frown, squint, scowl, grimace, sneer, leer, furrow your brow, raise an eyebrow, lift both eyebrows or wiggle them, set your jaw, grit your teeth, bite your lips, stick out your tongue, bat your eyelids, purse your lips, blush, flush or turn crimson, assume a solemn expression or an apologetic look, roll your eyes with a disgusted or fed-up look on your face, give a puzzled look, or blink rapidly.

"Do you smile softly or uneasily, smirk, beam, grin mischievously or lasciviously, sprout a predatory grin or an evil rictus (halfway between a grin and a grimace)? A laugh can be a giggle, guffaw or titter, a droll or mirthless chuckle, a bray or chortle, a snicker or snigger, or you could crack up, belly-laugh, and roar or howl with laughter.

"When you speak, talk, say, declare, or announce, it's useful to specify your tone of voice. Is it ominous, a growl, shout, roar, or a scream, or do you cry, squeal, whine, whimper or snarl? You can also purr, whisper, murmur, or speak in a voice husky or hoarse with lust. Or sometimes you will just cough, snort, tsk, groan, moan, sob, sniff, choke, gulp, swallow hard, grunt, or even blow raspberries."

Mamakie: "Some authors advise writers to avoid adverbs, but in a pinch, it can come in handy to be able to speak, look, or act adoringly, lovingly, hatefully, pleasantly, cheerfully, kindly, cruelly, calmly, enviously, warmly, coldly, openly, slyly, happily, miserably, impatiently, and so on. Adverbs tend to 'tell, not show' because they assume you already know what adoringly looks like, but they're so easy to use that it is tempting to overdo them."

Mahir: "Yeah, be careful not to restate the obvious. For example, you shouldn't write something like:

'Are you alright?' he asked worriedly.

'Damn you!' he shouted angrily.

'I love you,' she said affectionately.

"That's just poor writing because it's pretty obvious from the dialog that they are feeling worried, angry, or affectionate. BUT... if your adverbs add to or vary the meaning of the dialog, then go for it. For example, it would be acceptable if you wrote something like:

'Are you alright?' he asked sarcastically.

'Damn you!' he shouted laughingly.

'I love you,' she said sorrowfully."

Mamakie: "Also, to avoid overusing adverbs, take full advantage of the rich possibilities of your body language. You can wiggle your bum, nod, wobble, bobble, waggle or shake your head, spin around in surprise, cross your arms over your chest or place them akimbo, put your head in your hands, bite your nails, drum your fingers on a table, pick a stalk of grass and stick it between your teeth, chop the air with your hand for emphasis, scratch your head in puzzlement, and rub your forehead or stroke your chin or beard in thought."

Take full advantage of the rich possibilities of your body language.

Mahir: "Right, but again, avoid being repetitive, such as writing:

'No,' he says, shaking his head."

Mamakie: "Sure. And don't forget about hand gestures. Even without scripted animations, you can wave, raise a hand and wiggle your fingers, flick a birdie or flip someone off, facepalm, give them the thumbs-up, point, raise a victorious fist or clench a menacing fist with white knuckles, snake your hand out to pat their hand… or bum… poke them with your elbow, or even flick a beetle at them.

"Take-backs can also be both fun and useful. I sometimes correct myself in character with phrases like, 'I take that back,' 'That didn't come out right,' 'Scratch that,' 'Did I actually just say that?,' 'Was that out loud?' and 'That wasn't meant for your ears.'"

Tell a Story

Mahir: "Roleplay is all about telling stories, and roleplay in virtual worlds is about participatory, collaborative, immersive storytelling. Zander Greene says, 'The traditional ways we tell stories require an inherent separation between the storyteller and the story receiver. But with gaming culture and now with the emergence of user-defined virtual platforms, we can put you into the story.'[18]

"As you may know, table-top RPGs have Game Masters (GMs) who help move the story along. However, few roleplay regions in virtual worlds have GMs as such, although some have moderators who suggest and coordinate skeleton storylines on which players can expand.

"Some follow a 'canon'—official lore taken from works on which the region is based, such as Gor, Hogwarts, Lord of the Rings, or Star Trek, although even those often allow roleplayers to stray from canon. However, many—or perhaps most—roleplay regions, like Virtual India, are not plot-driven but character-driven, also known as play-by-post (PbP) roleplay.

"This is also called 'free-form' roleplay because roleplayers are free to make up the storyline as they go along, like an ongoing improv theater production. As they do, they weave various threads into a growing, increasingly complex tapestry as their storylines meet, combine, and twine around each other.

An easy way to develop stories is to alternate positive and negative situations in cycles of success-failure-success-failure.

"You come to realize that you're only one character in a far-flung, evolving story that somehow involves—to a greater or lesser extent—the entire community of practice that shares the roleplay region and sometimes beyond. You don't have to develop only one thread; some players have several going simultaneously.

[18] The Drax Files: World Makers [Episode 4: Fantasy Faire/RFL]: youtu.be/yjzG9g8PNFs.

"Ultimately, this tapestry of stories doesn't revolve around any one character; rather, each character revolves around the story, and it's important to keep that in mind. We're all on a collective, interactive journey, and you never know where the road might lead. Some roleplay stories may last only a day, others a month, and a few may go on for years.

Chiptag: "Even without being actual Game Masters, the owners and managers ('Admins') can introduce roleplay elements into their regions, such as new players or scripts, which practically force players to respond. For example, Virtual India's region Leaders have created extreme weather events such as monsoons, cyclones, floods, and droughts. They have also introduced rogue beasts of prey with special powers—making them very hard to stop—to terrorize the villages, and have rescripted certain diseases, making them more or less frequent or virulent.

"When they made the flu and diarrhea contagious, a terrible epidemic broke out that required the concerted efforts of all the healers to curb it. Medicinal herbs became scarce with the growing demand, and people would 'camp out' at collection sites to hoard herbs until the guards started arresting them. Some 'meanies' started spreading the contagion on purpose and had to be captured and forcibly quarantined. Then the Admins introduced a quest to obtain the vaccine, and players started completing it and seeking out healers to give them the injection."

Mahir: "Good point, Chiptag... So, let's see how stories are developed within such a context. First of all, they depend on the existence of short, medium, and long-term roleplay interactions among characters, known as 'character relationships' or CR for short. CRs can be anything from rivalries and enmities to friendships and romances. Bear in mind that CRs are among characters, not their players. IC enemies can and should be OOC friends, and IC lovers commonly have no OOC romance behind the scene.

Mamakie: "Just as a parenthesis, one of the longest-term CRs can be among members of a family roleplay. Whether you are a parent or grandparent, a baby, child or teen, another family member, or even the family dog or cat, family roleplay can mean a long-term, time-intensive commitment and should not be taken lightly. Well-roleplayed, family life can be satisfying, but it can also lead to heartbreak when a member decides it's time to move on, so please tread lightly. It is easy to roleplay family life poorly, too, once quotidian life sets in, so be creative and try new things to keep your RP interesting and exciting."

Mahir: "Good point. An easy way to develop stories is to alternate positive and negative situations. For example, after a romantic evening out, a couple has a big fight and then make up. After a major success, a character has a serious conflict with the situation and then finds a way to solve it. Keep it going in cycles of success-failure-success-failure, not in a straight line all the time.

"A more complex way to develop your story is to think about the 'story arc' or 'narrative arc,' which often consists of introducing a problem, solving the problem by making the character or relationship grow, and then the denouement. A story arc often relates to a 'character arc,' which is how the character grows and develops as the story progresses: initial state - overcoming a challenge - final state.

Make it Interesting

Arjun: /me butts in abruptly, "Um... Mr. Mentor, sir... I saw this on a profile once: 'I'm fine, so don't ask me how I am. If you expect me to RP with you, be creative and do something that grabs my attention.' At first, I thought it was a snotty thing to say, but yesterday I overheard this conversation, so now I'm not so sure:

Nisha: Hi Zaina
Zaina: How RU?
Nadin: waves
Nisha: Doing good and U
Nisha: Hi Nadin
Zaina: I'm fine
Nadin: Hello
Nadin: Here fine too
Nisha: Good to hear
Zaina: A little bored also...

Arjun: /me yawns, "Just a little bored?"

Mahir: /me laughs, "No wonder. They could have at least narrated SOMETHING interesting. What were they doing while all that chit-chat was going on? Looks like not much. Boring doesn't just happen—we MAKE it happen with this kind of drivel. I guess if the person addressing you like that is a friend, you can't just blow them off, but I don't put much stock in a stranger who comes up to me and starts the interaction with, 'Hi, how r u?'

"Roleplay will only be as good as you and each of your partners make it. Put effort and imagination into it. Otherwise, the old GIGO principle applies here: garbage in, garbage out. Starting a roleplay doesn't have to be complicated—it can be as simple as asking someone for a light or the time or as complex as your imagination will allow. Let's see a few examples of some interesting ways to start a roleplay, taken from actual situations:

> Roleplay will only be as good as you and your partners make it: garbage in, garbage out.

- A couple decides to check into a local hostel, which gives way to some interesting encounters with village members, including hunting excursions, wild sex in the public jacuzzi within chat range of others, and even being mistaken as intruders and attacked by a village guard.

- A young woman goes to the hunting grounds near a village, shoots a big cat, and shouts so the whole village can hear, "TAKE THAT, DAMNED CAT. DIE, BASTARD. I HATE YOU!" Then she runs into the middle of the camp and says, "Fresh meat, anyone? Warm and juicy, ready to sink your teeth into." The commissioner rebukes her for interrupting uninvited, and she replies, abashed, "Oh, I'm so sorry; I do crazy things when I'm angry." He asks why she is upset, and she explains that her boyfriend just dumped her. Everyone is introduced, and the story evolves from there.

- A boy sees a man standing in the middle of a high bridge over a churning waterfall and, instead of just going up to introduce himself, writes:

  Aahan: /me, alarmed to see a man standing in the middle of the bridge, furrows his brow and stretches out his hand, calling frantically to him, "Please don't jump, sir. Whatever it is, it can't be that bad. Life is too precious. Just come back, and we can talk about it."

  Parth: /me watches the water churn and froth as his eyes unfocus and his mind wanders. He hears a voice calling out frantically and looks up in surprise, then laughs heartily. "I wasn't going to jump, young man... I was just admiring the view."

  And as of that initial encounter, some good RP ensued.

- After reading a man's profile and seeing that he had an interesting philosophy of life, a girl goes within chat distance of his hut, near his totem, and posts:

  Pari: /me approaches the hut slowly, looking around, then murmurs to herself, "This looks like the totem my grandfather told me about. It must be here."

  [There is no answer, so Pari posts again]

  Pari: /me spies a firepit in the yard and musters her courage to go in and stretch out her hand over it. "Hmmm... it's still warm, so someone must be close."

  Nehal: /me is writing some letters at his table when he hears a sweet voice outside. He goes outside to see who it is and finds a lovely young woman in his yard. Approaching her slowly, so as not to frighten her, he says in a gentle voice, "Hello, I heard you talking to yourself."

  Pari: /me looks up to see a handsome young man. Could this be the one she was looking for? She had imagined him old and wrinkled, but her grandfather hadn't actually said so. She smiles, "Oh, hello. Are you the Wise Man of the Mountain?"

> *Nehal: /me frowns. How did she know that name? There was only one who called him that, and he hadn't seen or heard from him in many years. Could this beauty be somehow related to that friend? Well, only one way to find out, so he waggles his head and smiles back, "Well, I don't think I'm wise, but I do live here. I'm Nehal. Please take a seat by the fire and warm yourself."*
>
> *Pari: /me smiles back and sits, warming her hands at the fire. She looks up at him bashfully, then averts her gaze from his and says, in a small voice, "My name is Pari, and my grandfather told me to look for the Wise Man of the Mountain, who would teach me the secret of life."*

This creative opening sparked some interesting exchanges over the course of several visits as their RP grew and evolved.

"Those are just a few examples, but they show that roleplay can include any and all facets of life, real or imagined. Here's a suggestion for all of you. Instead of logging in just to see what happens, start your time inworld with a few interesting things in mind that you want to do and new ideas you'd like to explore. The scene may not go the way you want, of course, but at least you will have thought of something creative to contribute to it."

Mamakie: "Remember, you won't learn to roleplay just by talking about it. Yes, you should observe other players, take notes, and log chats so you can go back and study them, but then practice, practice, practice roleplaying yourself..."

Mahir: /me claps his hands and rubs them together, proclaiming, "Okay, time for the test," and hands out the instructions.

Arjun reads the instructions, which are basically to summarize what he learned from the class, and writes:

- Roleplaying is not just a game—it's an art form that we can practice and cultivate.
- Instead of worrying about how literate your posts are, add layers to your dialog, such as body language, action, appearance, environment, and context.
- Try to make each post reveal something about your character while moving the story forward.
- Develop a list of terms to use, especially for the body language and action layers.
- Roleplay is only boring if we make it so. Be creative and think of interesting situations to roleplay.
- Think about how the story can evolve, but be open to it going in a direction you didn't plan on.

Arjun turns in his notecard and, after a few moments, a message appears in his Local Chat:

> Dharma Guide: Congratulations. You have passed the Advanced Emoting class and advanced to Level 15 - Artist. You now have the right to a plot of land in the Communal Garden. Please check your Karma Tag for your next quest.

Arjun opens his Karma Tag, clicks on 'Quests,' and gets the following message:

You have a new quest available: Gardening	[Accept]	[Cancel]
You have a new quest available: Diary Farming	[Accept]	[Cancel]
You have a new quest available: Cooking	[Accept]	[Cancel]
You have a new quest available: Making Music	[Accept]	[Cancel]

Wondering why he has received four quests at once, Arjun accepts the first one and reads:

> Dharma Guide: You have accepted the quest "Gardening." To complete it, cultivate and harvest at least one of each type of crop plant available where farmers dwell. Happy farming.

Arjun grins and comments to the students around him, "Looks like we've gone from hunter-gatherers to the agricultural revolution already."

"Sweet," a student answers. "It'll be a welcome change of pace after all that shooting and killing things... not to mention getting bitten, mauled, and shot at."

Mamakie hears the students talking as she passes by and stops to say, "Yes, the next few quests may be easy for most of you, but bear in mind that their main purpose is to familiarize you with the region and its economic system, meet more of its residents, and have more opportunities to practice roleplaying."

Simlipal was obviously the farming village, so that must be where the supplies were sold. Yes, this promised to be a pleasant, relaxing change to all the nervous excitement of the last few quests. With those happy thoughts, Arjun poofs for the evening.

Why are you here, Arjun?

To cultivate roleplay as an art form.

CHAPTER TEN

THE GOOD LIFE

Status:	Artist
Level:	15
HP:	19.6

Virtual India RP Group:

Group Notice Sent by: Mahir Mukherjee

Subject: Community Radio Weather Alert

Good evening, Virtual India. This is Mahir Mukherjee with a weather update. Yesterday evening, the India Meteorological Department issued a severe monsoon warning for Virtual India.

The IMD radar in Sanjay spotted a large storm cell forming over the South Sea and moving rapidly northward. It hit the region early this morning and has started to flood the southern districts.

Flooding is expected to rise and include the Western and Eastern River basins at Simlipal and Sanjay. Extreme caution is recommended when traveling in those areas. The monsoon is expected to continue throughout the week.

"Citizen Tagore, good to see you up so early," Chris exclaims with a grin when Arjun logs into the Landing next morning. "Ready to sink your hands into some good, rich soil... um... I mean MUD?" He wears yellow galoshes with a matching raincoat, pants, and hat, and carries an enormous electric-green umbrella.

Arjun claps him on the back, slicks back his wet hair, and wipes rain from his eyes, squinting up at the downpour. "I can't think of anything I'd rather be doing right now... well... aside from one of the beauties we saw on the beach the other day. But is this really the kind of weather we want to start farming in?"

Chris: "Well, maybe we won't have to water our crops." ((Although the farming system probably doesn't take weather into account - hehe))

Gardening

The two boys trot off chuckling through the rain, pass the Communal Garden where several farmers in rain gear are already hard at work, then splash across the partially submerged Simlipal Bridge where they wave and call out to the fisherfolk wading along the inundated banks, and stride into the teeming Simlipal village. They soon find the U-Farm Gardening Store with its shovels, rakes, hoes and other gardening implements, packets of seeds, bags of fertilizer, bottles of agrochemicals, and sundry other items.

They duck into the store out of the rain. Under the windows at the front, Arjun finds seedbeds of wheat, sugarcane, corn, and squash ready for planting in a garden plot for fifty coins each. He buys one of each and reads the instructions that come with them. It turns out that, monsoon or no, he will have to water and cultivate them three times a day for three days to get the best harvest, so Arjun also buys a watering can and a hoe.

Equipped, they return across the bridge to the Communal Garden. It is divided into small plots with signs indicating their owner's names, some with plants and others barren. They find the plot with Arjun's name, just large enough for his four seedbeds. He lays them out and, to start them growing, clicks on them and then on 'Tend' in the menu that pops up. He tends each seedbed once, getting the message, "This crop has now been tended 1 of 9 times." Then he tries to do it again to save time but gets the message, "This crop has already been tended. It can be tended again after 2 hours have elapsed."

Animal characters can't speak, only emote animal sounds, movements, actions, and maybe some feelings.

Just then, the boys see a deer come out of the dripping woods and start grazing in the Communal Garden. Its tag identifies it as Wendi—a Virtual India wildlife. They try to shoo it out of the garden, shouting at it to go forage in the woods and leave the crops alone, but it paws at the ground as if it were about to charge at them. Chris picks up a stick, and it finally turns and bounds back into the woods. Intrigued, Arjun opens a group IM with Chris and Wendi to ask what it's like to RP as an animal.

Wendi: "It's really challenging. We can't speak, only narrate animal sounds, movements, actions, and maybe some feelings. When you're an animal, you have to really BE an animal. And if you're wildlife, it's even harder. We shouldn't write general posts like:

/me postures so they see she's not afraid of them and is ready to charge

"Instead, we need to be more creative, specific, and descriptive, like I did:

/me, sensing the boys' intention to deprive her of a delicious meal, paws at the ground with her front feet, throwing up dirt. She snort-wheezes loudly, jerking back and forth menacingly, her tensed muscles rippling as she prepares to lunge at them.

"You did a great job. Most people don't really know how to roleplay realistically with an animal. They either admire us and try to befriend us, or, in the case of the large predators, treat them as dangerous and try to avoid them, so we don't get that many good roleplay opportunities. I guess roleplaying a domestic animal might be a little easier, but wild animals don't really go around with toys in their mouths trying to get humans to play with them."

Arjun: "Can animals actually harm humans? Wouldn't you have to be a red-tagged warrior to do that?"

Wendi: "Some predators, such as big cats and bears, actually do have red tags and can attack others in melee using claws and fangs. But even those of us who wear yellow tags can always use animations, sounds, and text-based roleplay to at least act like we're defending ourselves, as I just did."

Arjun: "Okay, so once an animal downs its prey, what can they do with it?"

Wendi: "Big predators can drag their human or animal prey using the scripted leashing system. It's not realistic for an animal to use a leash, but it helps simulate dragging off their prey. It's easier just to use narration, and the prey is supposed to go along with them, moving their avatars according to the animal's posts, just like in any other capture roleplay. But they sometimes have to IM their prey to explain what's expected of them, hehe."

Chris: "What about when a fish, for example? I saw a beautifully coloured fish avatar in the river once and had no idea how to roleplay with it."

Wendi: "Hmmm... that IS a hard one... You could just admire its pretty colors, roleplay with others about what kind it is, or maybe even try to catch it and eat it... Oh, speaking of being realistic, you can't swim underwater for long unless you're a fish, and you certainly can't fly unless you have wings."

Arjun: "Thanks a lot, Wendi. Roleplaying and IMing with you has been a learning experience."

Wendi: "Any time. Thanks for the roleplay."

On a whim, Arjun tries to tend some of the neighboring crops. Some give him the same message, "This crop has already been tended. It can be tended again after 2 hours have elapsed." Others, apparently ready to harvest, say, "This is not your crop to harvest." One says, "This crop has already been tended three times today. Please come back tomorrow," but a few give him the message, "This crop has now been tended [#] of 9 times," depending on the progress of each.

Arjun: /me passes his hands over a patch of wheat, feeling the long awns caressing his palm, his pleased expression far off as if remembering a happy memory. "I like that I can tend other people's crops but not harvest them," he muses, then frowns, "Why haven't I received a message saying the quest is completed yet?"

Chris: /me picks caterpillars off some of the plants, squashes them under his feet, then looks up at Arjun, "You have to harvest all your crops to complete the quest. If you don't tend them three times a day for three days, you won't get a full harvest and will have to start all over again."

Arjun: /me finds a neighbor's corn patch to tend, "Interesting... while the hunting quest was about speed and agility, this one is about patience and persistence."

Chris: /me snips dead leaves off a squash plant with his fingernails and throws them on the compost heap "Yeah, but check your Quest menu just in case. If I remember correctly, this time, you can do others while you wait"

Dairy Farming

"Oh, yes, I forgot about that," Arjun says as he opens his Quest menu, which says:

You have a new quest available: Dairy Farming [Accept] [Cancel]

You have a new quest available: Cooking [Accept] [Cancel]

You have a new quest available: Making Music [Accept] [Cancel]

He accepts the Dairy Farming quest and reads the message in Local Chat:

Dharma Guide: You have accepted the quest "Dairy Farming." To complete it, take two small planks and a set of steel hoops to the highland steppes and have a milk bucket made, use it to milk the cows and goats there, and make cream, butter, and cheese with the milk. Happy dairy farming.

Arjun: /me reads it again and scratches his head. "Hmm... another quest that doesn't sound too difficult, just a lot of work." He gets out his map and points to the northern provinces. "The highland steppes... that must be Khangchendzonga. I guess there's a bucket maker in the village... But I only saw wild mountain goats there. Am I supposed to catch and milk them???"

Chris: /me laughs "Noooo, they raise domesticated animals too... But you'll probably have to give the farmers something in exchange for letting you milk their cows and goats"

Arjun: /me thinks for a while, then his face brightens. "I know. I can have two buckets made and then trade one of them for the milk. Since they're dairy farmers, I'm sure they would appreciate that."

The boys run to the Simlipal kiosk for the planks, then northeast to the Namdapha blacksmith shop for the steel hoops, and from there westward to Khangchendzonga Village, where Arjun looks around until he finds a shop where all kinds of buckets are made and sold.

The bucketsmith, a Mr. Cooper, tries to convince Arjun to buy a more high-tech hermetic bucket that will keep the milk longer, but Chris says there is no point in wearing out a fancy, expensive bucket just to collect milk since Arjun will be using it right away to make cream, butter, and cheese. Rather, he can use the simple bucket for milking and the hermetic one for storing processed milk later if he wants. They finally agree on the price, and Arjun gives Mr. Cooper the materials for two simple buckets. He 'sits' on the workbench, and a generic animation starts, but he then emotes the bucket-making process in great detail.

Mr. Cooper: /me cuts the planks into staves and joints the edges of each stave at an angle. "This angle has to be just right so that the walls of the bucket will be as tight as possible." He rounds off the backs of the staves with a kind of draw knife. "I use this backing iron so that the staves will fit neatly into the hoops, evening out the pressure all around." After clamping the two handle staves onto either side of the lower hoops, he inserts the rest of the staves until they all fit snugly, then adds the upper hoops and hammers all hoops snugly into place.

Arjun: /me watches Mr. Cooper work with fascination, his eager eyes drinking everything in hungrily, trying to learn as much as he can from him.

Chris: /me cuts two lengths of rope for the bucket handles, then gets the broom and starts sweeping up the wood shavings

Mr. Cooper: /me uses a special tool to cut an inside groove into the base of the staves. "This is where I will fit the 'heads' or bottoms of the buckets." He cuts round shapes with a bandsaw and uses a shaver to taper the edges so they fit into the grooves. Then he takes off the bottom hoops, spreads linseed paste into the grooves to seal them, and pushes the round bottoms down until they pop into the grooves. He fits the bottom hoops back on snugly and uses a shaver to round and smooth the outsides of the buckets. Finally, he inserts the lengths of rope into the holes in the handle staves and weaves the ends into themselves to form the handles. "There you go, Mr. Tagore. Two brand-new milk buckets," he announces proudly, handing them to Arjun.

Arjun: /me beams as he takes the buckets and pays one silver coin for each.

Chris: /reaches out to help Arjun carry the buckets as he heads for the door chuckling "Come on, mate, we need to find some udders to squeeze"

Arjun: /me follows after him, shaking his head and making a face. "That's udderly disgusting, Chris."

On the outskirts of town, they find a farm with cows and goats, and trade the extra bucket for permission to milk them. They use the cream separator, cheese factory, and butter churn to make the products they need, while the farmers suggest how to emote each part. Soon a message appears in Local Chat:

> Dharma Guide: Congratulations. You have passed the Dairy Farming Quest and advanced to Level 16 - Dairy Farmer. Please check your Karma Tag for your next quest.

Arjun: /me turns to Chris. "This is strange. I did the Gardening quest first, but this level is 16 – Dairy Farmer. Is that a mistake?"

Chris: /me laughs "No mistake. Everyone wanted to do other quests while waiting for their crops to grow, so that's how the devs worked it out. Cooking is level 17, Music is level 18, and then Gardening will be level 19."

Cooking up a Storm

Two quests in one day had been quite enough for the boys, so they meet up the next day at the Landing. Arjun opens his Quest menu, which now says:

You have a new quest available: Cooking [Accept] [Cancel]

You have a new quest available: Making Music [Accept] [Cancel]

He accepts the cooking quest and reads the message in Local Chat:

Dharma Guide: You have accepted the quest "Cooking." To complete it, take two bronze ingots from the mining town to the desert people to make a cooking pot, then prepare at least four different dishes. Happy cooking.

Arjun: /me scratches his head. "Why do we need to cook our food? I mean, why not just eat it raw?"

Chris: "For a few reasons. Many foods can't be eaten raw, and most go bad after a week. Once they're cooked, you can eat them and they last longer. Also, it's like packing HP: cooked meals give you more health points each time you eat. That's useful when you're in a hurry like during a fight. Plus, cooking adds more HP to the total for each dish."

Arjun remembers seeing metal bars for sale at the Namdapha Trading Kiosk, so they go cross-country to the northeast, happy to be out of the rain. There, Arjun buys two bronze ingots for one silver each. They take the scenic route back through the highland steppes of Khangchendzonga, the green slopes of Gangotri, and the steep mountain passes of Hemis to avoid the floodplain, and finally south to the Nomad Camp of Rajasthan, which, being a desert district, is also out of the monsoon area.

Chris (to the Virtual India group): Is there a bronzeworker available in Rajasthan for the cook pot quest?

Bisman: I'll be there in a few

Chris: Thanks, Bis

Soon they find the bronzeworker's shop, where a man politely introduces himself as Bisman. He wears brown jutti sandals, pajama pants, a kurta shirt, and a Patka turban over his joora topknot, all of dark blue cotton. Arjun gives him the ingots, and the two boys watch as he works the bronze bars into a cooking pot.

Bisman: /me heats the first bar in the forge, then beats it into a flat, round shape for the thick base of the pot. "A heavier bottom is better because it spreads the heat more evenly, so you won't burn your food," he explains. Then he heats the second bar and puts it through the roller several times to make a long, flat rectangle, which he curves to together for the sides. Finally, he welds the bottom and sides together, beats the weld to round the joint, and polishes the finished product, handing it to Arjun with a smile. "There you go, son. That'll be fifty copper. Oh, and I'll throw in a brazier and some recipes for free."

Arjun pays him five silvers and the boys walk to the Rajasthan Trading Kiosk, where Arjun buys four wheat, two corn, one squash, and two sugarcane. He clicks on the brazier to light it, places the cooking pot on top and clicks it to get it started. He rezzes the four wheats and one of the corns, waits a few minutes, and gets a 6-HP loaf of bread. Repeating this with a whitefish, a yellowfish, a coconut, and the squash, he gets an 8-HP fishstew. Finally, he uses a slab of meat, a monkey tripe, a chicken, and the other corn to make a 10-HP meatstew.

Raising an eyebrow at the idea of using a cooking pot to make fruit dishes, Arjun just shrugs and tries it after turning off the brazier. He rezzes a banana, pineapple, mango, grape, apple, and kiwifruit to make an 8-HP tutti-frutti, and then prepares a 6-HP fruitjuice with the sugarcane and an orange, litchi, kiwifruit, and watermelon, all the while posting the cooking process to local chat. While he is getting ready to make another fruitjuice for Chris, a message appears in Local Chat:

> Dharma Guide: Congratulations. You have completed the Cooking Quest and advanced to Level 17 - Cook. Check your Karma Tag for your next quest.

Making Music

While the boys sip their fruitjuice at a table under a parasol in the central square, Arjun accepts the next quest and reads the message in Local Chat:

> Dharma Guide: You have accepted the quest "Music." To complete it, visit the meadow people to receive three instruments and learn to play them. Enjoy.

Arjun thinks back to the places they had visited and guesses that 'meadow people' probably refers to Gangotri Village, which lies in a wide, green valley nestled between the northern mountain range, and Chris concurs. The straightest route would be up the Western River to Gangotri bridge, but Arjun wants to tend his crops, so they splash across Sanjay Gandhi to do that, then to the rising Eastern River to take a canoe to the Khangchendzonga dock.

It is raining here, too, but the flooding has not reached this high up. In answer to Arjun's questions, Chris explains that region admins can adjust water levels to enable flooding and dry up rivers during a drought.

They pass the Bahá'í Lotus Temple, pausing to admire its graceful white petals and listen to the lovely a cappella chorus. Again, the words of the song interest Arjun, so he writes them down:

Whatever objects appear in this world
are but pictures of the world of heaven.
This life is like a swelling wave,
a mirage of drifting shadows.
Can a distorted image on the desert
serve as refreshing waters?
No, by the Lord of Lords!
Never can reality and its mere semblance be one.
Wide is the difference between fancy and fact,
between truth and the phantom thereof.

They continue northward to the village square, where they find Commissioner Janus. Now more informally dressed, in an all-white pajama, he sits cross-legged on a rug under an awning out of the rain, playing a sitar. When he stops, they exchange greetings, and the boys ask him for directions. He leads them to the music shop, where Arjun buys a sitar, tabla drum, and bansuri flute.

Janus shows him how to play each instrument and then invites the boys to make music with him. Arjun plays the drum, Chris the flute, and Janus the sitar. The combination is magical, as each instrument contributes to the beauty of the whole. After a while, they switch instruments and play some more, changing again after another round of music. In this way, Arjun is able to try all the sounds each instrument makes. As they play, Arjun asks Janus if he could explain the words of the two songs he has written down at the Lotus Temple.

Janus: "According to the Baha'i worldview, what we perceive as the 'real' world is just outer pictures of the REAL real world, like a swelling wave, a distorted image on the desert, drifting shadows, a phantom of reality, a show, vain and empty, a mere nothing. The world *looks* like reality but is actually a mere illusion, like 'images reflected in the water, seeming as pictures to the eye.' Since reality and the mere semblance of reality can never be one, the 'divine Kingdom' is the REAL world, and what we call RL or the real world is only its shadow stretching out, has no life of its own, and is only a fantasy."

Arjun: "That's fascinating. Hindu philosophy also describes the world as 'lila' or Gods' 'play,' in which we become so involved that we mistake it for reality. It also sees it as a 'maya' or illusion that our limited senses perceive as real, 'Indra's net of jewels,' God's dream, to which we reincarnate in different avatars to play out our karma. And Buddhist writings speak of the illusory nature of the 'real' world as 'a mirage, a cloud castle, a dream, an apparition, without essence, but with qualities that can be seen' in which 'nothing is as it appears.'"

Chris: "Plato also compared the contingent world to shadows cast on a wall by a real or ideal world that lies beyond our sensorial grasp—a difference between form and essence. Some Christians also believe in 'intelligent design,' where the

Creator can be compared to a programmer, the initial 'Logos' (Word) to the operating system or program, the 'book of life' or 'scroll of deeds' to our chat transcripts, where everything we do is recorded, and in which Jesus appeared as an avatar—for instance, 'became flesh and dwelt among us.'"

Janus: "Yes, and modern-day thinkers, like Nick Bostrom with his 'Simulation Argument,' even speculate that we could actually be living in a virtual world created by some outside intelligence. This is only posed as a thought experiment, but it does reflect those religious traditions and early philosophies in some ways. They say that the contradictions found in physics, such as general relativity, quantum mechanics, entangled entities, quantum tunneling, curved space, dilating time, dark matter/energy, anti-matter, and so on, could be due to us trying to perceive the physical world as real and not as a simulation."

Arjun: "I like to imagine the basic laws of nature as an operating system, subatomic particles as bits, atomic elements as variables in an equation, and molecules as bytes. Even cells have been compared to batteries. The human body has fifty trillion cells, each of which has a negative charge on the inside and a positive charge on the outside, making each cell a 1.4-volt battery, for a total of 700 trillion volts of electricity in your body."

Chris: "And let's not forget genes, which are basically codes that design every living thing. Also, our brains are like holographic computers. Our senses only capture a small fraction of all stimuli, and our brains interpret it to build an 'image' of reality, running at about 100 million billion (10^{20}) operations per second."

Janus: "Michel Foucault says that 'discourse' is the social 'program' modeling our thought and perception of the world, which is where 'memes' came from, as the sociocultural equivalent to 'genes'. Those who have assimilated other cultures realize that there is more than one way to perceive life and the world."

Experiencing a virtual world through an avatar is a fitting analogy for our relationship to the 'real' world.

Arjun: "If all this is true, then experiencing a virtual world through an avatar could be seen as a fitting analogy for our relationship to the 'real' world. It would be a good way to train our minds to think of it in this way."

Chris: "Okay, but does that mean we shouldn't take the 'real world' seriously?"

Janus: "No, I don't think so. Like Lawrence LeShan says in Alternate Realities, 'A reality is real to you when you act in terms of it... It's a valid reality when, using it, you can accomplish the goals acceptable to it.' This kind of thinking seems to be popular among many people who have spent some time in virtual worlds. I often read people's profiles, trying to understand what virtual reality means to them, and some have said things like:

- <My avatar> is what I'd be without the constraints of the real world. It's the real me, my soul.
- Avatars are the real people; we are just the meat and bones that allow them to exist.
- (My avatar is) the me that's more 'me' than I can be, myself, in real life.
- The body is different, but the mind is the same.
- In SL, I both lose and find myself.
- I'm not 'playing' Second Life; I'm in it.
- I enjoy the infinitely precious gift of meeting someone's mind as represented by their avatar.
- First Life compels my second, and Second Life compels my first. The looking glass between the two is crystalline, absorbs the light and darkness...

By this time, they have finished playing all the songs available in each of the instruments since they had been able to play and chat at the same time. A message appears in Arjun's Local Chat:

> Dharma Guide: Congratulations. You have successfully completed the Music Quest and advanced to Level 18 – Musician. You will have no more quests until you complete the Gardening Quest.

The boys thank Janus effusively for the music and reflections, take their leave, and head back to the Communal Garden to tend Arjun's crops for the third time that day. Luckily, the flooding hasn't reached the garden... yet.

"You know," Arjun muses, "they were right to say that some of these quests are really easy, but I've realized that their purpose isn't to turn this virtual world into just one more videogame. I'm only half-way through, but I've already learned a lot about the region, met some really awesome people, and had gobs of chances to practice roleplay, which seems like the real reason for these quests."

They spend the next two days hunting, foraging, fishing, gardening, practicing with the cooking pot, playing music, and hanging out at pubs to get out of the rain. On Tuesday, Arjun buys another set of plants for his garden plot and is laying them out after harvesting his first crop when a message appears in his Local Chat:

> Dharma Guide: Congratulations. You have successfully completed the Gardening quest and advanced to Level 19 – Gardener. Please check your Karma Tag for your next quest.

He accepts the next quest and reads the message in Local Chat:

> Dharma Guide: You have accepted the quest "Advanced Roleplay." To complete it, go to the Betla Town Hall on Monday at 2:00 pm SLT. Pay attention, as you will be tested. Good luck.

CHAPTER ELEVEN

MIXING IT UP – I

Status: Gardener
Level: 19
HP: 18.5

Virtual India Group

Group Notice Sent by: Mahir Mukherjee

Subject: Advanced Roleplay Class

Due to flooding, this week's Advanced Roleplay Class cannot be held at the Betla Town Hall, which is under 1.5 meters of water, and has been changed to the Namdapha Community Centre. Our apologies in advance for any inconvenience this may cause.

Hanging out at the Landing, Arjun half-listens to the daily gossip when suddenly he gulps and goes pale. People are saying Eswa is pregnant. Eswa? Sweet, lovely Eswa, to whom he had repeatedly confessed his undying love? She had rejected his advances every time, saying she loved him like a brother. A lump in his throat, Arjun runs through the forest, not knowing where his feet are taking him. Arriving at the mining area, he sees Eswa smiling and chatting with friends, and his heart sinks to see her so happy without him. He enters the mine and opens an IM:

Arjun: /me ducks into the mine when he sees Eswa, hoping she hasn't seen him, takes up a pickaxe and starts beating furiously at the rock with all his strength, hot tears streaming down his face.

Eswaria: /me watches Arjun run past and calls out, "Arjun, what's wrong???"

[Arjun ignores this, hoping to draw her into Local Chat range]

Arjun: /me grunts and sputters with each blow of the pickaxe, "TAKE THAT, DAMNED ROCK, AND THAT, AND THAT, DAMN YOU!"

Eswaria [in Local Chat]: /me hears Arjun cursing the rocks—it's impossible not to hear him—and follows him into the mine. "What's wrong, Arjun?"

Arjun: /me looks up at her, tears forming long streaks through the dirt on his face. "Oh, hi, Eswa" -tries to smile- "How are you and the baby?"

Eswaria: /me smiles gently... "For now, everything's fine... but tell me, why are you crying? What's made you so sad?"

Arjun: /me turns his head away to hide his tears, and goes back to striking the rock. "No, it's nothing, sweetie. I'm just a foolish boy with foolish dreams, is all..."

Eswaria: /me takes a tissue and gently reaches out to dry the tears from his cheek. "Tell me, Arjun... what's the problem?"

Arjun: /me roughly turns his head from the tissue and strikes the rock harder, biting his lips until he tastes blood. "No, it's nothing. Please, just let me be, Eswa."

Eswaria: /me, now pissed off, grabs Arjun's shoulders and forces him to turn around. "Arjun didn't make my baby... Is that it?"

[This was powerplay, but Arjun let it slide]

Arjun: /me puts down his pickaxe and turns to face her, unable to hide his tears any longer. "No, Eswa, they're just tears of joy. I'm so happy for you."

Eswaria: "Oh gods, Arjun, but not tears for me? I want you to be happy. You're like a brother to me."

Arjun: /me gazes at her lovingly, and the tears start to flow again. "I am. I'm very happy for you, sis. Really I am."

Eswaria: /me smiles gently and reaches up to ruffle Arjun's hair.

Arjun: /me wipes his face with the back of his hand, smearing the dirt and tears

Eswaria: /me passes Arjun the tissue.

[A scripted tissue enters his Inventory, he 'Adds' it, and an animation starts]

Arjun: /me takes the tissue and wipes it on his face, smearing the dirt around even more. He blows his nose noisily into it, then stuffs it into his belt. "Thank you, Eswa. You're a real friend."

Eswaria: /me wobbles her head from side to side in Indian style and smiles sweetly. "My pleasure, Arjun."

Arjun: /me picks up his pickaxe again and turns back to the rock, striking it more reasonably now, glancing furtively at her from time to time.

Eswaria [in IM]: Damnit, Arjun. Hahaha. You had me worried. I thought something was really wrong. -looks at him with a big smile and winks-

[Arjun ignores this message also, being OOC]

Arjun: [in Local Chat] /me looks away, bites his lip, and keeps hitting the rock, his face a study of concentration.

Eswaria: /me raises a questioning eyebrow.

Heavy vs Light RP

Mahir: /me turns to the class. "I asked Arjun to share this roleplay scene to introduce today's first topic about heavy versus light roleplay."

Arjun: /me chuckles self-consciously, folds up his transcript and stuffs it back into his pouch, then turns and winks conspiratorially at Eswaria, grinning.

Eswaria: /me blushes crimson red and hangs her head, smiling self-consciously. "He was so convincing... I really didn't know what to think. When he IMed to thank me for the RP, I was so relieved."

Mahir: /me chuckles. "A lot of the roleplay is what I call 'RP lite' or 'chit-chat roleplay.' But a 'deep' or 'heavy' player works with emotions so well that some may think their feelings are real... that they are really crying, laughing, angry, in love, and so on.

"Just like an actor tries to be convincing, nothing makes serious roleplayers happier than to be so credible that other players are left wondering whether the love or lust, anger or hatred, joy or sadness expressed in the scene were for real.

"Be careful doing this with inexperienced roleplayers. If they haven't learned to separate the fiction of roleplay from reality, it can lead to hard feelings, from anger to heartbreak IRL. And when you are at the receiving end of highly emotional roleplay, don't invest your RL emotions in it. Don't get angry IRL, don't fall in love IRL, and whatever you do, don't let your heart be broken IRL when the IC 'love of your life' runs off with another partner." He turns to wink at Arjun.

Mamakie: "That's true, but on the other hand, we read books and watch movies in part for the emotions they evoke. Roleplaying can achieve the same. So instead of trying NOT to get emotionally caught up in the roleplay, why not embrace the emotions, savor them, enjoy them. After all, that's why we're here, isn't it?"

> *Mamakie: [in IM] /me looks around at each student until her eyes meet Arjun's, then raises an eyebrow as if to ask, "And* why are YOU here, Arjun?*"*

Mahir: "Okay, maybe that's why 3D landscaper Kriss Lehmann says, 'Second Life is really strong on the emotional bandwidth. Your brain doesn't really tell the difference between what happens on your screen and what happens around you. The people you meet, the places you go... those actually make real connections.'"[19]

Mamakie: "So if you feel RL emotions in your RP, don't fight them, use them. They are your friends, not the enemy. Turn them into wings to make your RP soar. Submerge yourself willingly in what your character and the situation is making you feel, and take advantage of the inspiration it can provide to make your RP come alive and go above and beyond anything you've done before."

---

[19] The Drax Files: World Makers [Episode 1: Kriss Lehmann]: youtu.be/Gbu2HN_aY7w.

Do the Unexpected

Mahir: "You can also enrich your roleplay by doing the unexpected. You don't always have to follow a linear path; your roleplay can go back and forth, up and down, or sideways. Try adding unexpected twists and turns to throw the other players off. Here are a few examples from actual roleplay to get you thinking about how to create your own unexpected turnarounds:

- In the heat of cuddling, a woman suddenly stops her partner and says he is going too far too fast. Nobody had done this with him before, so it takes him off guard and forces him to be more creative in his roleplay.
- To his 'surprise,' a warrior loses a fight he had 'expected' to win, which 'hurts his pride.' He insists it was beginner's luck and that they should skirmish again. He loses again and 'admits' that his opponent is the better fighter.
- A young man plays a Don Juan macho stance with a girl until this façade crumbles and he admits he is trying to learn to be more assertive with women. But it isn't coming naturally, so he asks her for advice (which she gladly gives).
- A young lady gets upset at something trivial her partner does and storms off, just when he thought everything was going so well.
- A broken-hearted lover begs his captors to put him out of his misery when they had expected him to struggle and beg for his life.
- A couple is cuddling lazily on the porch when suddenly the old wicker chair they are sitting on collapses under their weight and they fall to the floor.
- A warrior lockpicks a home whose frightened occupants had been engaged in erotic roleplay, then takes out a guitar and starts serenading them.
- A couple is cuddling on a beach towel, when suddenly she jumps up and runs away laughing, calling back, "You can't catch me!"
- A man tries to explain a concern to his wife, but she continually 'misinterprets' his meaning and intention, taking offense where none was meant, and ends up twisting the whole talk into a knot that could be either hilarious or tragic.

"You don't have to plan it out each time; don't let the paralysis of analysis bog you down. A lot of roleplay is just shooting from the hip. Go with what you feel, but don't let the roleplay always follow the straightest, easiest path. Stretch your limits within what is 'realistic.' Challenge your beliefs about what you can and cannot—or should and should not—do. As Robert Frost wrote, 'Two roads diverged in a wood, and I… I took the one less traveled by, and that has made all the difference.'"

Mamakie: "Roleplay is like any other skill, such as dancing—the more you practice, the more it comes naturally to you. As you gain experience, you'll feel more comfortable and at ease with it. As someone wrote in their profile, 'Roleplay is dirty and nasty, visceral and uneven. It's surprising and wonderfully imaginative. We make mistakes, and we learn. We try to drive a scene and then find it's not going where we thought, so we adapt. If you remove that beauty, it's nothing more than a flat story with no emotion or energy.'

"Remember, the sky's the limit. As long as it's not completely against your character definition, push the envelope. Don't be shy. Go from tender and gentle to wild and passionate, then back again. Go from seducing eagerly to pushing away angrily and back again. Be bold. Be creative. Keep your roleplay partners wondering what you'll do next. Stretch the boundaries of your imagination."

> A lot of roleplay is shooting from the hip. Go with what you feel, but don't always follow the straightest, easiest path.

Mahir: "But also bear in mind that others may also do something unexpected. Not everything will turn out the way you want, so be flexible and adapt your roleplay to whatever happens. That's what's so great about it—you never know what people might do next." -chuckles- "Heck, most of the time, I don't even know what *I* will do next. So just go with the flow, and discover the story together."

Using Non-Player Characters (NPCs)

Just then, a cute little scripted beagle puppy ambles onto the scene.

Chiptag: *tosses a ball for Pooch* Fetch, boy

Pooch: *scampers off to fetch the ball, his tail wagging his hindquarters*

Chiptag: *crouches down to take the ball and pets the puppy* Good boy

Pooch: *puts his paws on his legs, panting happily, and slobbers on his knee*

Chiptag: *pushes him off, making a disgusted face* Ew, you slobbered on me

Pooch: *prances backward, barking at Chiptag to throw him the ball again*

Arjun: /me watches the exchange in amazement, "How did you DO that?"

Chiptag: *laughs and makes Pooch sit* I just wear a 'name replacer' or 'chat replacer' HUD.' type 'Name=Pooch,' and whatever I write is posted under Pooch's name. The one I use is simple, but others even impersonate NPCs in IMs

Dorketta: raises a timid hand and squeaks "Excuse me, Chiptag, but... um... what's an en-pee-see?"

Chiptag: *smiles amicably at Dorketta and nods understandingly* Oh, sorry. I shouldn't use acronyms without defining them first. NPC means 'non-player character,' which in virtual worlds means any character that isn't managed by a roleplayer—like Pooch here, who is just a scripted puppy from my Inventory

Mamakie: "Some NPCs are actual avatars doing chores or posting preset phrases, without a player managing them, in which case, their tags should say they're NPCs. Others are 'dummy avatars,' either the old prim or new animesh ones. Some homes have dummy babies, maids, babysitters, guards, and so on. Here's how an NPC maid could be used without needing a chat replacer:

Mamakie: /me turns to the (NPC) maid and snaps her fingers, "Maria..." The maid prepares three glasses of juice and passes them around. Mamakie takes a sip and turns to smile at her guests, "So, you were saying...?"

Mahir: "Some regions have NPCs set up for roles such as a barman or store clerk. Even if they are not scripted to say or do anything, you can make them emote and speak. In this example, the person playing Zaina also uses a chat replacer to impersonate a clerk scripted to buy and sell items:

> *(NPC) Clerk: /me leans his fat torso on the counter, looking at the young woman with beady eyes full of lust, a smile twisting his red face into a grimace. "There's my pretty girl. What can I do for you today, sweetie?" He lowers his voice and winks, "And what will you do for me in exchange?"*
>
> *Zaina: /me smiles innocently, pretending to be oblivious of his lascivious gaze and words. By acting naïve and gullible, she had gained his trust and gotten him to share several secrets. She chuckles to herself, "He thinks I'm weak and ignorant. If he only knew that behind this soft exterior lies a warrior"*

"You don't even need to have a dummy NPC present. We've discussed writing props into existence, so why not NPCs? For example, in a bar, write a barman into existence . They're minor characters, but that's no reason not to make them distinctive and memorable. Here's what happened when a couple entered the only place open one night—about the most awful hamburger joint you can imagine. I've taken out the dialog between the boy and girl for the sake of brevity.

> *(NPC) Waitress: /me, an overweight redhead in her early twenties, wearing black leather and chains under a grimy, once candy-striped apron, waddles up chewing gum with her black-lipped mouth open, the expression on her heavily pierced face clearly saying 'don't fuck with me,' and drawls, "Hey y'all. What'll it be?"*
>
> *Girl: /me tries to ignore the smell of stale grease that permeates the place and forces herself to smile at the waitress. "What's the house special tonight?"*
>
> *(NPC) Waitress: /me smirks. Did this girl think she was in an actual restaurant? Then she drawls facetiously, "Well, let's see... We's got sum reeeeel special hot dawgs 'n hambuggahs wid fries. How's dat sound?"*

Girl: /me almost looks like she'd rather throw up, but swallows hard and forces her voice to sound cheery. "Oh, that sounds great. I'll have a hamburger, but no fries please... Oh, and a Diet Coke."

Boy: /me gulps down his bile and stammers, "Ahm... the same, but a beer for me, if you have it."

(NPC) Waitress: /me nods and blows a bubble, which bursts around her black kisser, then licks it off before drawling, "Awll righty. Cummin' right up," and saunters off, enormous hips swaying.

Girl: /me takes out a handkerchief, wipes the dust and grime from her seat, and sits down daintily before smiling and saying... [dialog]

(NPC) Waitress: /me ambles back and plops the food on the table in no particular order, "Here ya'll go. Two buggahs, a Diet Coke an' a beer. Anything else, or does y'all want da bill awready? It IS gettin' kinda late, ya know."

Boy: /me blinks at the woman chewing like a cow. "The bill, please." Then he mutters to the girl, "Some customer service..."

Girl: /me forces a smile at the waitress and rearranges the food on the table, "Nothing else for me. We won't be long, promise." She nods pointedly at the boy.

Boy: /me frowns at the grimy glass, drinks his beer straight from the bottle after wiping the top with a napkin, and pushes his greasy burger to one side with distaste.

Girl: /me opens her burger and inspects it carefully, pulling some dead things out of it and placing them in a little mound on the table, trying not to look too disgusted, then starts nibbling at it around the edges.

(NPC) Waitress: /me saunters off and soon comes back to slap a stained piece of paper with some scribbles onto the table. "Here's ya bill. Let's wrap it up now, okay, folks? It's 'bout closin' time."

Girl: /me looks askance at the 'bill' and pays the waitress, then turns to the boy... [dialog]

(NPC) Waitress: /me finishes wiping the grime around the tables and starts clattering pots and pans noisily as if to say 'get the hell out of here already' without actually saying it...

[...and so on...]

> Write NPCs into existence anywhere. Just because a place looks empty doesn't mean it's meant to be.

"NPCs can be written into existence anywhere—as librarians, nurses, street vendors, students, you name it. Just because a place *looks* empty doesn't mean it's meant to be. High schools usually have hundreds of students, so although there may only be three PC students in a class, that doesn't mean there aren't many more. You should assume they are present as NPCs, even though you can't see them.

"Here's part of a scene where one student impersonated another (NPC) student to interact with her in class. As you will see, this confused the teacher and required an embarrassing explanation after the fact, so it's advisable to at least give your roleplay partners a heads-up before using invisible NPCs.

> *(NPC) Max: /me slides Jane a folded-up paper while the teacher isn't looking, then sits back, innocently facing the front.*
>
> *Jane: /me takes the paper under her hand and opens it, finding two carefully-rolled joints and a scribbled price. She grins, then slips a bill into the paper, folds it up again, and passes it back while the teacher isn't watching.*
>
> *(NPC) Max: /me takes the paper, glances at the bill, nods, and slips it into his pocket while the teacher isn't watching, all while looking forward innocently, then pokes Sally in the back with his pencil with a mischievous grin.*
>
> *Sally: /me spins around, glares at him and growls, "Stop pestering me, Max."*
>
> *Teacher: /me turns around and eyes the class sharply. "Beg your pardon?" She looks around, seeing no one else but the three girls in the room. "Who, pray tell, is Max?"*
>
> Jane: ((Sorry, he's an NPC student. I should have consulted with you first.))

Mahir: "In regions using group IMs to supplement roleplay, players impersonate NPCs for roles such as operators. If you don't have a chat replacer or one that will work in IMs, just put ((NPC Name)) before a post to indicate it's not you but the NPC speaking. For example, if Chiptag were impersonating a 911 operator in a group IM chat, we might do this:

> *Mahir: /me, panting, picks up the phone with trembling fingers and dials 911. "Come on, come ON, answer already."*
>
> *Chiptag: ((NPC George)) hears the old black analog phone ringing and sighs, lazily pulls his feet off his desk and takes the control to lower the TV volume. He noisily clears his throat, picks up the receiver, and says, in his most official-sounding voice, "911. What's your emergency?"*

Mamakie: "Another use of chat replacers is 'doubling.' If I have to go AFK, I'll ask Mahir to double for me. He will use the name replacer to post under my name so the scene won't be interrupted. But be forewarned—the SL Terms of Service prohibit 'spoofing' – impersonating other users without their permission."

Roleplaying in Personal IMs

Arjun: /me raises his hand, "You said some regions use group IMs. I've seen that here but wasn't sure of the rules. Also, can I roleplay with my friends in IMs?"

Mahir: "Thanks for that question, Arjun. That was actually our next topic. Let's start with personal IMs and leave group IMs for later. According to roleplay convention, personal IMs are used for OCC messages. But as I've said before, roleplay has no hard and fast rules, so nobody can tell you not to roleplay in IMs if you wish. Some people ONLY roleplay in Local Chat, but that's their choice."

Mamakie: "Mahir and I sometimes share erotic IMs while cuddling when we are with a roleplay group. You can also emote that you whisper something to another character and then use IMs as the whisper. Be sure not to ignore Local Chat, which should take precedence. Part of gaining confidence in your roleplay comes from doing it in front of others in Local Chat."

Mahir: "But let's say you're at the Landing and Local Chat is crowded with chit-chat, or you're using a chatty scripted object like a Trading Kiosk that fills Local Chat with repeated messages like this:

> *Virtual India Trading Kiosk: Make sure you have rezzed an item - checking...*
>
> *Virtual India Trading Kiosk: Normal trading day. Standard rate.*
>
> *Second Life: An object named [Virtual India Trading Kiosk] gave you this object: 'copper coin'*
>
> *Second Life: An object named [Virtual India Trading Kiosk] gave you this object: 'copper coin'*

"In such cases, you may want to roleplay in IMs until Local Chat is quiet enough to be used again comfortably. Another situation for roleplaying in IMs is when your partner goes outside chat range, so you can continue at a distance."

Chiptag: *unsheathes his mobile phone, holding it up for the group to see* Sometimes I use IMs to roleplay calls or text messages to people on my mobile phone

Mahir: /me snorts "This is rural India, Chiptag—there's no mobile service here"

Chiptag: "Hey, we're not in the 19th Century anymore, Mentor. According to the region's charter, this is *modern-day* rural India. Mobile phone penetration in India was already close to 90% in 2020, with well over a billion subscribers, and most of those were in rural areas."

Mahir: /me growls angrily, "Well, that may be, Chiptag, but it's against the region's rules. Using communication devices makes it too easy, so get off your lazy arse and go out to roleplay with people in Local Chat."

Chiptag: *laughs nonchalantly, re-sheathes his mobile phone, and winks conspiratorially at the rest of the group*

> IMs can disengage you from Local Chat and make you look like an AFK zombie, which is frustrating for others.

Mahir: /me scowls at Chiptag, then turns back to the group, "One problem with IMs is that having several private discussions going on at the same time can disengage you from what's happening in Local Chat and make you look like an AFK zombie, which is frustrating for others. There's also a risk of the lines becoming blurred when you roleplay IC in IMs and accidentally talk OOC in Local.

"That's why many people try to minimize IM conversations and ignore random IMs entirely when they're roleplaying, and some even say so in their profile. Others use automatic responses such as 'I'm roleplaying. Please approach me IC in Local Chat,' or 'Before you send that IM, ask yourself whether you could say it IC in Local,' or even 'I give preference to Local Chat over IMs to discourage their use.' That also lets people know you're not just ignoring them."

Chiptag: "I may have mentioned this before, but some of the most serious roleplayers even go to the extreme of making their accounts unsearchable, automatically or individually rejecting friend requests, and even turning off the 'eyes' on their friend list, so people won't IM them just to say hello every time they log on. This allows them to concentrate 100% on 'face-to-face' roleplay in Local Chat."

Arjun: /me pipes up, "Should you use double brackets for OOC messages when you're roleplaying in IMs?"

Mahir: "Another good question, and again, according to roleplay convention, you wouldn't, but I'm sure it wouldn't hurt if you did."

Mamakie: "That's actually one of the problems I have with roleplaying in IMs. I've been in situations where I wanted to say I didn't feel comfortable with where an RP was going, but I also thought it wasn't right to use double brackets in IMs, so how do I keep the IM in character and convey my OOC message at the same time? It can get really confusing.

"It's also a good idea to minimize the use of OOC IMs during roleplay in Local Chat, to avoid breaking the other players' focus. Some players have gotten into the bad habit of keeping up a running commentary on the roleplay in IMs between posting in Local Chat. Although IMs can help when you need to coordinate something, it can also distract players from concentrating on writing their posts.

"Especially if the scene is emotionally intense, you may not want to see comments that would detract from experiencing the scene to its fullest. It takes time, effort, and concentration to get into character and stay there, and receiving OOC messages all the time makes this all the more difficult.

"Bear in mind that we suspend disbelief to immerse ourselves in a play, movie, novel, or roleplay, so try not to do anything that might break that magic for yourself and the other roleplayers. If you want to write a critique of the roleplay, do it in a notecard or other document, then share your impressions with the other players after the scene has ended."

Mahir: "Well, we've gone over the two hours allocated for this class, so let's meet again in two days to continue."

CHAPTER TWELVE

MIXING IT UP – II

Two days later, the class meets again for the second half of the Advanced Roleplay Class. Mahir summarizes the last class and asks whether there are any questions before proceeding.

Roleplaying in Group IMs

Mahir: "Okay, the last class ended with roleplaying in personal IMs. I'd now like to move on to roleplaying in group IMs. Sometimes your RP group isn't within Local Chat range, but you want to keep them up-to-date on what's happening. That's where filler posts can come in handy—to fill others in on the roleplay, whether with a quick summary or a full description of what has transpired. For example, a worker at a fast-food joint can IM the group about how she is getting the place ready to receive customers:

> *Waitress: /me arrives early at the taco place and changes into her new uniform, giggling at what the tee-shirt says, 'If you don't like TACOS, I'm NACHO type.' She starts her shift by dusting off surfaces, sweeping floors, polishing tabletops, and making sure she has enough ingredients prepared for the day, then starts doing her college homework while she waits for the first customers to arrive.*

"There are many uses for group IMs. A couple might IM the group about arriving for a jalapeño-hot date at the taco place. The witness to a crime or other emergency might IM about calling 911 and providing first aid until the authorities arrive.

"Someone away on a journey might use a narrative post to share important occurrences of the trip related to the group's story, or the member of an RP group might just use a mood post to set the scene, tie it together, and move the story forward. These posts are not for the characters *per se* but rather for other players' benefit and enjoyment."

Chiptag: "These group IMs will most likely be missed by whoever is not inworld at the time, so some roleplay groups use platforms such as Discord (discordapp.com) for this kind of thing, since it allows access to the history of all threads' at any time, without needing to go inworld to receive them."

Mamakie: "Another method is to compile notecards of each scene to share with roleplay group members. However, if a member isn't present, they may risk metagaming with that information because it's hard to 'unknow' something once you know it. That's why some prefer to share the information IC so that they can use it without metagaming.

"You can write a post saying that you're telling the group about something and then share a notecard instead of posting a lengthy explanation. Speaking of which, please DO NOT include private IM communications without express permission from the other party or as needed to report an issue to a Moderator."

Mahir: "We commissioners often have IM chats about administrative issues, use of region resources, absent or sick villagers, and so on. But a lot of that, such as village development and defense plans, can be discussed IC by couching them in IC terms. For example, prim allowances can be building permits, going on the Marketplace can be shopping in the city, and so on."

Use group IMs to start a story by sending out 'lures' to a roleplay group so that anyone who feels so inclined can respond.

Mamakie: "Another good use of group IMs is to start a story by sending out 'lures,' which are often IMs to a roleplay group so that anyone who feels so inclined can respond. Lures are simply initial IC posts, often a paragraph or more, describing a scene or situation framed as a roleplay idea, followed by an OOC invitation for others to participate. In the invitation, you can state how many players can participate and whether the roleplay will be continued 'on-site' in Local Chat, through IMs at a distance, or in a separate group chat. Here's an example I saw just recently:

> *Sarah: Early one Monday morning, after catching a private jet back home, Sarah signs the papers to inherit and manage her recently deceased father's company. Walking into the office to check her mail, she notices a blank envelope reading 'URGENT! OPEN NOW! IMPORTANT!' Sitting at her father's desk, she opens the seal and reads... ((Your input here. One player needed on site))."*

Mahir: "When you answer a lure requiring you to go to a specific site, let the group know via a group IM so that the lure won't be answered by more people than it calls for. If you send the lure poster an initial IM before going, start with an interesting emote revealing something about your character and that advances the roleplay, not just 'Hey, where are you?' or 'Be right there.' For instance, in Mamakie's example, you would IM back with the letter's message, maybe giving her some news she can't ignore, and ask her to meet up in a dark alley to discuss it.

"When responses are to be given in IMs, tell the group when you start IMing with the person posting the lure. If more than the allotted number responds, they will have to choose whom to roleplay with. Please don't get upset if you're not accepted; there will always be another chance.

"Finally, lures MUST NOT be used to draw people into traps because that would be using OOC means to gain unfair IC advantages. If fighting might be involved in the roleplay, make that clear in the OOC invitation so that the other players can decide what color Karma Tag to use if and when they respond."

The whole point of having to eat, collect food, cook, and trade is an excuse to roleplay.

Mamakie: "Yes, and I will not tire of saying—NEVER attack anyone who has just logged or TPed in. Give them time to rez and get ready before commencing or resuming a fight. In other words, don't be a dick."

Using Notecards in Roleplay

Arjun: /me sits and listens with interest, taking notes and nodding. "If I might ask both of you a personal question... What are the worst roleplaying mistakes you have ever made? Your answer might help us to avoid making the same mistakes ourselves in the future."

Mamakie: "Good question. Mamakie was the village cook when I started here, and she wrote the commissioner a full report about what stocks were available, how much had gone bad, difficulties with the stocking system, ideas to improve it, and even ended it with conclusions and recommendations. As you might guess, the commissioner was not happy about this. He explained what should have been obvious to me—that the whole point of having to eat, collect food, cook, and trade was an excuse to roleplay, or better yet, a context within which to roleplay. He then gave me the task of using each point of my report as an opportunity to roleplay with him and other village members. That actually took me several days.

"So, here's my recommendation about writing letters and reports: don't do it—unless it's for a quest or something OOC. It's a piss-poor replacement for roleplay. Rather, talk to the person. And don't just sit there giving a long report without waiting for a response, like Mamakie tried to do before the commissioner stopped me. Take your time, share it little by little, wait for an answer, and make it a roleplay conversation. Of course, this is not a hard and fast rule, just a recommendation based on my own experience."

Urstud: "I've seen notecards used to describe package contents. For example, a man who visited his partner in jail emoted passing her a package and then shared this notecard with her, enabling her to roleplay using the items in jail:

> Package for <name> in jail
>
> - plain white brief-style underwear x 3
> - plain white tee-shirts x 3
> - plain sports bras x 2
> - tracksuit bottoms, female
> - flip-flops
> - towel, hand
> - towel, larger
> - foam earplugs
> - pencils x 2
> - notebook (moleskine pocket)
>
> [The above unpacked with store receipt]
>
> - small set of A5 stationary, envelopes, and stamps
> - a photo of us (taken from a frame at home)

Mahir: "Good point, Urstud. Objects are also available for leaving notes for people, which will give notecards when you click on them. And believe it or not, notecards can even be used for spreading diseases. Not long ago, an epidemic spread throughout the region when someone started sharing the following notecard with other players:

> Important RP info
>
> Congratulations (or not). You were recently in contact with a person (or surface) infected with an unknown but potentially serious disease. If you choose not to be infected, please disregard this notecard.
>
> Symptoms for infected patients:
>
> -- Headache [1 SL day after transmission]
>
> -- Chills and fever (severe enough to potentially cause hallucinations and abnormal behavior) [3 SL days after transmission]
>
> -- Weakness, loss of appetite, coughing up blood [1 week after]
>
> -- Weight loss if left untreated [11 SL days after transmission]
>
> IF LEFT UNTREATED (and if you OOCly choose), this disease can cause death. However, with appropriate medical treatment, it should clear up in 4-7 RL days.
>
> Please note that this strain of the disease can be transmitted through airborne particles or exchanging bodily fluids. If you have physical contact with, cough on, or exchange bodily fluids with someone after becoming infected, please share this notecard with them.

"When people went to the health clinic, they were instructed to take a medical chart (notecard) from a pile, complete it, and deposit it in a box. A form was even available for victims who were brought in DOA to be given to the medical examiner and mortician. These are only a few examples of the many creative uses you can give notecards to enhance your RP."

Pre-scripting Roleplay

Mahir: "So far, we've discussed spontaneous roleplay, which may have been decided on beforehand in general terms but not scripted or choreographed. You want to be careful about pre-scripting your roleplay. At one roleplay region, Mahir became so frustrated and angry at his boss that I sat down and wrote out a long tirade for him to spout as soon as he got a chance. When the time came, he started posting my script, paragraph by paragraph, like this:

> Mahir: /me's face contorts and turns an angry red, his eyes squeezed shut, fists tightened at his side, a guttural hissing sound coming from his clenched, bared teeth, like an overheated steam boiler. Suddenly, all the frustration and anger pent up inside exploded in a torrent of high-pitched yells. "Boss, I'm not going to take any more of this from you. I've busted my butt for you ever since I came on board, given back hundreds of times more than I've taken, filled the storeroom with all kinds of supplies, cooked dozens of meals for you and the rest, filled your coffers with gold, jewels, and coins..."
>
> Mahir: /me fights back angry tears and continues, hoarsely, "And what have I gotten back in return? Barely a kind word from you or anyone else." He mimics his boss's voice, "'Thank you, Mahir...' 'Good job, Mahir...' 'That's great, Mahir...'" He scoffs bitterly, shaking his head, "Practically the only kind words I've heard from you were when you wanted to 'fuck'—to use your own gross term—one of the women here. Instead, you criticize me for whatever I've said and not said, done and not done..."

"By that time, my boss IMed to tell me to stop chain-posting and that he refused to roleplay with something that it was obviously prewritten. But being the tempestuous, rebellious youth that I was..." he laughs, "...I was undeterred by this and selected a couple more paragraphs from my tirade to post, to which he said he had heard enough, got up, and left."

> Writing even semi-para posts in real time can tax an audience's patience, so pre-script events as much as you can beforehand.

Mamakie: "Well, when you throw a tantrum, you don't really want to listen to anyone else, but he may have been right, in this case at least. Roleplaying is about creating something together, a give and take, not a monolog. If you're like me and need to collect your thoughts before a foreseeable situation arises, you might make some 'notes to self' as a support for your roleplay, but not a complete script. There are obvious exceptions to this, of course, such as giving a speech or teaching a class, but in general, it's not considered good roleplay. The good thing, though, is that you kept your drama IC and didn't take it OOC. That's key when roleplaying."

Mahir: "Yes indeed. Other situations in which pre-scripting your posts is not only allowed but expected are events staged for an audience, such as weddings, ceremonies, rituals, and so on. They require considerable preparation to build the actual setting, develop a program of each character's actions, and even pre-script certain posts as necessary. You may want to see the event as a theatrical production, even if it is not advertised as such. I recommend loading an outline of the script to a service such as Google Docs so that all the players can contribute to developing it and everyone can see the latest version in real time. You can also use Discord or another service to discuss ideas, as they keep the history of the discussion.

"In preparing the setting, the players should agree what props to use and which ones will have animations or will only be emoted. If animations are used, be sure to choose them carefully beforehand and write their names and locations into the shared script to avoid bumbling around looking for the right animation during the event. Remember that you can write anything into existence. If you want smoke rising from an object, for instance, and don't have or don't know how to make a smoking object, you can just emote something like '/me watches the smoke rising from [the object] and gasps,' or some such.

"Taking the time to write even semi-para posts in real time can tax an audience's patience, so I recommend pre-scripting as much as you can beforehand. For instance, in the case of a wedding, the presiding player and the couple would pre-script their posts, including vows and other speech, along with the associated emotes. Once you have decided on the sequence of actions in your script, I suggest you roleplay the event beforehand and then edit the transcript and insert the posts into the script. This tends to make everyone's posts more spontaneous and realistic than writing them out in a vacuum. During the actual event, each player can then simply copy-paste their posts into Local Chat. But even then, you will want to remain flexible and edit your posts before hitting 'Enter,' adapting them to any foibles, interjections, or sudden inspirations."

Avoiding OOC Drama

Arjun: "I don't know whether this question is appropriate here, but I've seen profiles saying people don't want any 'drama.' I may be misunderstanding the term, but isn't that what roleplay is all about—creating a drama? Aren't we all like actors in an on-going play on the stage of this roleplay region?"

Mahir: "That's a great question, Arjun, and very much in line with this subject, so thanks. The dictionary defines drama as 'a composition intended to portray life or character or to tell a story, usually involving conflicts and emotions, through action and dialogue, as in a theatrical performance.' Sounds almost like a definition of roleplay, right?

Drama is great as long as you keep it IC and don't let it go OOC.

"But there's a big difference between IC drama and OOC drama. Conflict is fine as long as it's kept IC in Local Chat and everyone realizes that it's part of the roleplay. People whose characters are grumpy, nasty, offensive, or even anti-social IC may be gentle and friendly IRL. True roleplayers know the difference and act accordingly.

"The real problem, and what most people call 'drama,' is when a character's bad IC behavior crosses the line into OOC conflict. This kind of OOC drama is often caused by hurt feelings over issues such as arguments about the 'correct' way to roleplay, jealousy or possessiveness, disagreements about rules of combat, or people feeling slighted or offended in some way IRL."

Mamakie: "One of the main sources of OOC drama is arguments about how to roleplay. As we have emphasized several times, aside from each region's norms, there are no hard and fast rules for roleplay, only several conventions and best practices. If someone has a different roleplay style from yours, criticizing them will only upset them or start an argument. It's better just to set a good example of what you think is the right way and then let others decide whether to follow it or stick to their own.

"If others make mistakes, remember that nobody is perfect... well, except maybe for me." -laughs- "Other things that bother people and can be a source of OOC drama are being a Mary Sue or Gary Stu, always calling attention to oneself, ignoring other characters, trying to be the center of attention (the protagonist or main character syndrome), forming exclusive cliques, bullying (both IC and OOC), metagaming, godmodding, disrespecting others, nit-picking or being pedantic about rules, and so on."

Mahir: "Another source of OCC drama is arguments about the rules of combat. Each RP region has different combat rules, leading to some confusion, so it's important to know and follow those rules. We will discuss this in greater detail in another class on Capture Roleplay (CARP).

"Don't be too hard on others who break the rules, especially if they do so unwittingly or understand the rules differently from you. If you MUST insist on a rule, send them a COURTEOUS IM explaining the rule and asking them to please follow it when roleplaying with you. Don't get into an argument if they don't accept your request but agree to disagree and carry on with the RP, which is the ultimate reason for getting into a CARP situation in the first place."

Mamakie: "Remember that behind every avatar is an RL person with real feelings and emotions. For particularly intense scenes, you can put their minds at ease by giving them an OOC heads-up beforehand, periodically checking in to see if they're alright with what's happening during the roleplay, and finally thanking and congratulating them for their roleplay afterward.

"The key here is R.E.S.P.E.C.T. Your IC enemies should be your OOC friends, so try to keep it that way. Be gracious and courteous when you IM them. Thanking them for the RP will help bring you both back to reality, will make them feel appreciated, and will encourage them to continue improving, especially if they're new to roleplay."

The key is R.E.S.P.E.C.T. Your IC enemies should be your OOC friends, so try to keep it that way.

Mahir: "This IM can be as brief and simple as 'Thanks for the RP' or something more elaborate, highlighting specific parts that you especially liked, such as 'You're a worthy opponent, and I loved the creative way you handled the capture scene. It was a lot of fun, and I enjoyed it immensely. I hope we can roleplay again sometime soon.'"

Mamakie: "The less you know about the person behind the keyboard—and in my humble opinion, for roleplay purposes, the less you know, the better—the more important it is to be patient, lenient, and give them the benefit of the doubt. For all you know, they may be suffering from a painful loss, depression or anxiety, have autism spectrum disorder (ASD), bipolar disorder, or just be having a bad day. No amount of virtual damage to an avatar can compare to the real mental damage you can do to the emotionally vulnerable person behind the keyboard if you're not gentle."

Mahir: "If YOU start to feel upset and emotional IRL about something in the roleplay, open a courteous IM and try to resolve it NICELY with the players involved. It's better not to air your grievances with others in Local Chat. The LL Terms of Service forbid 'posting interpersonal disputes or personal negative commentary publicly when such communications should occur through private channels of communication.'

"Also, please don't complain to the Admins right away—there's little they can do about it, and they already have enough on their plates. If you get angry and report others without good cause, they will see you as immature, and others will start avoiding you. I've received complaints from people about someone's CHARACTER being mean or rude when they should have made those complaints IC to that character in Local Chat. That's why it's so important to know the difference between IC and OOC and keep the two separate in your own minds and in your roleplay. If their CHARACTER is rude, that is not necessarily their real-life personality."

Chiptag: "Of course, there are all types of people. Some are drama-llamas, and some are just nasty jerks, ranging from grumpiness to outright trolling—immature users who hide like cowards behind the anonymity of the web. The key is to avoid getting emotional, upset or stressed IRL. And whatever you do, DON'T FEED THE TROLLS by answering them in kind or arguing with them.

"There's no excuse for anyone to intimidate, insult or bully you OOC, but if they do, do NOT respond in kind. Rather, report them through the 'Help' function in your Karma Tag, then ignore them and find someone else to roleplay with. If they insist or stalk you, you can block them by right-clicking their tag or name in chat and clicking on Mute – Block, or by clicking on the 'Block' button in the lower right of the '2nd Life' tab of their profile.

"You also have the option to activate 'Send autoresponse to MUTED avatars' under Preferences – Privacy – Autoresponse 1 to send them a message next time they IM you, saying they have been blocked. Another way to enhance your privacy is to deactivate the 'Show in search' function in the '2nd Life' tab of your profile, which you can detail further in the first three options of Preferences – Privacy – General.

"If you get a lot of pesky friend requests from mere acquaintances, try Comm – Online Status – Reject all friendship requests. If you're tired of friends IMing you all the time, uncheck the boxes under the eye icon ('Friend can see when you're online') in your Friends List (Ctrl-Shift-F).

"Another important function few seem to know about is under Preferences – Privacy – LookAt, where I recommend checking all the boxes so that people won't see where you are looking, but you can see where they are looking if they haven't done the same. This is especially useful for women, as men will often interpret women looking at them as a come-on."

Mamakie: "If you're tired of roleplaying with your partners, please don't feel you have to 'ghost' them, which means simply disappearing and cutting off all communication with them. This is a cowardly, hurtful thing to do. Talk to them. Tell them you no longer want to roleplay with them, that you want to change directions, or whatever, but be upfront about it. Ghosting is a BIG no-no in the roleplay community.

"Of course, you're not responsible for how others will respond emotionally to your RP, but be aware that some people have a harder time keeping IC and OOC separate or are more sensitive, emotionally vulnerable, and susceptible than others to getting their RL feelings hurt. If that's something you care about—which I assume is the case—then try to avoid triggering potential causes for OOC drama."

Mahir: "Another source of OOC drama is 'roleplay burnout,' which can happen if you spend too much time roleplaying—you get fatigued, and your patience wears thin. Just like when seriously practicing any other artistic activity, it's important to take good care of yourself, eat properly, get enough exercise and sleep, and maintain a good balance of activities in your life. There's no point trying to be positive and creative when you've just pulled an all-nighter and have a major 'roleplay hangover.'"

Mamakie: "The first rule of roleplay is to have fun, but everyone has a different idea of fun—whether it's exploring, daily village life, eroticism, fighting and capturing or being captured, or whatever. So if you find that it's no longer fun for you, stop and do something else for a while, either here or in RL. If people let you down, betray or even kill you in roleplay, don't take it seriously or personally—it won't mean anything once you log out."

Are You Welcome?

Mahir: "Okay, we need to discuss one more sticky issue—the joys and perils of roleplaying in non-RP sims. If you do it well and people enjoy it, the effect can be like when actors play out an unexpected scene in a public space. But where roleplay isn't appreciated, where friends just get together to shoot the bull and have a good time, you may be about as popular as a mime crashing a family reunion and could be thrown out on your arse.

"To illustrate this, let me share some RP transcripts where the players were asked to stop roleplaying or leave the event. In the first case, a teenage girl, her hair in a tangled mess, goes to a Blues venue wearing flip-flops and an oversized flannel shirt only half-covering her panties and bra. Amid the usual greetings and chit-chat, she starts posting things like this:

/me strolls up, flops unceremoniously onto a chair, and glances around the venue, flicking her hair back, a bored look on her face. "Same ole, same ole, I see."

[Someone asks if she will be dancing]

/me lights a joint, takes a long drag, and lets it out slowly. "It's too early in da mornin' fo' dat much effort, ma friend."

[The DJ asks the crowd what they want to hear]

/me saunters over to the bar and slides onto a stool, looking around with a sour face and rolling her eyes, then slaps the counter and shouts in a raspy voice, "Hey, DJ, any chance I can hear da clinking o' some ice in a glass o' whiskey? What's a girl gotta do ta git a drink 'round here anyways?"

[A man sits at the bar next to her]

/me swivels around on the stool to check out the scene and spies a hot dude at the bar to her left. She grins to herself, licking her lips, and drawls, "Hey dude, ya seen da bartender anywheres 'round here?"

[He answers and gives her a beer]

/me takes the beer and checks out the man as she sips it. A little smile flickers across her lips as she flutters her eyelashes, trying to decide whether to ask him to dance or wait to see if he will ask her.

[He laughs and asks her to dance]

/me chugs the rest of the beer in one swig, lets out a little burp, and hops off the stool to stand in front of him, trying to dance despite her unsteady state. "Damn, I thought ya'd nevah ask."

[The DJ plays some Latin dance music]

/me shouts out, "Yeah, DJ man, now ya talkin'." She fumbles in her shirt pocket, finds a quarter, and flips it at the tip jar. "Here ya go, sexy... Dat's all I got. Keep da change, an' don' go spendin' it all in one place, ya hear?"

[They dance a while, the man leaves, and she dances alone for a time]

/me dances alone, looking around and sighing, "Looks like there's no single guys here who know a good thing when they see it." Finally, she loses her temper and stomps her feet, clenching her fists and shouting out, "WHAT'S A GIRL GOTTA DO TA GET A GUY TA INVITE HER TA DANCE 'ROUND HERE????"

[Snide remarks about whether she's 'a good thing,' and someone suggests that she should dress for the event]

/me sniffs under her arms, looks down at her shirt, and picks a dried blob of ketchup from it. "Watcha mean, dress? I actually changed my shirt ta come here... and I only worn it three days b'fore dat."

[People laugh, and she starts flirting with the DJ]

/me pulls a used bubble gum from behind her ear, pops it into her mouth, and gazes at the DJ with big, longing, puppy-dog eyes as she chews with her mouth open and pops bubbles, mumbling along with the song while looking up at the DJ as if she were singing the words to him.

[The DJ returns the flirts]

/me turns and winks at [the club owner] as she pops an extra big bubble. "Hey, Mom, can I take him home wid me after dis set? I promise ta brush him 'n clean up aftah him."

[At this point, the club owner IMs her]

Owner: There are places to roleplay and places not to roleplay.

Girl: I thought SL was ALL about roleplay.

Owner: No, SL is not all about roleplay at all.

Girl: It's all RP for me. That's why I use a lot of 'emotes' so people will know I'm IC :-)

Owner: I know a troll when I see one, and you're being a troll.

Girl: Aw, c'mon. There's a BIG difference between a troll and an actual roleplayer.

Owner: Really?? What is the difference, pray tell? Bugging people is trolling.

Girl: I see roleplay as an art form and practice it whenever and wherever I can.

Owner: Do you think you are roleplaying here? Who are the other roleplayers? You should try to roleplay with people who are into that. There are many in SL. I think you would be good.

Girl: Oh, I do, but I'm always looking for new, interesting venues to try.

Owner: I have had bossy teens in my life. Three of them. Been there, done that, got the tee-shirt.

Girl: OMG, no wonder you got upset.

Owner: Not really. I just didn't like your attitude, but good roleplay :-) You do need to move on to a better place for your skills. We are all old people here... Go and roleplay with some younger people.

Mahir: "The girl finally got the message and left, but it's interesting to note that her roleplay was so effective that the owner actually got upset at her 'attitude' and put her in the category of 'bossy teens' and not in the other 'old people' in the group.

"This next case is a scene Mamakie and I played out at a Western-themed dance venue. I was wearing a tuxedo, and she was elegantly dressed in a formal gown with a character tag saying 'High-class lady.'

Mamakie: /me glides in, hand-in-hand with Mahir, then pulls back on his hand, furrowing her brow. "Oh, no, darling, this place is too packed. Let's go back to that other place."

Mahir: /me looks around and answers excitedly, "But it's ROCKING here."

Mamakie: /me looks down her nose at the people around her. "Are you sure it's safe?" She clutches her purse closer, her eyes darting around warily.

Mahir: /me steps closer to her. "Come on, baby, let's dance. Everything will be alright."

Mamakie: /me takes a deep breath and shrugs, "Oh, alright darling..." then tweaks his cheeks. "Anything for my coochie-coo."

Mahir: /me holds her tight, stroking her smooth, silky skin as they dance.

Mamakie: /me wraps her arms around his neck and shivers with delight as he strokes her bare back.

Mahir: /me feels her warmth, taking in the sweet smell of her perfume, and slips his hand down, feeling the smooth roundness of her bum.

DJ: lol

Mamakie: /me feels his hands roaming down to her bum and reaches down to pull his hand up again to her back, whispering in his ear, "Behave yourself. People will see us."

Mahir: /me squeezes her tighter, pressing against her. "I don't care baby. I just want to hold you tight."

Mamakie: /me slaps his hand, looking around nervously at the people nearby.

Owner: Please do that in IM, guys.

DJ: Yes, please.

Mamakie: "We did take it to IMs because we think it's important not to give roleplay and roleplayers a bad name by being obnoxious. Does anyone have any other examples of roleplaying in non-RP venues?"

Urstud: -looks at EyeCandey and Dorketta, sees them urging him on, and raises his hand "The three of us went to a topless dance party and decided on a scene where the two women would get into a fight over me. Like you said, Local Chat was full of greetings, chit-chat and canned gestures. Here's an edited transcript:

EyeCandey: :giggles as Urstud whirls her around, 'Hey, you're making me dizzy'

Dorketta: dances past Urstud and pinches his ass, winking and puckering her lips at him

Urstud: -turns to look at Dorketta, grinning and rubbing his ass

EyeCandey: :bares her teeth at Dorketta and growls, 'Hey, you leave my man alone'

Dorketta: shoves EyeCandey out of the way with her hip and turns to Urstud, grinning, "Hey there handsome, why not dance with a REAL woman?"

Urstud: -looks from one woman to the other, uncertain what to do

EyeCandey: :stops dancing and turns to face Dorketta, reaching out to tug her hair. 'Hey, bitch, no dumb blonde is gonna take away my man'

Owner: wtfff?

Dorketta: cries out as EyeCandey pulls her hair, and aims a slap at her face

Urstud: -stops dancing and backs away, watching the two women fight

DJ: The Cat Fights are on Fridays

EyeCandey: :yelps at the slap and aims a scratch at Dorketta's face with her fingernails. 'Come on. I may be small, but I'm wiry. Let's see whatcha got'

Dorketta: dodges her fingernails, grinning, and aims a slap at her tits

EyeCandey: :growls in pain as Dorketta slaps her bare breast and aims another scratch at her face

Owner: RP is mostly best for RP places

DJ: Agreed. We are here to enjoy the party. Please take RP where RP belongs

Mamakie: "Thanks for that example. It was a good scene and you roleplayed it well, but the fact is that most music and dance venue owners are trying to make money, and they don't want people doing things that might disturb the party atmosphere and affect their bottom line. So as a last word of hard-learned advice, if you want to RP in places like that, try something very low-key with short posts first to see how people respond, before going deeper. Better yet, IM the owners or DJs to ask whether they would object to your roleplaying a little scene during the event. Like I said, we don't want to give roleplay and roleplayers a bad name."

Most dance venues are trying to make money, and disturbing the party atmosphere can affect their bottom line.

Mahir: /me hands out a notecard "Okay, time for your test."

Arjun opens the notecard, which has the usual question: "Summarize what you have learned today in a few short sentences," and writes:

- Do not be afraid to evoke intense emotions in your roleplay.
- Shake things up from time to time by doing something nobody expects.
- Use a name replacer to impersonate NPCs during a scene.
- Roleplay in personal IMs can be used, but sparingly and only when necessary.
- Roleplay in group IMs can be used for sending out lures and fillers.
- Be careful of people's feelings, and don't let IC drama turn into OOC drama.
- When roleplaying in non-RP sims, take care not to bother or upset non-roleplayers.

Why are you here, Arjun?

To learn to be more creative and push the limits.

CHAPTER THIRTEEN

COLLECTING RESOURCES

Dharma Guide: Congratulations. You have passed the Advanced Roleplay Class and advanced to Level 20 - Citizen. You now have a capacity for 25 HP and a new category in your Region Map HUD: Resources. Please check your Karma Tag for your next quest.

Status:	Citizen
Level:	20
HP:	24.8

Dharma Guide: You have accepted the quest "Mining." To complete it, take a small log and iron ingot to the blacksmith to make a pickaxe, then mine 10 nuggets of each type of metal and have them smelted into ingots. Enjoy.

The mining area is northeast of the Landing, so Arjun and Chris pass by the Communal Garden to tend their crops and chat with other farmers, then cross the Simlipal Bridge, greeting some fisherfolk in the shallows below. They cut through Simlipal Village, stopping along the way to buy five small logs at the trading kiosk, then pick their way through the pine forest to the Namdapha Village. There Arjun buys five iron ingots, then takes everything to the blacksmith. Meanwhile, Chris has been IMing the Virtual India group chat.

Chris: Any smithy available to make a pickaxe for the mining quest?

Baldomar: Be there in a minute

Chris: Thanks Bal :-)

Arjun: /me approaches the blacksmith's shop loaded down with five small logs and five iron ingots and dumps them heavily on the smithy's worktable with a weary sigh, wiping the sweat from his brow with the back of his hand. "Good morning, sir... um... I'm Arjun, and this is my friend Chris... um... I'm doing the mining quest and want to have five pickaxes made 'cause... um... I hear they wear out after 100 uses, so... um... I might as well have more than one made, right?"

Baldomar: /me stops his work, raises his safety goggles to his forehead and wipes grimy hands on his leather apron, then winks at his friend Chris and turns to nod seriously at Arjun, sizing him up shrewdly "You're absolutely right, Arjun," he growls in a gruff tone. "I'm Baldomar. You must have heard of me because I'm the best. My work is guaranteed, but it's not cheap. That'll be two gold coins each."

Chris: /me looks from one to the other but holds his tongue

Arjun: /me gasps in dismay. "What? One thousand coins?" he exclaims. Baldomar was asking twice the going rate, so he would have to offer much less to get him down to the right price. "Where would I find that kind of money? Do I look like a tourist to you? I'm not asking you for the materials, just for the work. I thought you'd ask me for something more like five silvers each."

Baldomar: /me chuckles and shakes his head. "You might get one of those youngsters who don't know an anvil from a sawhorse to charge you fifty copper, but I'm the best blacksmith in the region... I tell you what I'll do... Since Chris here is my good friend, I'll let you have them for 150 each. Deal, buddy?"

Chris: /me raises his hands defensively and backs away, shaking his head "Hey, leave me out of this... This is just between you two"

Arjun: /me eyes the blacksmith doubtfully, "I'm asking for five pickaxes at once, which saves you time and effort..." Then he grins as though seeing through the smithy's ruse and states with greater confidence, "How about this... I pay you 100 coins each, just because you're Chris's good friend, and you invite us both to some fruit juice after we're done to call it even," then adds with a smirk, "Deal, buddy?"

Baldomar: /me laughs mirthlessly and nods grudgingly as he fires up the forge and turns on the bellows. "Your friend drives a hard bargain, Chris." He lowers his goggles and takes up some long tongs and a heavy hammer, then holds each bar in the forge until it is reddish-orange and, taking it to the anvil, beats it into shape. "Some folk think that being a good smithy is all about brute strength, but they're dead wrong," he bellows over the racket. "It's mostly about knowing how to hit at just the right time, with just enough force, at just the right angle, using just the right hammer..." He puts the piece back into the forge for a while and wipes his sweating brow with his long, rough cotton sleeve. "Of course, you have to be strong enough to control the hammer just right, but you also need a delicate touch, mind you... Sorta like dealing with the ladies, you know?"

Chris: /me takes a shaver and one of the small logs to the carpentry workbench and starts shaving it into a handle "Baldomar has been in this business ever since I can remember. He really is the best around..." he tells Arjun, then comes closer to whisper confidentially "...if you don't mind his attitude"

Mining

They continue talking as they work, Baldomar fussing and fuming at everything under the sun and the boys mostly listening while shaving the logs into handles until the blacksmith finally fits the heads to the handles and gives Arjun his five pickaxes. They then sit to rest and have their fruit juice while Arjun reluctantly counts out the 500 coins for Baldomar.

After taking their leave, Arjun opens his Region Map HUD, which now shows several black dots around the village indicating the mines for tin, copper, gold, silver, and iron. There is also a coal mine in Sundarbans near the Raider Castle, a ceramic clay mine in Hemis, a salt mine on Rajasthan's western beach, and a diamond mine in the northern hills, but those don't seem to be part of this quest.

The boys visit the tin mine first. Chris shows Arjun how to mine, placing a collecting basket near it, wearing the pickaxe, and 'sitting' on the rock, upon which he starts swinging at it vigorously to the sound of iron striking stone and rubble hitting the ground. Arjun gets a few pieces of sterile rock before the first chunk of copper ore enters his basket after a few minutes. At this rate he calculates it will take him about half an hour to collect ten pieces of ore.

Just as he is going to suggest that his atman could be doing something else in the meantime, Arjun stops swinging his pickaxe and leans on it, panting, and has to 'sit' on the rock to start again. "So much for AFK mining," he chuckles. He then tries to add another pickaxe to save time, but it detaches, and a message in Local Chat says: "You can only use one pickaxe at a time." He tells Chris, who only nods and explains that all tools are scripted that way in Virtual India, unlike other regions, where he once had twenty pickaxes going at the same time.

Once Arjun has his 11 nuggets of tin ("one extra for good measure"), they climb the slope northward through the pine forest to the copper mine and repeat the process, then eastward to the gold mine, southeast to the silver mine, and due south to the iron mine. Finally, they take their stock for the blacksmith to turn into bars in his enormous smelter.

Baldomar: /me stops his work with a sigh and looks at the baskets blankly. "Where's your coal?" he growls testily, scowling at Arjun.

Arjun: /me blinks stupidly. "Coal?" he echoes, glancing at Chris in confusion.

Chris: /me snaps his finger and stamps his foot "Oh bugger, I forgot. You also need two pieces of coal to make each ingot"

So they trudge southward, stopping for a moment at the old stone Christian church to listen to the haunting Gregorian chants, then on to the coal mine. An hour later, they return to the blacksmith, beads of sweat tracing rivulets through the black coal dust on their contented faces, having filled a basket each with coal.

Baldomar: /me shovels the coal into his refractory-cement smelter and fires it up, then dumps the first basket of nuggets into a clay-graphite crucible and stands back to wait for it to melt. "Each bar takes more or less ten nuggets to make, so it's a good thing you got a little extra," he admits. As soon as the nuggets have melted, he skims the slag off the top, pours the molten metal into a graphite mold, and lets it cool while he starts on the next metal using a clean crucible.

Shortly after the last ingot is ready, a message appears in Arjun's Local Chat:

> Dharma Guide: Congratulations. You have completed the "Mining" Quest and advanced to Level 21 - Miner. Check your Karma Tag for your next quest.

By now, it is well past noon, so they go to the Namdapha tavern for lunch. Checking his Karma Tag, Arjun sees that his HP has dropped from 24.4 to 8.3. "Why have I lost so much HP?" he asks Chris.

"Heavy manual labour uses much more HP than the normal rate," Chris replies, "and we've been working hard, sooo...." he chuckles.

"Oh yes, I think you said something about that before," Arjun says. He gives Chris his fishstew and eats his tutti-frutti, for 8 HP each, and they top that off with some raw food to buff all the way up. His Karma Tag now reads:

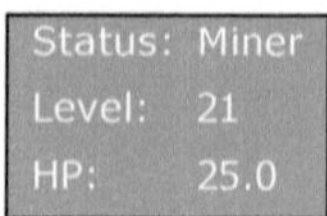

Logging

"What's your next quest?" Chris asks the next day at the Landing.

Arjun accepts the next quest and reads the message in Local Chat to Chris:

> Dharma Guide: You have accepted the quest "Logging." To complete it, take a log and iron ingot between Jnana and Shringara to make an axe, then fell enough trees to collect small, medium, large, and extra-large logs and planks, plus a bundle of scrap wood. Good luck.

Arjun frowns. "Between Jnana and Shringara? I don't see them on the map." He looks to Chris who just hums a little tune and looks around distractedly. Arjun searches his 'memory' for a while and finally lights up. "Of course. Jnana is knowledge and Shringara is erotic love, so the Temple of Knowledge and the Love Temple." He checks his map and waggles his head, grinning at Chris. "Between them is Indravati Village. Let's go."

They set off at a southwesterly trot through the pine forest, across Simlipal Village and the Bridge, stopping briefly to tend their crops and buy another log, and then find the axesmith's shop in a small, dusty, run-down corner between two streets in Indravati.

Arjun hands over an iron ingot and the log, and watches as the axesmith fashions the ingot into an axe head, tempers and sharpens it, then shapes the log into a long, strong handle and fastens the blade to it. Arjun pays special attention to how the axesmith fully emotes everything he is doing. Handing the axe to Arjun, the man winks at him and grins, "Don't cut your foot off with it."

Thanking him, the boys walk north into the jungle, and Arjun clicks on the trees until he finds one that says 'extra-large.' "Might as well do the hardest one first and then the easier ones as I get tired," he chuckles.

"Yeah, but you'll need to cut two extra-large trees, one for the log and another to cut into the planks."

Arjun takes a deep breath and, under Chris's instruction, wears the axe, clicks the tree again to choose 'Fell,' then 'sits' on it. He starts swinging the axe with long, heavy strokes, making chopping sounds, while a hovertext shows his progress. "What's the wood for?" Arjun asks between blows of his axe.

> Scripted chores usually take a few minutes –plenty of time to write detailed posts.

"Well, you can sell it at a kiosk, but you also need both logs and planks to make tools and lots of other things, and eventually even to build your own house," Chris replies. "I suggest you keep all your wood for now until you're ready to build your home. It's a quest you can do later," he explains.

After what seems like a long time, during which Arjun has to stop to rest and eat a snack three times, the tree turns into a huge log that falls sideways with a horrible groaning, crunching, crashing sound. "Wow, that's pretty impressive," Arjun laughs as he takes it into his Inventory and goes to look for the next tree.

Chris [in IM]: Now that you understand the technique, let's practice emoting how you would fell the other trees. Bear in mind that the whole purpose for the roleplay support system is to provide situations for roleplay. An extra-large tree takes a good five minutes, which is plenty of time to write detailed posts.

Chris: /me chops off the bark around the base to give him better access to the wood, then starts cutting out an open wedge shape on the side he wants the tree to fall. Once he is about half-way through, he goes around to the other side and cuts out another wedge shape a little above the first one until the tree starts to lean. "TIIIIIIMBEEEEEER," he shouts as he runs in the opposite direction.

Arjun: Good job. While you were doing that, I watched a short video online about how to fell a tree with an axe, so let me try.

Arjun: /me sharpens his axe with a whetstone first. "Like anything in life, you need to sharpen your tools to avoid having to work harder than necessary," he explains. Then he clears away the underbrush and branches within reach of his axe. "Safety first, right?" He removes about two feet of the bark all around, then uses downward and upward chops to slice out a wide face cut. He places his axe head against the cut, sights down the handle, and adjusts the cut to make sure the tree will fall in the right direction. "Don't want it to break any others as it falls," he chuckles. Next, he starts on the back cut about two inches above the bottom of the face cut, making sure it's parallel and leaving about ten percent of hinge wood to hold the tree as it falls. "You might want to stand back now, Chris," he pants as he starts cutting gradually into the hinge wood until it starts to groan, then steps away and shouts "TIIIMBEEERRR" as the tree slowly topples in the exact direction he wanted it to go.

Chris: /me stands back as the tree starts to fall, then pats Arjun on the back, giving him a wide grin. "Good job, mate. I'll clean this one up while you go for the next one." He starts cutting away the branches and stripping off the bark while Arjun tackles his next tree

Once Arjun has all the logs he needs, the boys go to the sawmill to have one of them cut into planks. The carpenter puts the extra-large log on the mill and cuts it into two extra-large planks. He then cuts one of these into two large planks, one of these into two medium planks, one of these into two small planks, and one of these into scrap, emoting what he is doing all the while. Soon afterward, a message appears in Arjun's Local Chat:

> Dharma Guide: Congratulations. You have successfully completed the "Logging" Quest and advanced to Level 22 - Logger. Please check your Karma Tag for your next quest.

A Scorpion Sting

Contented with a good day's work, the boys take a short-cut toward their favorite spot at the Papikonda Spa for some refreshments, when suddenly...

> Karma Tag: You feel a painful sting or bite. Could it be a scorpion? A viper? A poisonous centipede? Your HP will go down faster until you find a cure. Create a good roleplay story about it, describing it however you want.

Arjun: /me screams as a searing pain shoots through his foot like being stabbed with a red-hot skewer. He jumps back and sees a big black scorpion scuttle away through the underbrush as he slumps to the ground, clutching his foot and crying out "Owwwww, dammit! I've been stung. I think it was a scorpion."

Chris: /me, alarmed at Arjun's yelling, kneels beside him and looks at the foot where a nasty red spot is growing and swelling, then jumps up, cups his hands around his mouth and shouts desperately:

Chris: shouts: **"HELP! WE NEED A HEALER! CAN ANYBODY HEAR ME? HEEEEEEEEEEELP!"**

> *Karma Tag: You now have 21.5 HP*
>
> *Elaine: entered chat range (17.64 m)*

Elaine: /me is tending her herb patch at the Communal Garden when she hears a desperate shout for help. She immediately drops her hoe, grabs her healer's bag and runs toward the sound. "What happened? I'm a healer—how can I help?"

Arjun: /me clutches his throbbing foot, which is now swollen like a club and turning purple. He fights back tears and clenches his teeth in pain, "My foot. I think a scorpion stung me."

Chris: /me beckons the healer over, "Oh, thank the gods, Elaine. Arjun needs help, fast." He points to Arjun's foot and moans as he sees it swelling more and changing colour. "Can you do anything for him?"

Karma Tag: You now have 21.0 HP

Elaine: /me kneels next to Arjun and inspects his foot. "Yes, that looks like a scorpion sting. Did you see what it looked like?" She rummages in her bag and pulls out a strip of pain relief tablets and a gel icepack compress. She passes Chris the tablets and a water bottle, "Give him one of these now and make sure he takes one every six hours for the pain." She then drapes a cloth over the icepack and places it gently over the swollen area. "This should help bring the swelling down."

Arjun: /me winces and gasps as she lays the icepack onto his swollen foot, then moans through clenched teeth, "It was big and black. I saw it running away." His vision is starting to cloud over, and he lies down to keep from passing out.

Chris: /me helps Arjun lie down, then folds up his own shirt and places it under Arjun's head, murmuring in soothing tones "Take it easy bro, you'll be alright. Elaine is the best healer I know. She's the director of the Health Clinic." He takes the tablets and water bottle from Elaine and helps Arjun take one of the tablets

Karma Tag: You now have 20.5 HP

Elaine: /me selects a vial of antivenom and a syringe, pierces the rubber top and pulls back the plunger to draw the liquid into the barrel. "Hmm... okay, so it was probably a giant forest scorpion. They're big, ugly, and aggressive, but not as venomous as some others. You're lucky it wasn't a deathstalker, or you might already be dead. Okay, breathe deeply now." She would take Arjun's arm, cotton swab it with alcohol and inject the antivenom straight into his vein.

Second Life: secondlife:///app/agent/Elaine gave you this object: Antivenom serum

Arjun: /me sits up a little to take the tablet with a swallow of water, then lies back again and looks at the syringe with horror. He's always hated injections but he lets Elaine take his arm and looks away, screwing up his face as he holds his breath against the jab, then starts panting heavily as the cool liquid flows into his arm. "Yeah, I feel really lucky right about now," he moans.

Karma Tag: Rez your food now. You have 60 seconds. If you rez more than you need, it will go to waste.

Arjun rezzes the antivenom serum to the ground, and the system takes it, the same as food.

Karma Tag: You have been successfully healed.

Chris: /me would help Elaine to hold Arjun still for the injection, then smirks at his reaction to the shot and laughs at his comment "Well, good thing you're not gonna die on me, bro, or I'd have to find another noob to mentor and start my quest all over again"

Elaine: /me puts away the vial and syringe, closes her bag, and stands up. "Well, I'm done here. Arjun, I want you to take it easy for the rest of the day and keep taking those tablets. Keep that compress on as long as it's still cool. If you have any complications, you can usually find me at the clinic. Thanks for your help, Chris." She turns and walks back to the Communal Garden to fetch her hoe.

Elaine: left chat range

Arjun lies still until the medicine takes effect, then Chris helps him stand and hobble over to the Pub for dinner. As they eat, Arjun accepts his next quest:

Dharma Guide: You have accepted the quest "ERP Class." To complete it, go to the home of Prajapati Daksha's daughter and the god whose consort she is on Wednesday at 2:00 pm. You will be tested, so pay attention. Good luck.

Arjun: /me raises an eyebrow "ERP?"

Chris: /me looks up, faking surprise "Arjun, you're supposed to cover your mouth when you burp, and say 'excuse me'"

Arjun: /me chuckles, "I'm not burping, stupid, I'm asking what E.R.P. means."

Chris: /me chuckles with a twinkle in his eye "Oh, that's LOADS of fun" then adds, with an air of mystery "You'll see tomorrow at the class..." then thinks better of it and adds "...but I'll give you a hint: The E stands for 'Erotic'"

Arjun: /me gulps and turns as red as a beet, "Oh... um... so... this class is gonna be about... SEX?" He whispers the last word and casts a bashful glance around to see if anyone is watching.

To Arjun's chagrin, there is Eswaria shaking her head and smirking at him. Next to her, EyeCandey is puckering her red kisser and fluttering her long eyelashes suggestively. Dorketta is gazing at him with forlorn longing and wringing her hands at her clunky prim waist. Arjun wishes the ground would open up and swallow him. He quickly passes Chris his report and logs out, still blushing.

Why are you here, Arjun?

*To do grunt work like mining and chopping wood and try not to die or make too much of a fool of myself *laughs**

CHAPTER FOURTEEN

EROTIC ROLEPLAY

Prajapati Daksha's daughter' turns out to be Rati, the goddess of sexual pleasure, and 'the god whose consort she is' proves to be Kamadeva, the god of love, so the class would be held at the Love Temple.

At 2:00 pm, Arjun strolls into the Love Temple with wonder. Several students are already there, talking in hushed voices and gawking at the erotic scenes depicted in paintings and carvings along the walls, giggling softly to each other. At the head of the long hall is a portrayal of Kamadeva and Rati locked in a passionate embrace, in front sits a long stone altar, bathed in bright sunlight, where a couple is trying some of its animations.

Sex is one of the most common activities in virtual worlds, but also one of the worst roleplayed.

Abashed at the scenes' brazenness, Arjun backs toward the end of the hall and bumps into something hard. Turning, he sees an enormous marble phallus towering above him, its head reaching half-way to the soaring ceiling. A gleaming white liquid flows from the tip and pools at the base around massive testicles, where blue and pink poseballs invite visitors to make their 'offerings' of passion and ecstasy to Rati and Kamadeva.

"They say the gods bless this place, and women who have sex here are almost certain to get pregnant," says a soft, musical voice at his shoulder. Startled out of his reverie, Arjun turns to see Eswaria's lovely face close to his, her dark eyes bright with an emotion he can't quite make out.

"I... um... I'll make sure not to have..." *gulps* "...sex here then," is all that Arjun can think to blurt out, to which Eswaria smirks and turns away. Admiringly, regretfully, he watches her graceful figure retreat as she returns to mingle with the group. "I'm such a dork," he murmurs, kicking himself.

"Now then... ERP," proclaims Mahir as he strides through the entrance, arm in arm with Mamakie, and the group gathers around. "ERP stands for erotic roleplay, which is a subset of MRP, or mature roleplay. Erotic Roleplay can be anything from cuddles and intercourse to BDSM and rape.

"Sex is one of the most common activities in virtual worlds, but it's also one of the worst roleplayed, as we will see. There is a BIG difference between good ERP and the kind of cyber-sex or pixel-porn most people engage in. We hope this class will change that to some degree. Let's start with a bad example, and then we'll analyze it and see how we can improve on it."

[Animation: sitting and kissing]

Mahir: kissing her pushing his tongue into her mouth UR so hot babe

Mahir: tugging at her nipples making them hard

Mamakie: Mmmmmm

[Animation: lap sit]

[Animation: hard ride]

[Animation: sweet caress]

Mahir: stroking her body forcing his hand between her legs feeling she is wet

Mamakie: /me moans and grabs his stiff throbbing cock

[Animation: missionary]

Mahir: thrusting his huge thick cock into her tight pussy making her scream

Mamakie: Ohhhhhh

Mahir: exploding into her making her pregnant

Mahir: "Okay, okay, we may be exaggerating here a bit, but you get the point."

Urstud: "I don't think you're exaggerating at all, Mentor. In fact, that's pretty much what goes on most of the time."

Dorketta: raises a timid finger and squeaks, "I don't see what's wrong with what you did. It looked fine to me... I mean... not that I would know, but..."

Mahir: "Okay then, see what we did wrong. We're flipping through animations and letting them do all the work, the narrative is scanty and far too general, and we're powerplaying all over the place. There's really very little to work with except for what you see in the pixels, which makes it more pixel-sex than actual ERP.

"I also used netspeak, chain posted, used the '-ing' form of verbs instead of third-person present, left out punctuation, didn't differentiate between narrative and dialog using something like '/me' and quotation marks, and somehow spoke while I had my tongue down her throat" –laughs–

Animations versus Emotes

Mahir: "Let's look more closely at each of our main mistakes. One was letting the animations roleplay for us, and as Mamakie illustrated, all some people do is moan and groan. The animations were doing a lot more than what we described, when it should have been the other way around. Our narrative should enrich the animations and go beyond them, not be replaced or overshadowed by them.

"There are many animations for cuddling and sex, BUT… are they really necessary? From what I've seen, the better the animations, the worse the roleplay. Some of the best ERP I've seen used only static poses or none at all, while some of the worst involved the highest-quality animations. Instead of writing a story together, some just seem to be watching virtual pornography scenes.

"Now, I'm not here to criticize that choice, but I WILL say that it's not true roleplay. Granted, people want to feel eroticized by ERP. That's kinda the point, anyway, isn't it? And I won't deny that today's mesh bodies and heads and mocap animations do offer a lot of good eye candy. But in my humble opinion, if you just want to see naked bodies having sex, then go watch a porn flick."

-laughter around the circle-

"Seriously though, most of you have read erotic literature, which incites you to turn words into images in your mind. Well, ERP is about creating that kind of writing together, evoking images with verbal descriptions in a play of give and take, building on what the other writes, each taking it a step further. Try to write detailed descriptions, and not just what the animations are doing, which is already pretty obvious.

> Write detailed descriptions, not just what the animations are doing. Take your time and involve all the senses.

"You can describe highly nuanced actions and movements. For example, don't just TELL me you're kissing or stroking me—paint a picture in your imagination and then describe it in detail and make me really FEEL it. Tell me HOW are you touching me: roughly or gently, with powerful paws or trembling fingers, digging in your fingernails or with a feather touch.

"Likewise, a kiss is not just a kiss—it will mean something entirely different depending on where and HOW it's given. Are you brushing your lips softly along my shoulder or pressing them eagerly to mine, running the tip of your tongue slowly around the curves of my ear or seeking my tongue greedily with it? Are our tongues dancing a passionate tango? Or maybe you're nibbling and sucking on my neck or some other part of my body.

"Take your time and try to involve as many sensations as possible. Explore all six senses, not just sight and touch, but also what you hear, taste, smell, and that *je ne sais quoi* that moves deep within you. What does it feel like to be touched and to touch in a certain place and manner, and how does your body respond to it? How do you look, and what do you see and let be seen? What are you smelling or tasting, and what does it compare to?

"Also, what sounds are you making and hearing? Sweating bodies slap together, beds creak and groan, coitus makes wet noises, and even caresses and kisses can be heard. As in RL sex, ERP is more about actions than dialog, but if your character is going to speak, then emote how their voice sounds. Is it harsh and demanding, hoarse or husky with lust, sweetly murmured or breathily whispered in an ear?

"Body parts can be described creatively, evocatively, using analogies and similes, or in anything from vulgar language to scientifically correct terms. For example, if a male character is rude and crude, he might 'grope' or 'fondle' his partner's 'boobs' or 'jugs,' but if he is more refined or romantic, he is more likely to 'caress' or 'stroke' her 'breasts' or 'bosom.'"

Mamakie: /me cuts in, "I've seen guys write things like '/me thrusts deep into her with his enormous, thick cock, as only an awesome lover can do.' Roleplay is not for flattering yourself but for describing a scene and giving your partner some fun, so please don't be that person. It's tacky and just... EWWW. Besides, even if size matters, oversize kills the fantasy."

Mahir: /me laughs, "I'll keep that in mind for next time."

Mamakie: /me smirks at Mahir then turns to the class. "Finally, there are feelings and emotions. How does the scene make you feel? Lustful or romantic, angry or enamored, fearful or sad? And how can you emote it in such a way that your partner will perceive what you are feeling without having to read your mind?"

Mahir: "In a word, don't settle for GIGO (garbage in, garbage out). The more you put into your roleplay, the more you will get out of it. But PLEASE keep it real. This is especially for the ladies. Moaning as soon as you are barely touched is so cliché, tacky, and unrealistic. Please refrain.

> The most realistic, convincing responses are those you couldn't avoid even if you tried.

"The most realistic responses are those you couldn't avoid if you wanted to... the involuntary gasp, the soft whimper that escapes unbidden, being unable to stifle a moan, crying out in surprise, or not being able to suppress a giggle or laugh.

"Other uncontrollable responses are sweating, tearing up, breathing harder, and heart beating faster. When in the throes of ecstasy, your body will do things you couldn't control even if you tried. Sure, it's *mostly* fiction, but that doesn't mean you shouldn't tell the truth. Be real. Be convincing. Be a true roleplayer."

Mamakie: "Speaking of realistic, if you roleplay anal sex, don't penetrate your partner with no preliminaries. The sphincters will fight it, making it uncomfortable for you and your partner. Take your time to open and relax those muscles, using lots of lube. For example, start by slowly inserting one finger, then another, then a third, and when you get to the fourth, your partner will be open and horny as hell. It's more realistic, way sexier, and makes for much better roleplay."

Mahir: "Good point. Now some exercises to turn general emotes into detailed descriptions. I want to hear from EyeCandey, Urstud, Eswaria, Arjun, and Dorketta, in that posting order:

/me kisses her or him

EyeCandey: :turns her face toward his, eagerly lifting her parted lips to his and gazing longingly into his eyes

Urstud: -returns the gaze and tenderly presses his open lips to hers, feeling their wet warmth

Eswaria: /me breathes more deeply, inhaling his manly scent, her eager tongue hungrily seeking his

Arjun: /me caresses her tongue with his, tasting the sweetness of her mouth, his heart beating wildly

Dorketta: sucks greedily on his tongue, whimpering softly as her racing blood flushes her cheeks and neck

Mahir: "Good, let's try another one."

Mahir: /me strokes her or him

EyeCandey: :slides her warm hands from his shoulders to his chest, then down his side to his hips, where they linger, kneading his bum

Urstud: -raises his left hand to caress her cheek gently as his right hand slips from her waist, up over her ribs to just below her breast

Eswaria: /me feels goosebumps run up and down her spine as she digs desperate fingernails into his bum, then up his back and back down again, drawing long, pink scratch marks along his skin

Arjun: /me runs gentle fingertips, trembling with emotion, up her smooth belly to her breast, where he circles her areola with a feather touch

Dorketta: moves her hand up his inner thigh to his balls, which she cups and fondles, then over his cock and gently down, shuddering with excitement

Powerplay and ERP

Mahir: /me chuckles, "Good job... except for one thing, which I want to discuss with you now. Another mistake Mamakie and I made—and which some of you came close to making just now—was powerplay, which we've discussed in other classes. For example, I pushed my tongue into her mouth, tugged at her nipples, and forced my hand between her legs. Then she grabbed my cock, and I shoved it into her vagina. All that is powerplay because we are not only acting but also dictating the results of our actions—that is, how they would affect our partner.

"Not only that, but we even posted each other's responses, which is worse. She said that my cock was stiff and throbbing, and I wrote that her nipples were hard, that she was wet, and that she screamed and got pregnant. Don't tell your partners what they're doing, feeling, or how their body is responding. Let them decide that."

Don't tell your partners what they're doing, feeling, or how their body is responding. Let them decide that.

Mamakie: /me laughs, "By the way, if a woman screams during sex, either you're paying her waaaay too much, or she is in terrible pain. Keep it realistic. Also, keep the ERP fluid, which means that each partner waits for the other to post and then adds another post that follows naturally from that one and adds something more to the scene, as we've already discussed."

Mahir: "I like to take a minimalist approach—one baby step at a time, letting the other person take the next baby step from there. Granted, it takes longer, but hey, why rush it? Take your time, and build up the erotic tension slowly. Otherwise, she might decide to slap my face if I suddenly grab her tits, and men who go straight for the pussy rarely get second dates."

Dorketta: interrupts, looking around with a silly grin and wobbling her head "Yeah, I like to savor it slowly, like a good wine. Fast sex is highly overrated; slow sex is my favorite"

Mahir: /me laughs, "I like to mix it up, but in any case, it's darned difficult to avoid a certain amount of powerplay in ERP, even for seasoned roleplayers. Technically speaking, it's powerplay whenever you touch, kiss, stroke, or scratch, instead of emoting things like, 'raises her parted lips to his,' like EyeCandey did, or 'WOULD move her hand down TO stroke...' like Dorketta did.

"It takes a lot of concentration to avoid powerplay in these cases, and a lot of attention by each partner to respond to the other's attempts, saying how they are received. Even so, the interaction can be so intense that the lines often get blurred. The important thing is to TRY to avoid powerplay—especially at key points such as penetration, and ESPECIALLY in cases of forced sex or rape."

EyeCandey: :raises her hand and grins, 'I love it when a man takes me in his strong arms and manhandles me. It soooooo turns me on.' She hugs herself and shudders with pleasure at the thought.

Mahir: /me chuckles, "If you agree to give control to your partner and you don't ask him to change directions afterward, then whatever he does to your character with your consent is not considered powerplay, but this is usually only the case among players who know and trust each other well. If you're with a new partner, you should be especially careful to go slow and write that you're ABOUT to do something or INTEND to do it without actually doing it until you see how your partner responds. For example, with Eswa, I'd write:

Mahir: /me raises his hand TO stroke her cheek gently with the back of his hand.

Eswaria: /me takes a step away from him and scowls, raising her hand to ward him off.

"Okay, so Eswa has chosen to reject my advance. But if you're with a partner you know well, both of you can relax a little because you pretty much know what the other will accept. For example, if I'm with Mamakie, I'd feel fairly safe to write:

Mahir: /me raises his hand AND strokes her cheek gently.

Mamakie: /me smiles and places her hand softly on his, then turns her face to press soft lips into his strong, warm palm."

Eswaria: /me raises her hand. "What if you see that a man has an erection but hasn't emoted it yet? Would it be wrong to mention it?"

Mahir: "Well, strictly speaking, if something hasn't been introduced in a post, it doesn't exist. The pixels are just props, not an actual part of the roleplay. However, a pixel penis wouldn't have an erection unless its owner had raised it, usually by way of a HUD, so although it may not be perfect roleplay form, he probably wouldn't complain if you mentioned it.

"That said, I do know of a case where a warrior was dry-fucking a young man he had captured, who emoted being in terrible pain. The warrior thought his victim's penis was erect because, although flaccid, it was lying against his upturned tummy. He posted something about asking the young man why he was complaining if his penis was hard, showing that he liked it. In this case, the victim asked him to void this post and change it because he did feel that it was powerplay."

Mamakie: "Yes, that can happen, so be careful. Conversely, as soon as something is posted, it exists and can be used by all roleplayers in the scene, even if there's no pixel prop for it. You can literally roleplay anything into existence out of thin air—within reason, of course. For example, if a man loses his digital genitals from his Inventory (stranger things have happened), he's free to write them into existence until he can replace them."

Dorketta: raises a timid finger and pipes up in a high, nasal voice "Yeah, but so much for the eye candy... Um... and what if they powerplay and we wanted the roleplay to go in a different direction? Any suggestions for that?"

Mahir: "Well, that's the thing about roleplay—you never know what direction it might take. You just have to go with..."

Mamakie: /me interrupts him and chuckles, "I think I know what Dorketta is getting at. If your partner powerplays and you don't want to go along with it, but you don't want to IM them and complain, you can post resisting their attempt and doing something else. Eswaria has a great example of what she did when her partner went for full penetration in one go, but she wanted to do something unexpected and toy with him a little. Would you like to share it, Eswa?"

Eswaria: /me riffles through her notes and pulls out the transcript. "Sure... here's just a snippet. It shows how I handled it and what effect it had on him." She grins mischievously through her blushing. "In this scene, I'm riding him."

Man: /me shifts under her, his pelvis pressing upward, gently pulling her down onto his rod until he is a good way inside her.

Eswaria: /me resists his strong pull to only take in his glans at first, gazing down at him with a mischievous grin, and would start moving up and down on his bulging knob, taking him in a little deeper each time, clenching and unclenching her walls. "You like that? You want to go deeper?"

Man: /me blinks, taken by surprise at first, but happy at her initiative. A girl of spirit! The moment he feels her resisting, he relaxes his hands, not forcing her, and grinning, "Oh, I like it very much. How about a bit deeper, hmm?"

Eswaria: /me grins down at him, her face showing how much she loves to be in control and watch him squirm under her. Suddenly she drops her pelvis all the way down, taking him in fully, then pulls up again, almost to the top, and lingers there, moving slowly up and down on his glans and watching his expression with an amused little smile. "You like that?" she asks in a voice husky with lust. "What will you give me if I do it again?"

Mahir: /me takes out a handkerchief and wipes sweat from his forehead and cheeks. "Good example, Eswa. You have combined resisting his powerplay with the unexpected. We discussed surprising your partner in general terms, but it's especially good in ERP. Here are a few more examples of unexpected twists:

- In the heat of heavy petting, a woman suddenly tells her lover that she is menstruating and cannot 'go all the way' with him this time.
- A man tries to insert a finger into his lover's vagina, and she involuntarily pulls back, remembering a bad experience from her past.
- A woman feels her lover start to pulsate inside her and his body tense. Knowing he is close to cumming, she stops moving and grins evilly at him, "Now, let's see how long you can hold it, hmm?"

"Okay, now let's look at some examples of obvious powerplay in ERP and think about how it could have been done better. This takes two to make it work, so I'm going to ask Urstud and EyeCandey to show us some alternatives. Don't use the furniture this time, just your posts. Here's the bad example: '/me tugs at her nipples, making them hard.'"

Urstud: -raises his hands to cup her soft breasts and tease her pink nipples between thumb and forefinger

EyeCandey: :arches her back, raising her jugs to his touch, and feels her nubbins harden at his teasing

Mahir: "Good. Here's another: '/me forces his hand between her legs and feels that she is wet'"

Urstud: -moves his hand down over her mound to massage her clit, then would slip two fingers down between her labia to the opening of her vagina

EyeCandey: :spreads her knees to give him access, swiveling her pelvis toward his hand, and whimpers softly as her core warms and her juices start to flow

Mahir: "Excellent. Next example: '/me grabs his stiff, throbbing cock'"

EyeCandey: :explores down his belly to his groin, where she finds his manhood and would wrap her fingers around it, squeezing and pumping it, slowly and gently at first

Urstud: -feels his cock twitch with excitement at her touch, engorging and stiffening in her hand

Mahir: "Very nice. One more: '/me thrusts his cock into her tight pussy, making her moan'"

Urstud: -would roll over on top of her and press his swollen knob between her legs, feeling her wet warmth and eagerly seeking an opening, murmuring, "Spread those pretty legs and let me in, babe"

EyeCandey: :instinctively pulls back her pelvis as his cock approaches her inner sanctum, then realizes what she is doing and instead opens her knees and swivels her pelvis up to take him into her hot, wet sheath, trembling with excitement and anticipation, 'Take me, love, use me...'

Urstud: -would push his cock in one inch, then withdraw it and push it in two inches, playing with her inch by inch and increasing the sexual tension until the full length of his rigid shaft would slide deep within her tight warmth. He groans into her ear as his cock twitches with pleasure, "You're mine, now, wench"

EyeCandey: :whines as he teases her, then gasps with pleasure as his thickness slides deep into her, stretching her walls deliciously and bottoming out against her cervix. She pants hoarsely into his ear, 'Yes, I'm all yours. Fuck me hard, Urstud'

Urstud: -would thrust deeper and faster, his sweating body slapping against hers, his breathing labored, his heart pounding, his head spinning, his cock throbbing with pleasure as he groans into her neck, "Oh babe, I think I just died and went to heaven"

EyeCandey: :raises her legs to wrap them around his hips and pull him deeper into her in time with his thrusts, bucking her pelvis upward with each of his downward strokes, feeling how his glans bumps against her cervix as the bed jerks and creaks, 'Oh babe, YES! Fill me with your hot seed!'

Know your Furniture

Mahir: /me interrupts, chuckling, "Okay, okay, let's give these two some privacy now... That was great. Their posts were rich, evoking what each one was doing and feeling; they also used all six senses and even added some appropriate dialog. They avoided powerplay and instead wrote things the other could pick up and build on, step by step."

Mamakie: "I especially liked EyeCandey's initial hesitancy and Urstud's toying with her instead of just penetrating her in one go. That made the scene much more realistic and added some exciting erotic tension."

Mahir: "Yes, indeed... Now then, another mistake Mamakie and I made, and which many people seem to make, was flipping through the animations, trying to find just the right one for the sequence we wanted:

[Animation: lap sit]

[Animation: hard ride]

[Animation: sweet caress]

"If you really wanna show your prowess as ERP connoisseurs, get to know your furniture beforehand. REALLY. Take the time to go through it and see what each animation does. Ask a friend to help or take an alt and make notes of how the two interact. Think of logical sequences for the animations to come up with interesting, fluid progressions.

Avoid flipping through animations to find what you want. Get to know your furniture beforehand.

"If your avatar is an unusual size (large OR small), adjust and save its positions in advance so you won't be fiddling with adjustments any more than necessary during the actual roleplay. Don't you at least owe your partners that much? I mean, after all, they ARE putting up with your BO 'n stuff, right?"

–laughter around the circle–

Chiptag: "By the way, it's a pain to adjust your height for each piece of furniture if your avatar floats above it in all the positions. Instead, simply lower the 'Hover Height' slider in your 'Quick Preferences' button at the lower-left corner of your screen. That will take care of the Z (up-down) axis at least. Also, make a note of which way you move on the X and Y axes, indicating the plus and minus directions. That way, you won't bumble around when the moment of truth comes."

Mahir: "Thanks Chiptag. Now, if your partner is more familiar with the furniture, give over the controls in an IM. And if it's new to both of you, then whatever you do, PUHLEEEZ don't go flicking through the animations during the actual roleplay, looking for just the right one. It makes me sea-sick, and you don't want me throwing up all over our love nest."

-laughter around the circle-

"It's far better to send a friendly IM saying, 'Okay, then let's just explore, see what it does, and adapt our RP to whatever comes up.' OR—and this is not optimal—you COULD ask your partners to close their eyes for a moment until you find the animation you want. But if you don't find the perfect one, be creative and don't let that limit your ERP."

Urstud: /me raises his hand. "The problem is that even if it's your own furniture, it can have so many animations that it's impossible to memorize them all. I was making notes of each animation for my furniture, but ended up with pages and pages of notes and was lost when I used someone else's.

"But then I found that you can buy 'Adult Furniture Guidebooks' for the most common adult furniture at marketplace.secondlife.com/stores/217863. They have photos of the avatars' positions for each animation, so that you can quickly see what's available and choose the one you want. You can either wear the book as a HUD or rez it nearby, and it even comes with XYZ axis indicators to save you fumbling around with the adjustments."

Animations and Powerplay

Mahir: "That's a great tip, Urstud. We should definitely check it out. Now, assuming you know your furniture (PLEASE do), then the next point is that animations can be seen as a sort of scripted powerplay, in the sense that when you change animations, you force the other avatar to do something their player would not necessarily have chosen to do.

"To compensate for this, you can work up to the next animation in your description before switching to it. This makes a lot of sense anyway because it's highly unrealistic to go straight from sitting next to each other on a couch to whamming and banging energetically on the floor."

-laughter around the group-

"It would be much better to roleplay a gradual transition, like this:

[Animation: Cuddles - sitting side by side, hugging and kissing]

Mahir: /me grabs his heart dramatically, feigning a heart attack, and falls to the floor moaning, "Oh, Mamakie, my heart is bursting for your love."

Mamakie: /me lies down on top of him, rubbing her wet pussy against his thigh, whispering, "I want you, Mahir. Take me now!"

[Animation: MF Sex - Missionary]

Mahir: /me rolls over on top of her and eagerly presses his hardness against her pussy, searching for an opening.

[note: to actually penetrate her here would be powerplay]

Mamakie: /me opens her legs and thrusts her pelvis toward him, feeling his long, thick shaft sink into her, and gasps with pleasure.

Mahir: /me starts to thrust rhythmically...

"Of course, your actual roleplay would be much more detailed and specific, and would involve more give and take between the two, but that's enough to show you how it can flow much better than just switching animations all of a sudden without a smooth transition from one to the other.

"You can only do that if you know what the next animation will make you do. We might even have found an intermediate animation for when I lie on the floor and she lies on top of me. So, use the Adult Furniture Guidebooks and KNOW YOUR FURNITURE.

"Oh, also notice that I changed the animation AFTER her post and BEFORE mine. It's better not to change animations while your partners are writing, as that could oblige them to change their posts. It's frustrating when you're about to post a response to one animation, only to find yourself in a completely different one."

Mamakie: "Right, and keep in mind that you don't have to use all the hundreds of animations in your new ultra-hyper-super-duper sex bed. I've found that it's plenty to use two or three cuddles, maybe preceded by just sitting and chatting first, one or two foreplays, one or two sex positions, and one or two final cuddles for the afterglow.

"Speaking of which, please be sure to have a nice, long afterglow. That's especially important for us ladies. Don't just get up and leave, gentlemen, once you've shot your wad. We need to be reassured that it was more than just a matter of getting your jollies and that you're still there for us.

Take your time and squeeze all the RP juice you can out of each animation before going on to the next one.

"Take your time and squeeze all the RP juice you can out of each animation before going on to the next one. You don't have to change positions every time you post. Let the erotic tension build up gradually. The whole point of the furniture is to encourage better RP, so there's no point in switching to another animation before exploring all the roleplay possibilities offered by the one you're on.

"Besides, if you go through all the animations the first time, it won't be as interesting and exciting next time (supposing there IS a next time - hehe). Less is more. Fewer animations means more exploration of each one. And the less you use now, the more novel things you'll be able to explore together in the future."

Who Are You to Me?

Arjun: /me raises his hand and blurts out, "Since you told us about stories being based on 'character relationships' or CRs, I've been trying to find specific CRs to play with different characters to see how that works out and to make the RP deeper and more interesting. For example, my character is crazy in love with this girl..." He glances furtively at Eswaria.

Eswaria: /me looks away as if distracted.

Arjun: /me frowns and shakes his head in frustration. "...but she only wants a platonic relationship with me. That tension has opened up some interesting RP situations."

Mamakie: "Yes, it can be useful to think about the kind of affair your characters have. Is it dominant-submissive or on an equal standing? Is it a one-time fling or a traditional way of bonding? Is it a secret affair or a long-lasting, exclusive bond? Also, what is your character looking for in the relationship? Love or money, gratitude or revenge, a baby or a quick-and-easy release? Are you playing cat and mouse or passionately surrendering to each other?" She smirks at Arjun. "Is this an impossible love...?"

Arjun: /me blushes and looks around furtively to see if anyone else has noticed.

Mamakie: /me continues, "...or a match made in heaven?" She beams at Mahir.

Mahir: /me beams back lovingly at her.

Instead of going for long-term relationships from the start, squeeze all the RP juice you can from each encounter.

Mamakie: "The possibilities are endless, and taking them into account will add depth and nuance to your roleplay. Mind you, not every acquaintance will become a long-term relationship. You might roleplay only once with some characters and a few times with others. So instead of going for a long-term CR from the start, squeeze all the RP juice you can from each encounter.

"Then, if a longer-term relationship does evolve from that, be creative and keep it alive by stretching yourself and constantly reinventing your story with new ideas and unexpected actions. Just remember that in true roleplay, the relationship is between two CHARACTERS, not between two PLAYERS. If you want a real-life relationship, then leave the RP region after the session, go to an OOC area, and get to know each other OOCly, but please don't do it here."

Mahir: "Exactly, but going back to what you said, Arjun... You realized that your tastes and preferences don't have to coincide for good roleplay to be possible. Some of the best stories arise from conflicting interests. Another example is a dominant older man who wants a submissive femboy, where the femboy is anything but submissive. You might think that wouldn't work out IRL, but it could lead to some very interesting situations indeed in RP, so don't limit your roleplay partners to those who exactly fit your likes. Give yourselves the chance to explore new situations, like Arjun and Eswa have done.

What about BDSM?

Urstud: -raises his hand "You have mentioned a dominant-submissive relationship a few times, but just in passing. Could you say more about that?"

Mahir: "Ah, yes, thanks for reminding me. I did want to say a few words about BDSM, but first a caveat. Since much of the sexual roleplay in real life has at least some BDSM elements, many just assume that ERP and BDSM are synonymous. As we have seen, this would seriously limit the true scope of ERP.

Now, as some of you know, BDSM a combination of the abbreviations B/D (bondage and discipline), D/S (dominance and submission), and S/M (sadism and masochism). Some also say that the S/M can refer to a slave-master relationship. BDSM can include a wide range of activities, usually involving a dominant partner (the 'dom(me),' 'top,' or 'master/mistress') and a submissive partner (the 'sub,' 'bottom,' or 'slave').

"If the character relationship involves dominance/submission (D/S), the sub is expected to have complete respect for and submission to the dom(me), with no room for disobedience or even disagreement—within their RP limits, of course, which should include a 'safe word.' On the other hand, discipline will not involve anger when the dom(me) realizes that the sub's submission is actually a gift. A D/S roleplay can often be temporary, lasting for only one or more scenes, while master/slave relationships tend to be longer term.

"Most BDSM roleplay I've seen in virtual worlds uses scripted devices, such as leashing collars and other accessories. These are driven by menus with various permission levels, grab/post/release functions, RLV (restrained love viewer) restrictions such as sight (blindfolds), speech (gags), or movement (bindings), and other options such as animations, clothing, and so on. Open collars and relay HUDs also drive several BDSM 'machines' such as cages, crosses, slings, and more.

"Many of these devices have good animations and other effects, even posting their own descriptions in Local Chat. But remember that such accessories and machines should only be seen as props, not as substitutes for actual roleplay. Bear in mind that you don't HAVE to use ANY scripted items for BDSM roleplay, as they can all be written into existence.

"Of course, part of the interest of roleplaying in virtual worlds is the eye candy—the ability to illustrate what you're doing with pixels and code. BUT, if you don't have the handcuffs you need in your Inventory, you can always write them into a post. Even when you DO have them, the pixels and code should NEVER be a substitute for emoting them.

"If the sub is using a scripted gag and blindfold, for example, then the dom(me) should not only activate them but also describe putting them on, such as: '/me pushes the ball gag into her mouth (or places the blindfold over her eyes), tightening the strap firmly around her head.'

"As I mentioned before, some 'chatty' scripted BDSM items will put canned posts into Local Chat. For example, a diaper will not only change color but will also say when your character is peeing or pooping, when the diaper is dirty or leaking, when it's being checked or changed, and so on.

"If you can turn these chats off, I would recommend you do so. If not, you may not want to repeat the exact same descriptions in your posts. Instead, a good roleplayer will add more detail, such as describing sensations, smells, how their body language communicates their feelings of repulsion or humiliation, and especially the process of changing the diaper. Again, the virtual diaper is there to stimulate roleplay, not to replace it.

"It's piss-poor roleplay for a dom(me) to simply put a sub on a 'fuck machine' without emoting it. Describe how you lubricate the machine or the sub, lower them onto the anal plug (gently or forcefully, for example), bind them to the braces, make sure the phallus is positioned correctly, turn on the machine, change the speed, and so on. In turn, this gives subs a chance to write their responses about what is being done to them.

Don't let your scripted props roleplay for you. Take your time and squeeze all the roleplay juice from each prop with descriptive posts.

"Some BDSM machines have moving parts, such as folding tables that put subs in different positions. Again, manipulating the table should NOT be limited to clicking the menu but should also involve emoting what you do and say, your tone of voice, how your facial expressions and body language convey your feelings, and so on.

"Other BDSM machines can have fixtures added, which should also be written about. For example, one treadmill has a cross-piece holding an electric shocker. Dom(me)s should describe fastening the beam to the machine, turning it on, and explaining how it works, while subs will write how they are experiencing it. A good rule of thumb is to post whatever you do BEFORE activating the scripted action.

"In sum, the general principles applicable to BDSM are the same as for all ERP—and all roleplay for that matter. Don't let your furniture, machines, accessories, and other scripted props roleplay for you. Good roleplayers will take their time and try to squeeze all the roleplay juice from each prop and activity by using carefully crafted, descriptive posts. And remember: without emotes, there is no true roleplay."[20]

---

[20] For a sample BDSM roleplay, see "A BDSM Scene" in the next chapter.

ERP Etiquette

Mamakie: "On that note, we'd like to end with a few words about ERP etiquette. It's a topic that some may feel a little uncomfortable discussing, so let's just get it out in the open now. First and foremost, you would do well to clarify how much time you'll be able to give your undivided attention to each other. A good ERP session can take AT LEAST half an hour and easily up to two hours for para-roleplayers. It's frustrating to have to stop in the middle because one of the two had a prior engagement. If you try to pick it up later, you may find that the flame has gone out and will have to be rekindled.

"As always, announce beforehand OOC that you have to leave, and try to roleplay your exit—don't just poof in the middle of a session. In one scene, for example, the man was telling the woman how much he needed her, to which she answered, 'You know what I need?' then giggled, 'I need to pee,' and ran to the bathroom where she poofed, having first IMed him that she had to log.

It takes a lot of concentration to get into character and stay there, a lot of focus to write good ERP, and OOC IMs can be distracting.

"Remain in character throughout the session, use Local Chat by preference, and keep IMs to an absolute minimum from beginning to end. It takes a lot of concentration to get into character and stay there, a lot of focus to write good ERP, and OOC IMs can be distracting. Personally, I feel it breaks the magic when someone starts talking about RL feelings during a session.

"Avoid chain-posting. It's frustrating to be writing your response to 'strokes her breasts' and then receive another post saying 'lowers his hand to stroke her bum.' Of course, you can and should write a second part to your emote to address their second post, but RP convention AND etiquette dictate that you take turns posting—this applies even more to ERP.

"If you get an inspiration right after hitting 'Enter' and wish you'd added something else to your post, you can post '((Cont...))' immediately, and your partner will know to wait before posting, but please don't abuse this possibility.

"This is especially important when there's more than two of you. And yes, threesomes, foursomes, or more take longer but can be LOADS of fun. In such cases, you should agree on a posting order and strictly respect it. If it's your turn to post and you don't want to take any action for the moment, don't stay silent, leaving the others waiting for you. You can always write something like '/me watches the others with wide eyes, drinking in the scene.'

"Also, respect others and their limits, likes, and dislikes. The fact that you're in an adult RP region does NOT give you a right to help yourself, no matter how horny you may feel. Who knows? They may have a friend, work partner, child, or significant other looking over their shoulder. An IC 'no' may mean 'yes' sometimes, but an OOC 'no' means NO.

"Public adult furniture is available in the six adult-rated sims of the region: Rajasthan, Gir, Indravati, Betla, Papikonda, and Sundarbans, where it's acceptable to have sex in public areas. The other six sims are rated Moderate—Hemis, Gangotri, Khangchendzonga, Namdapha, Sanjay Gandhi, and Simlipal—where sex is only allowed in private homes, with sight and sound turned off to potential outside observers.

"As for the adult sims, some like being watched and watching, while others are shyer. How to know who's who? You could IM them and ask or wait for them to IM you and say whether it's okay to lurk, but that might break their concentration, so it's not the optimal solution. A better approach would be for us all to assume that if a couple is using the all-access sex furniture in adult-rated public areas (as opposed to private dwellings), they won't mind being watched and may actually enjoy it. Most of us understand that one good way to better our art is to watch other roleplayers.

"Now, as the voyeur, if you come across a couple having sex openly in a public area and want to watch, then just sit or stand quietly within chat distance unless they post something in Local Chat that would include you in the roleplay or invite you to take part in an IM. Otherwise, you can either just stay there lurking or move away discretely.

"What if you're the ones having the ERP? If you don't mind being watched or no-one is around, it's fine to do it just about anywhere in an adult region or district (sim). But if you're within chat range of where other people are roleplaying, remember that ERP often involves a lot of steamy text in Local Chat, so try to take a few things into account.

"If something else is already happening in such an area, you obviously wouldn't just barge in and start ERPing with no regard for what's going on. But if you're just sitting around in a group and want to emote that you're cuddling with your partner, it's fine if you can integrate that into the group RP with something like:

> *Mamakie: /me snuggles closer to Mahir, feeling his warm chest and belly against her back, and raises her arms to wrap them around his neck, smiling at Arjun. "I hope to meet that girl sometime. She must be very a special person if you like her that much."*

"However, if your cuddling leads to sex, then it would be better to excuse yourselves from the group and go out of chat range to avoid interrupting people or making them uncomfortable. Please don't just start your ERP in IMs and ignore Local Chat. If you're not going to roleplay with the group, it's better to leave."

Chiptag: "You can see when you're entering or leaving chat distance by activating your Radar under Preferences – Chat – Radar. Although it's not as precise, you can also watch the 'whisper,' 'speak,' and 'shout' circles in your mini-map (Ctrl-Shift-M), using right-click on the map and selecting 'Chat distance rings.'"

Mahir: "If you share a dwelling with others and set your 'Home' there, please set it where you won't accidentally log in on top of a couple in the middle of an ERP scene. If you do, you might step on some tender bits, besides disrupting their roleplay."

Erotic roleplay can give rise to IC and OOC jealousy, so find out whether your RP partner has a special someone first.

Mamakie: "Finally, erotic roleplay can give rise to jealousy, both IC and OOC, so find out whether the character you're roleplaying with has a partner, lover, or special someone. If so, and you still want to pursue it, ask whether the relationship is exclusive or open. If exclusive, respecting it could go a long way toward avoiding OOC drama, although you can always roleplay the jealous lover IC without being jealous OOC. If your partner is using a fertility system, ask whether a pregnancy is wanted or birth control should be used, then respect that choice."

Eswaria: "I've had partners who got upset when I've practiced ERP with others. If they loved me so much, they could have at least read my profile, which says, 'I practice ERP with different people and expect you to do the same.' But nooooo... when they realized our love was 'just' roleplay, they got mad at me OOC."

Mamakie: "Yes, that cannot be stressed enough. That kind of thing would never happen if people would just read each other's profiles and make sure their own are complete. You can also use the 'Notes' tab in people's profiles to write additional information on them that only you will be able to see, such as where you met, what they like and dislike, and so on."

CHAPTER FIFTEEN

THE ERP TEST

Mahir: /me looks at the time and gasps, "Oh, we've gone way over two hours. Let's stop there so you can take your test." He passes out a notecard. "There's a theoretical and a practical part. Once your theoretical test is accepted, you'll be told about the practical part."

The Theoretical Part

Arjun reads the notecard: "Summarize what you have learned about ERP and deposit the notecard in the urn at the Love Temple altar." He thinks for a while, looking over his notes, then starts to write, adding a few ideas of his own:

TEN COMMANDMENTS OF EROTIC ROLEPLAY

1. Thou shalt emote: Do not let the furniture roleplay for you. Do not limit yourself to dialog (chat-boxing) or sounds like *'Mmmm'* and *'Ahhhh,'* but rather use abundant emotes, at least as much as your dialog. There should be much more emoting than talking and making noises, especially in the case of ERP.
2. Thou shalt be detailed: Do not just say WHAT you are doing in general but also HOW and WHERE you are doing it. For example, do not just post *'kisses her'* or *'strokes him'* but say exactly how and where you are kissing or stroking them.
3. Thou shalt use all thy senses: Do not limit yourself to sight and touch—include hearing, taste, and smell. Touch can be hard or soft, warm or cool, and so on. How does your body respond? Emotes should be perceivable, tangible, and evocative. Others cannot respond to thoughts and feelings unless they are mind readers.
4. Thou shalt not powerplay: Do not force your actions on your partner. Start your action and state your intention, but let your partner say how

it affects them. Do not emote what the other person does, what happens to their body, or how they respond to what you do.

5. Thou shalt not chain post: Chain-posting means posting out of turn or more than once before your partner responds. Type everything you want to do and say in one post, then wait for the other person to respond before posting again. If there are more than two of you, establish a posting order and respect each other's turns without cross-posting.
6. Thou shalt know thy furniture: Avoid flicking through the menu. Know what each animation does beforehand or roleplay around whatever happens. Choose carefully to build a good story, and ensure smooth transitions by working up to the next animation. The partner handling the menu should change it just before or after their own post so that the change does not clash with what the other is writing.
7. Thou shalt not be an animation hog: Do not try to use as many animations as you can just because they're there. More is not better. Plan a sequence that uses a few good animations and squeeze all the RP juice you can from each one. Save the other animations for your next scene to keep things interesting and exciting.
8. Thou shalt be realistic: If your avatar is a human and not a caricature or a fantasy character, find out the normal range of human proportions and stick to them, especially for sexual traits. Many people don't like you to go straight for their genitals, and you don't make people orgasm just by looking at them. If a woman screams, she probably either saw a mouse or is in terrible pain. You can't French kiss and talk at the same time. Keep it real, and don't be a twink.
9. Thou shalt not be a drama llama: Much OOC drama is about romantic relationships, so be careful to avoid it. Unless you both agree to start an exclusive relationship, do not think that having ERP with someone gives you sole rights over them. Many practice ERP with several players and expect that others will do the same. The more people you practice with—especially if they are good roleplayers—the more you will learn and the better your roleplay will become.
10. Thou shalt have fun: The first rule of roleplay is that it should be fun—any kind of RP, and especially ERP. If your partner does not share your same kinks, respect their preferences. It should be fun for both of you.

A BDSM Scene

Looking around, Arjun sees an urn at the altar saying, 'ERP reports here.' He drags his notecard onto it, then goes to explore the temple while waiting for the results. Climbing the winding stairs to the upper level, he finds a balcony overlooking the gardens among the mangroves. Below he sees some students finishing their written tests and a few couples of diverse genders already cuddling on the blankets, pillows, sofas, and other furniture strewn around the garden.

'Hearing' a 'voice' behind him, Arjun turns to see a jail cell-like room built into the wall. Inside, Urstud stands over a naked EyeCandey, who is bound hand and foot to an X-shaped St. Andrew's bondage cross, two wires hanging from clamps fastened to her swollen red nipples. Arjun feels his stomach tighten at the unexpected sight but curiosity gets the better of him, so he goes to sit on one of the several cushions lying around the floor to watch and listen.

EyeCandey: :opens her eyes wide as he moves over her, and tries to raise her knee to stop him, but her leg is pinned to the wood. She arches her back, groaning, the wood digging into her back, 'Urstud... get off of me,' she snaps and groans louder as her arms are pulled even higher above her head

Urstud: -brings his legs up to ward off the blow, then settles himself onto her, looking down at her and reaches out his hand to catch her throat as he tries to hoist himself up onto her

EyeCandey: :sees him coming and stops wasting her energy but pants, trying not to whimper. 'Urstud, I have a nice cock cage for you... with needles... You'd better stop while you're ahead,' she says through her teeth as she watches him, trying to get more comfortable in the binds

Urstud: -moves closer and grins, "Not a full charge, but still..." He grabs one of the hanging wires, closes the other end of the steel contact, and reaches for the other one, clipping it to the first and holding it up for her to see

EyeCandey: :opens her eyes wide, 'Urstud!' she warns as he starts to mess with the contacts. Feeling the shock through her nubbins, she whimpers, digging her nails into her palms as she jerks, trying to pull herself from it, and cries out with a growl as she feels her whole body tingling

Urstud: -smiles wider and lets the taser hang from her nipples as he grabs her ankles and flips the cords around them, pulling her legs apart before tying them off "So much nicer..." -he chuckles- "...you look so much nicer like this"

EyeCandey: :takes a deep breath as her jugs ache. She feels her ankles being tied before she can pull away or kick at him and groans as her legs are forced open, knowing there is nothing she can do to hide her sex from him. Her head clears a little, and she jerks on her binds, feeling them cutting deeper into her wrists, leaving no room to struggle. 'I swear you'd better never be within 100 meters of me again, Urstud'

Urstud: -shakes his head and would slip his hand between her legs to rub and probe her roughly, his fingers tracing from her clit through her flower, all the way to her rosebud, before roughly drawing his fingers back

EyeCandey: :growls and tries to close her legs, making her ankles burn as she feels his fingers move to her clit... Unable to prevent her wetness, she closes her eyes with a whimpering growl, feeling his fingers exploring her pussy and rosebud, unable to pull away without causing herself more pain

Urstud: -shakes his head and, taking a third clip from the floor, dangles it before her, waiting for her to open her eyes as he raises his hand to crush her clit against her pelvic bone

EyeCandey: :hears something and opens her eyes, feeling him pushing on her swollen clit, making her core warm, but fights to keep any pleasure or discomfort from her face. She sees the extra clamp and opens her eyes wide, 'Urstud... don't you dare,' she hisses, shaking her head rapidly

Urstud: -chuckles and raises his eyebrows, kneeling between her legs, and would push her folds open to play with her clit and get it hard. The moment it is, he would snap the clip, letting this one close itself from full open

EyeCandey: :growls and pulls harder on her binds as she sees him kneeling before her and feels his fingers teasing her clit. She closes her eyes and turns her head, her chin on her shoulder as she tries to fight the pleasure and think of anything that would block it but feeling herself getting even wetter as her pelvis tries to move against his hand. She starts to take a long breath as she feels his finger move from her clit, then feels a sharp pain as the clip snaps onto it and lets out a scream, her clit throbbing as she gasps for air, tilting her head back as if the clip had knocked the breath out of her lungs

Urstud: -stands up slowly and smiles, watching how her body reacts. "Hmm... like that, do you?" he says as he leaves the wire hanging and walks around her. Stopping behind her, he would run his fingers between her butt cheeks and stroke her wet cunt several times before drawing his fingers back to her tight little rose and start to force a thick finger into it

EyeCandey: :pants, feeling the pain become more of an ache that refuses to settle. 'Fuck you,' she hisses between pants. She tries to follow him with her eyes, feels him stop her behind her, and takes a steadier breath, knowing he has no more clamps. She whimpers, feeling his fingers in her pussy, trying to avoid his touch, but is helpless and unable to move. She feels him moving his fingers out and to her rosebud, trying to close her butt cheeks around his hand to block him but feels his rough hand still pushing into her, making her whimper and gasp as she fights to stop him

Urstud: -chuckles, moves closer and would push his finger in harder as she resists, slipping his other hand around her and finding the clip, tugging on it each time he drives his finger deeper into her ass

EyeCandey: :feels his heat closer, knowing she can't move. She shakes her head, hearing him chuckle, and opens her mouth to threaten him, but only a whimpering cry comes out as she feels the fresh ache and tingling through her body, which responds more to the clamps than to his fingers, making her close her eyes tight. Tilting her head back, trying to fight the pleasure she is finding in the ache he is sending through her body, she gasps louder, feeling his finger move deeper into her rosebud, which loosens enough as not to be so painful, while her body starts to crave the attention she refuses to admit

Urstud: -chuckles, feeling her body react, and would slide his finger in and out of her ass several more times before pulling it suddenly from her and walking around, running his hands around her until he is facing her again

EyeCandey: :closes her eyes tighter, feeling him moving his finger in and out of her rosebud, making her clit swell around the clamp, making her whimper at the movement. Biting her lip, refusing to moan, she feels him pulling out of her and pants, trying to catch her breath, catching his eyes as she moves her head back down as he goes in front of her. She shakes her head slowly, wanting to find smartass words but trying to calm her body instead

Urstud: -grins wickedly, connects the last wire to the contacts, and would touch the switch for a split second

EyeCandey: :narrows her eyes at his grin and starts to shake her head when suddenly a quick shock hits her nipples and clit, making them tense and jolt as her head jerks back and she cries out. The shock turns to ache, making them hard and her body tingle as she closes her eyes, leaning her head against her shoulder and panting...

Arjun: /me had been watching with bated breath, appalled at the scene, his whole body tensing painfully. Finally, unable to take any more, he covers his ears and shouts, “Stop. Stop! STOP! You're making me sick to my stomach!”

Startled by his shouting, Urstud and EyeCandey stop their roleplay and come out of the cell to join him. To Arjun's surprise, they both look calm and happy. How could they be, after what they had been doing?

EyeCandey: :seeing Arjun upset, comes to sit next to him, wrapping an arm around his shoulders, and says, in a soothing voice, ‘It's okay, sweetie, we were just playing. If I hadn't liked what Urstud was doing, I would have IMed him and asked him to change direction’

Urstud: -sits next to EyeCandey, a gentle arm wrapped around her waist, and says comfortingly, “We were both happy with where the roleplay was going, Arjun. EyeCandey had control of everything I did. She could decide whether I captured her, whether I put her on the cross, whether I used electricity, everything.”

Arjun: /me looks up sheepishly, wringing his hands nervously and stammering in a wavering little voice, “You... you made it all seem so real... I... I thought...”

EyeCandey: :lets out a soft, tinkling laugh, tousling his long, unkempt hair playfully. ‘You thought he was hurting me? You're so sweet, but no, dear boy, I was enjoying it. We both were! Otherwise, we would have played at something else.’

Urstud: -nuzzles EyeCandey's neck and chuckles “To tell the truth, little brother, we decided on the overall story in IMs before we even started. And you know what else? Last time it was me on the cross, and she was making me squirm”

Arjun: /me laughs bashfully, “Scary stories have always made me uncomfortable... My head knows it's not real, but my heart doesn't understand and really feels disturbed.” He stands to go, “Sorry I interrupted your roleplay. Thanks for talking to me about it. I guess I should just avoid listening to that kind of thing next time.”

Urstud and EyeCandey stand also, and he pats Arjun on the back as she gives him a quick hug, saying, “Don't worry about it, darling. BDSM isn't everyone's cup of tea. That's why we have RP limits in our profiles, right?”

BDSM isn't everyone's cup of tea. That's why we have RP limits.

Eswaria Catches a Rasthar

Urstud and EyeCandey go back to their cell to finish their story while Arjun descends the stairs to stroll around the gardens, taking in the sights and sounds to calm himself. After a while, a message pops up on his screen:

> Dharma Guide: Congratulations. You have passed the theoretical part of your ERP test. You can now use the public adult furniture in the six adult-rated sims. For the practical part, put what you learned about ERP into practice and rez the transcript onto the urn at the foot of the Love Temple altar.
>
> NOTE: You don't have to go all the way; cuddling and light petting are sufficient, but use everything you learned to make it detailed and convincing."

While Arjun is reading, a Virtual India group IM also pops up, announcing a party at the Indravati village, and Arjun turns his steps northward. As he crosses the bridge over the Southern River, he hears dance music pulsing from the town square, where several people are gathered. People are making love on the furniture strewn tastefully around the garden—men with women, women with women, men with men, and even a foursome in one of the gazebos.

Arriving at the party, Arjun's heart jumps as he sees Eswaria dancing alone, dressed in sheer silks, radiantly desirable. He is about to approach her but stops cold when he sees her dance toward a tall, dark, muscular man dressed only in a short silk loincloth, long wavy black hair framing a perfectly chiseled face.

> *Eswaria: /me dances toward the most handsome young man at the party and smiles sweetly. "Hello, gorgeous."*
>
> *Rasthar: /me hears a musical voice and turns to see a radiant beauty dancing toward him. "Well, hello there, beautiful. Would you like to dance?"*
>
> *Eswaria: /me doesn't answer but only smiles sweetly as she raises her hands to his as she dances closer to him.*
>
> *Rasthar: /me would entwine his fingers in hers as their bodies dance close but not touching.*
>
> *Eswaria: /me feels the warmth of his body almost touching hers and sways with him, fingers enmeshed in his, their bodies in sync, and smiles into his eyes.*
>
> *Rasthar: /me inhales a sweet perfume from her glistening body, mixing with the scent of flowers, making him dizzy.*
>
> *Eswaria: /me reaches back and unties her soft silk camisk, raising it in her hands as she sways to the music, her bare torso brushing lightly against his.*
>
> *Rasthar: /me staggers slightly as if from the electric shock of her perky nipples just barely grazing his chest and lets out a low, appreciative growl.*
>
> *Eswaria: /me lowers her camisk to drape it around his neck to pull him closer.*
>
> *Rasthar: /me moves with the music, pulled toward the warmth of her supple, lithe body, touching then parting, over and over again.*

Eswaria: /me releases her camisk, which falls around his neck, and would let light fingertips trail along his broad shoulders, over his powerful chest, down the smooth ripples of his abs and to his hips, swaying with his body as she would slowly pull his pelvis toward hers.

Rasthar: /me feels his arousal grow as her pelvis presses against his and raises his hands to stroke her soft shoulders and supple back as they sway, transfixed by her dark, penetrating eyes.

Eswaria: /me shivers with pleasure as goosebumps run up and down her spine at the touch of his strong, warm hands, and smiles into his kind eyes, her pupils dilating, her lips partially open, breathing in his manly scent.

Rasthar: /me feels no need to talk, or the mood would be broken. Their eyes tell all as their bodies meet with the beat of the music.

Eswaria: /me feels his strong, hard body warm against hers and sways with him, dizzy with desire as the dance envelops her as if in a trance.

Rasthar: /me comes closer to slide his hands down her moist back and pull her lower back in firmly, lowering eager lips to hers, then releases her again.

Eswaria: /me feels a warm pulse of pleasure flutter like a trapped butterfly deep within her core, and a soft whimper escapes her throat as his soft, warm lips close onto hers, and she tastes the sweetness of his mouth. She turns slowly as he releases her and raises her arms around his neck, placing her head on his chest as she dances with her backside pressed against his front.

Rasthar: /me struggles with strong feelings as her soft, firm cheeks press against his bulge, and lowers his head to run his lips along her shoulder.

Eswaria: /me would run her fingers through his hair as she sways against him, pressing her bum against his hardness, her back arched, pink nipples hard with excitement, the blood running hot in her veins.

Rasthar: /me would slide his hands down her arms, brushing her armpits, stopping to feel for a slight stubble, then would lightly cup her shapely breasts that sway against the palms of his hands as she dances.

Eswaria: /me feels her skin tingle deliciously under the warm, gentle touch of his big, strong hands and lets out a long, moaning hum, raising her face to press her cheek against his as she sways against him, the corners of their mouths touching, then closes her eyes, smiling.

Rasthar: /me releases her breasts, allowing them to dance freely, and would place his arms around her waist, locking his fingers together along her belly.

Eswaria: /me would lower her hands slowly from his hair, over his cheeks, down his neck, then over her own breasts and stomach to place them gently over his hands, stroking them gently, urging them down toward her need as she turns her face to his and murmurs breathily, "My body wants yours..."

Rasthar: /me lets her push his hands down to her mons pubis, pressing her bum harder against his package that throbs to burst free as he nibbles at her neck, desiring... hoping... knowing that they will soon be together as one.

Eswaria: /me lays her head to the side to enjoy his lips teasing her neck, sighing happily at the reassurance of his strong arms enfolding her. She moves her hands on his to press the tips of his fingers down over her clitoris and whimpers as a warm wave of pleasure fills her core. She feels his hardness between her bum cheeks and moves her pelvis rhythmically up and down over it, her heart beating wildly with the thrill of expectation.

Rasthar: /me strokes her clitoris with a circular motion and, unable to contain his desire, looks around to see where they can go. The bushes may have poison ivy that would irritate her perfect skin, and the gods might disapprove.

Eswaria: /me turns her face to murmur into his ear, her voice husky with lust. "Please, take me away from here."

Rasthar: /me gently bites and sucks her long, slender neck, tasting salty-sweet as his fingers explore the softness of her labia under her silk, and whispers, "Yes, my home is not far. Shall we slip away quietly?"

Eswaria: /me overcomes her reluctance to break his embrace, turns to smile eagerly into his eyes, attempting to entwine her fingers into his, and whispers excitedly, "Yes, let's go while no-one is looking."

Arjun's heart sinks as they run off happily. "Damn, she's good," he mutters. Besides the knot of jealousy constricting his chest, he has a sinking feeling he could never rival the ERP skill she has just shown. No wonder she hadn't chosen him. He's wanted her since the Basic Roleplay class, but she's never wanted to be anything but his friend. "Of course not," he mutters bitterly. "Why would she want poor little crooked-tooth Arjun when she can have any stud she desires?"

Arjun Meets his Match

Arjun is just about to turn away and slump dejectedly from the party when suddenly, unexpectedly, his luck changes:

Zurie: ::casts a bored glance around the square until her eyes rest on a cute young man, and steps toward him to take a closer look:: Well... you look like fun ::she purrs::

Arjun: /me hears a voice next to him, turns to see who it is, and is met by a pair of sharp, olive-green eyes framed by an Arabian face of wild, hard beauty, like something out of 101 nights. She looks like a fierce warrior in her tight black-leather top, shorts, and boots, not to mention her various weapons. "Oh, hello," he stammers, looking for words, "Um... I'm Arjun."

Zurie: ::lets out a low chuckle as her eyes trail up and down his thin frame:: Arjun, huh? Sounds like a pastry. It's making me hungry ::she growls softly as she comes closer::

Arjun: /me opens his eyes wide. "Oh, are you a cannibal? I'm sort of skinny, but I do have lots of food if you're hungry..." That sounds lame, even to his own dorky ears, so he changes tack and grins mischievously, lowering his voice, "Oooorrrr... we could go into the bushes and..." then bends close and whispers something into her ear.

Great use of an unknown.

Zurie: ::smirks and looks him over slowly, running her tongue over her lips, and murmurs:: Oh, and now I'm hungry for something else. And no, not quite a cannibal, but from a bad place, that's for sure. Zurie's my name.

Arjun: /me tastes the name sweetly on his tongue, pronouncing it slowly. "Zuuu-riiieee..." then deepens his voice as if to make it sound more seductive. "Maybe we can go share our sob stories and show each other our scars..." He looks up, his youthful eyes sparkling, his voice back to normal. "Wouldn't that be fun?"

Zurie: ::grins and runs her hands slowly down his bare front:: And where might those scars be?

Arjun: /me would catch her hand half-way to his belly and draw it up to press his lips into her palm, "The ones on our skin aren't the worst, but the ones imprinted deeply on the heart... those are the scars that burn hot late at night." He gazes deeply into her enchanting eyes as he deepens his voice again, "Am I right, Zuuu-riiieee?"

Zurie: ::sucks in a breath and lets it out slowly as his lips touch her hand, and shivers, at a loss for words:: Definitely.

Arjun: /me grins mischievously as he spies the rifle in her hand and chuckles, "As long as it doesn't involve that little popgun you're carrying, Zuurriiee."

Zurie: ::raises an eyebrow and slowly slides her hand suggestively up and down the barrel of her rifle, curling one finger around it completely:: Popgun, huh?

Arjun: /me watches the gesture and feels an overpowering urge welling up deep inside him as he comes closer, blushing and mumbling, "Um... well... yeah... I mean..." then takes a deep breath, squares his jaw, and blurts out, "I don't know why, but I feel like I could follow you anywhere."

Zurie: ::holds his gaze and tilts her head, a smirk playing on her face as she hums, coming so close that their bodies brush, letting the pads of her fingers trail over his side:: Maybe you should reconsider that 'anywhere.' You don't know where I've been, hmm?

Arjun: /me suddenly feels the need to inhale deeply and smells her richly feminine scent as his skin prickles and twitches at her soft touch, "Um... could we go somewhere private? I'm embarrassed to be doing this out here in public."

Zurie: ::grins in amusement and lowers her head to run her lips along his neck, breathing in his smell of earth and man as she would trail kisses slowly up to his ear, and murmurs:: Alone? Are you sure you're not scared, baby boy?:: as she lifts a hand to place it lightly on his slender shoulder::

Arjun: /me shivers at the feel of her lips on his neck and his ear but tries to maintain his composure, turning his head until they are cheek to cheek, then gathers enough courage to murmur, again in that deep voice, "From one scared baby to another, I think we can handle ourselves alright, don't you?"

Zurie: ::chuckles against him before lightly nipping his turned cheek, stepping away and sliding the rifle firmly into its holster on her back:: We'll see, hmmm? I'm new here, so lead the way ::she grins, licking her lips, her eyes trailing over him::

Arjun: /me points toward the beach, "There's a lovely hammock hanging over the surf just beyond the Love Temple, where we could be alone and get to know each other better." He turns and walks slowly away, his hand brushing hers as he goes, as if he were about to grab it but had decided against it. "Follow me," is all he says.

Zurie: ::chuckles and follows the young man, her eyes not leaving his body as he moves smoothly in front of her, growling in appreciation::

Arjun: /me, arriving at the hammock, gestures for her to climb on, then clambers up after her and would recline comfortably against her with a sigh. "Tell me about yourself, Zurie. How did you get here, and what are your hopes and dreams?"

[Lying animation with him reclining his back against her front, by default. Neither knows this hammock, so they decide in IM to just roleplay around whatever it does.]

Zurie: ::hums and lies back, letting him fall back onto her as she wraps her arms around his front, her fingers grazing his warm skin delicately:: I came here to escape a life I didn't want to keep living:: she smiles sadly:: And yourself? What do you want? ::She leans forward and presses her lips to his shoulder::

Arjun: /me enjoys the warmth of her body against his back, her caresses making his skin tingle and twitch, and her breathing on his neck as he gazes out to sea. "I guess I found everything I ever wanted here. The love of friends... food... shelter... what else is important in life?"

Zurie: ::chuckles and begins kissing his neck, sliding her hand down his chest and stomach, grazing her nails around his waistband:: Sounds like the definition of contentment.

Arjun: /me reaches down to wrap his arm around her thigh and turns toward her, head back, semi-parted lips turned up to hers. "I guess all I'm lacking now is the love of a strong, capable woman..." He smiles up expectantly into those captivating eyes.

Zurie: ::smirks at him, a playful twinkle in her eye as she leans down toward his face to kiss his mouth once lightly, her warm lips barely touching his as she curls her leg around him, hand sliding down into his waistband, circling on the tops of his thigh:: Well, let me know when you do, hmmm?

[Animation with him lying beside her, caressing her front]

Arjun: /me turns and lies at her side, his head settling lightly on her shoulder, and whispers in her ear, "When you spoke to me at the party, something deep inside me said, 'Maybe she's the one.' –blushes– "I hope I'm not being too brash, telling you this..."

Ugh. Cooornyyy!

Zurie: ::grins and turns to face him, her eyes meeting his, holding his gaze while her fingers trail lower:: Not at all... If you never tried, it would never happen, would it? ::She bends her head forward to kiss his chest, sucking lightly and relaxing against his warm body::

Arjun: /me lightly strokes her tummy with gentle fingertips and, feeling his penis swelling uncomfortably inside his thong, loosens the ties to relieve the pressure, but it falls off entirely. "Why don't we get a little more comfortable and just see where this path leads us?"

Zurie: ::hums in approval and shrugs out of her constraining jacket, feeling his skin soft and cool against hers, then reaches down to find his shaft, a giggle escaping from her lips as she starts stroking it slowly, eyes greedily taking in his form::

Arjun: /me turns his head to place trembling lips against her soft, ivory shoulder, breathing harder, his heartbeat quickening. A twinge of pleasure shoots through his groin, making him gasp, but he manages to control his urge and pulls his hips back to release his penis from her grasp, whispering huskily, "Wait, Zurie, not yet. Let's go slow. I want to cuddle more before getting that intimate. Please... be patient a little longer..."

Hehe. Nice little surprise action there; bet she didn't see that coming.

Zurie: ::smiles and curls into him, pressing her body closer to his warmth and begins kissing and sucking the soft skin between his shoulder and neck, letting his penis slide from her grasp and curling her hands around him to trail them up and down his back, marveling at the feel of him:: To me, lazily petting you is part of cuddling, but this is very nice too. I apologize ::nuzzles into his neck and nips him gently::

Arjun: /me feels his back arch with pleasure at her touch and submits happily to her kisses while trying to undo the ties of her top with one hand. "No, I'm the one who should apologize. It's just that I'm inexperienced in the ways of love, and I'm afraid my seed might escape me too soon. I like being with you so much I don't want it to end quickly. You're such a lovely woman, and you make something stir deep within me that I can't explain."

Would Arjun really speak that formally?

Zurie: ::lifts up, turning her shoulder toward him slightly, and allows her top to fall away, shivering in the cool night air before snuggling into his side, pressing herself into his heat, a soft sigh escaping her lips as she reaches up to slide her fingers through his long, soft hair, tugging gently at the unruly locks:: You're right. This should last a good, long time, so we can enjoy each other to the fullest. You're definitely special...

Arjun: /me gazes with admiration at her young, firm breasts and proud nipples and, feeling the tug on his hair, lets it guide his head toward her breast, placing trembling lips against the warm, silky flesh, while his free hand wanders up her side to cup her other breast almost reverently. Then he starts kissing up her chest to her neck as he murmurs a little song, "You can't be special 'till you're special for someone... You can't find love until you give it away..."

Zurie: ::shudders at the feeling of his lips against her skin, her eyes fluttering shut with pleasure from his gentle touching, hands curling further into his hair, smiles at the tune and hums along, as his kisses reach her pale, slender neck, her lips grazing against his cheek, barely touching it, as she exhales warmly against it, her mouth trailing warm kisses along his jaw, lips sliding against the moving muscles::

Arjun: /me turns his head slightly until the corner of his mouth reaches hers and gently circles the areola around her nipple with a light fingertip, using a feather touch, hesitantly, as if fearing it would try to escape, raising his head to gaze into her eyes, his lips near hers, whispering, "You're so lovely, Zurie, all of you... inside and out."

Zurie: ::makes a small sound at the teasing touch of his fingertips on the swelled mound of her sensitive breast, then opens her eyes to meet his, melting into the dark brown pools before turning to kiss him sweetly, tasting his warm, soft lips as she curls herself around him and slides her foot up and down his leg teasingly, nibbling his bottom lip and pulling at it with her teeth:: As are you, Arjun, such a gentle spirit amid so much trouble.

Arjun: /me parts his lips to take her upper lip gently between his teeth, tasting the sweetness of her mouth and would lightly caress her belly. His manhood springs to attention as her thigh strokes against it. He suddenly feels the need to gasp for air, and with it, inhales the perfumed scent of her hair. His hand explores downward, discovering there a metal zipper that gives way to his tug. "This is what makes the trouble bearable, sweet Zurie," he gasps, coming up for air. "Human tenderness and warmth..."

Sweet, but careful with the powerplay.

Zurie: ::lets out a soft moan as he grazes his teeth on her lip and unwinds her hands from his soft hair to snake down his sides, needing to feel him warm and alive under her hands. She shivers as he unzips her shorts and arches her back slightly off the bed to slip them off, then raises her leg to run the silky skin against his throbbing member, gliding along it as her lips open, kissing him again fiercely::

Arjun: /me explores between her lips with the tip of his tongue, which meets hers. He presses his body against hers while curious fingers slip under her panties to explore the silky skin of her lower belly and groin. He pulls gently away from the kiss long enough to murmur in a trembling voice, "I can't believe I'm making love with such a beautiful, strong, fierce woman," then plunges back in to seek her tongue again with his...

Some time later, after a satisfied, happy Zurie has left him, Arjun edits his transcript into a notecard, cutting it short so as not to disclose the most delicious and secret of their intimacies. He then makes his way to the Love Temple, deposits his notecard in the urn, and, exhausted, poofs for the night.

Why are you here, Arjun?

To give and receive love. So many lonely souls in this world
just need a little human contact and warmth.
I know because I am one of them.

CHAPTER SIXTEEN

MAKING A HOME

Status:	Lover
Level:	23
HP:	24.8

In this chapter, we will be changing gears a little and summarizing several weeks of Arjun's virtual life to tie it into what happens afterward, so please bear with us. We start with Arjun lounging on his new porch, gazing out over the lush green of the Gangotri Valley. To his right, the sparkling Eastern River flows lazily toward the sea; to his left, the quaint cottages of Gangotri Village sleep under the noon-day sun, and beyond it in the distance, the graceful white petals of the Lotus Temple shine dimly through a light blue haze.

Arjun lowers his gaze to Zurie napping by his side. She had turned out to be rather dominant, and to make her happy, Arjun had assumed a relatively submissive role, although not in a strict sense, as he did not enjoy BDSM and was rebellious and defiant by nature. When she had called him her pet, he had reminded her—half in jest—that tiger cubs had sharp fangs and claws, and that he would not hesitate to use them if she didn't treat him right.

With one hand, he gently caresses the silky thigh that Zurie had lain over him during the afterglow of yet another passionate bout of love-making, and with the other, he softly strokes her auburn hair falling in rich waves over her bronze shoulders as she sleeps, a faint smile softening the otherwise fierce look on her strong face. His skin still tingles, and a pleasant ache lingers in his groin. Arjun takes a deep breath of satisfaction, his flared nostrils inhaling the musky scent of their mingled love juices combined with the earthy sweetness of his garden.

Choosing a Village

Arjun's first night with Zurie had gained him "Level 23 – Lover" and the "Villager" quest, which had consisted of joining a village and learning its rules. Through a process of elimination, he had chosen Gangotri for its rich cultural diversity, openness to free thought, and captivating landscape. Sanjay had no village, he had zero interest in living with the Raider scum of Sundarbans, Papikonda City was exciting but too busy and noisy, Namdapha was ugly and its miners coarse, the Gir Ashram was too strictly disciplined, the Simlipal farmers were too traditionalist for his inquisitive mind, the blatant eroticism of Indravati made him uncomfortable, and being a Betla fisherman was not his idea of fun. He liked neither the snows of Hemis nor the cold steppes of Khangchendzonga, which is where Eswaria had gone, attracted mostly by its inhabitants' courage and dare-devil games.

Living in neighboring villages, Eswaria and Arjun had visited each other but had never gone beyond a platonic, fraternal friendship. Arjun had been tempted by the vibrant, colorful life of the Rajasthan nomads, but that was Zurie's village and they had decided not to live together, preferring to visit each other's homes and remain free to develop relationships with other people. They cared for each other dearly but knew that steady relationships tended to last on average no more than three months in virtual worlds, and they didn't want theirs to become yet another statistic.

Building a House

Arjun glances around in approval at his lovely little cottage. Once he had reached Level 24 – Villager, he had accepted the "Resident" quest, consisting of setting up his home in or near his chosen village. When Commissioner Janus had shown him the only available building—a large townhouse half a block from the central square—Arjun had decided against it. It was lovely but had a land impact of 203 unfurnished, which was way over his budget. Instead, he had chosen this empty 30m x 30m corner lot on the village's outskirts. It was bordered at the back by a rocky cliff dug into the mountainside from which a narrow cascade fell, had a fabulous view over the valley, and was tastefully landscaped with trees and other plants, so he did not have to spend land impact points on lots of vegetation.

At one copper per meter, it would cost him nine gold coins per month, which he could pay for by selling about 100 items per week at the bonus rate. What he hadn't factored into this calculation was the drought season, which had hit him and everyone else hard. The rivers and swamp had all but dried up under the scorching sun, food plants had started producing much less and at a slower rate than ever before, and fish and animals were also fewer and harder to catch. This had made food scarce and had required much more effort to collect his 100 items.

Granted, more of the trading kiosks had been offering bonus rates due to the scarcity of produce, but Arjun had only needed one to get the best prices, so that really hadn't helped him much.

To make matters worse, the crocs and big cats had become hungrier and fiercer due to the lack of prey and had gone beyond their usual ranges to terrorize the villagers, even in their own homes. Arjun had responded to this threat by taking the path of the yellow spirit to help with the protection efforts, but that had made him susceptible to attack by desperate warriors who had robbed him of his earnings on more than one occasion. Not only that, but the incidence of diseases such as snake bites, scorpion stings, sunstroke, and respiratory ailments had seen an upsurge, which had also meant a significant drain on food resources. Then, as if to add insult to injury, the region had been plagued by sudden whirlwinds that ejected their victims from the region, who were unable to return for several hours.

Luckily, the drought had only lasted a couple of weeks before life returned to normal and Arjun could go back to building his home. He had scoured the Marketplace and inspected several structures inworld until he had finally decided to put together various structures to get just what he wanted. The main room was a five-sided hut with large roll-up doors on two sides and full-width shutter windows on all but one side. He added a mesh porch to the front door side and a lean-to greenhouse on the other door side for his vintage copper bathtub. Finally, he replaced the front door with a lock-pickable Kool RP Door—as per the region's rules—filling the extra space with stained-glass panels on either side.

The finished product was gorgeous, blended well with the surrounding landscape, and had a land impact of only 34. At a rate of one plank and two nails per LI, he had only needed 34 planks and 68 nails, which had taken him a few days to collect. Several good roleplay opportunities had arisen while he had been felling trees, mining the iron and having the planks and nails made, which he knew was the whole purpose of having to collect these resources in the first place.

Arjun would have to pay $5 Linden per week for each LI he rezzed, by increments of 100 LI, so the minimum would be about L$ 2000 (US$ 8.00) per month. With that much, he had been able to furnish and decorate his cottage tastefully, including several low-prim mesh indoor plants and a TV screen for music videos, and had even planted a little vegetable garden to bolster his income. That had meant depriving his atman of some favorite RL goodies from the corner store to fit the budget, but it was well worth it.

Choosing a Specialty

Soft music wafts through the porch door from his media screen, combined with the tinkling of wind chimes and the gentle shushing of the waterfall. Arjun heaves another deep, happy sigh and reaches again for the notecard describing his current quest. Commissioner Janus and his wife had visited to inspect his home, congratulate him on his lovely build, and welcome him to Gangotri Village. Soon after that, Arjun had reached Level 25 – Resident and been given a quest called 'Prospect,' comprised of choosing one of three specialties—tradesperson, healer, or warrior—and signing up to receive special training on roleplaying the various situations common to each.

Arjun had already gone to an introductory session for prospective tradespersons, given by the Commissioner of Simlipal, who had spoken to them on the pros and cons of the specialty. He had explained that scripted systems used to support roleplay are commonly of two kinds: combat systems (CS)—including scripted weapons, ammunition, hit points, and so-on—and economic systems (ES) that included growing/gathering and cooking food, collecting and processing other resources such as fibers, wood, and metals, and building objects to use within the system, plus the numerous machines and services needed to process those resources, all of which operates as an entire economy of supply and demand.

Several good economic systems were available. Some used actual mesh items that players could keep in their inventories and rez when needed, while others were based entirely on HUDs telling users how many items they had collected. The Virtual India Karma system was a hybrid of the two, with the HUD taking in mesh items as lists and numbers, not objects, then re-rezzing them as mesh objects as required, thereby eliminating the need to keep and sort the items in the Inventory and reducing the land impact and lag that could be caused by rezzing many scripted items.

The main problem with scripted economic systems is that, for psychological reasons that Arjun only partially understood, a human tendency to hoard leads players to spend more time merely gathering resources than actually roleplaying with them. The challenge of learning all the ins and outs of the system also tends to be highly motivating. However, this can become quite expensive as players purchase all the equipment and supplies needed for production, and people tend to collect everything until they learn how the ES works, realize its limitations, and grow tired of it. Some think they will be able to set up a profitable business selling the products, but due to the nature of the system, which requires relatively little ongoing investment and poses virtually no risk, there is always much more supply than demand, prices are extremely low, and actual sales are scant.

The Commissioner had pointed out another problem with publicly-available economic systems. When they are used in roleplay regions, large amounts of resources can be brought in from outside the region, flooding the market and eliminating the need to roleplay their production and marketing, which is the whole purpose of the ES.

That is why Virtual India has its own proprietary ES that will not work anywhere except within the region using the Karma HUD. The tools and equipment for the trades are not sold but only rezzed in specific places around the region, and only trained members of the Virtual India Tradespersons' group can use them. This prevents market gluts and ensures that the production and marketing of goods are achieved through actual roleplay and not in isolation, as ends in themselves.

The problem with economic systems is when players spend more time gathering resources than actually roleplaying with them.

Tradespersons are given exclusive access to operate the various workshops around the region, such as basketry, smithy, carpentry, butchery, pottery, spinning wheels and weaving looms, the stations for preserving and packaging fish, meat, and dairy products, the weaponry, fishing supply shop, and others, plus the six Trading Kiosks around the region. In addition to this group-only access, some resources, such as fruits and nuts, hunted animals, mines, trees, reeds, and fish, have open access to all players in the region, while others, such as personal garden plots and cookpots, have private access, available only to use by their individual owners.

The group had visited several tradespersons who had showcased their crafts. The carpenter had made a table for someone's house and the blacksmith a butcher knife, the weaver had spun thread, dyed it, and wove it into a tapestry, the potter had turned a jug on the pottery wheel, then glazed and fired it, and the butcher had prepared sausages and shared them with the students. What had struck Arjun the most was their highly graphic emotes describing each step of the manufacturing process. Each had emphasized the importance of not letting the carpentry table, forge, spinning wheel, weaving loom, pottery wheel, or butcher's table roleplay for them, but rather seeing the scripted equipment merely as props and the animations solely as a support for their actual roleplay, which was what they had written in their posts.

Arjun saw that this was a broad, interesting field that could also make him rich in RP money, but spending options were limited to the tools and resources needed to make even more money. That could get old really fast, so wealth was less of a motivation than the chance to enrich his learning and roleplaying opportunities. However, he wanted to explore the other specialties before deciding.

He went back to reading the 'Prospect Quest Instructions' notecard. Healers or shamans received specialized powers, tools, and training to cure the various illnesses that periodically struck people, such as colds and diarrhea, wounds and stings, high and low BP, plus things like drowning, starving, and injuries from fights, with an emphasis on healer roleplay.

Warriors received special training, weapons, and powers as fighters, whether in the role of bad guys such as Raiders or good guys such as Guards, and everything in between. They could wear the red spirit, which gave them the ability to use the scripted weapons system, but they had to follow strict rules and codes of conduct. Having to go through warrior training to get those powers was a way of ensuring that those rules and codes were followed and of preventing 'murderhobos' from just coming in to terrorize the region.

It was time to IM Mahir.

> Arjun: Hi Mahir. I've reached Level 25 – Resident and am ready to specialize.
>
> Mahir: Congratulations, Arjun. You did it in record time, and everyone agrees that you've done an excellent job on all your quests.
>
> Arjun: Thanks, Mentor. It's been a lot of fun. You, Chris, and the others have been extremely helpful and patient. This mentoring system saved my roleplaying career after my first two fiascos. How can I find out more about the healer and warrior specialties? I've attended an introductory class on the Trades already.
>
> Mahir: You should attend the other introductory courses then. The one for warriors is on Friday at 2:00 pm at the Arena, and the one for healers is on Monday at 2:00 pm at the Health Clinic.
>
> Arjun: Thanks, Mahir. I'll be there.
>
> Mahir: Good luck, Arjun.

Arjun: /me, smiling, turns to admire Zurie's lovely face and press his lips to her forehead.

Zurie: ::stirs from her sleep and props herself up on an elbow to look back at him with her large, olive-green eyes, searching his face as her fingertips would slowly graze his skin from navel to cheek. She then leans in to press her parted lips to his as her thigh would move up from his leg over his groin:: Are you rested enough for another round? ::she purrs softly, then grins tauntingly:: I seem to recall that I won the last one.

Arjun: /me growls contentedly, "Gods, you're irresistible," as he turns to gather her in his arms and hold her close and ravish her mouth with his...

Why are you here, Arjun?

Never mind that – I have more pressing matters to attend to right now.

Part III:

Arjun Finds His Role

CHAPTER SEVENTEEN

CAPTURE ROLEPLAY – I

Status:	Resident
Level:	25
HP:	23.2

Several warrior prospects stand around panting, chatting and laughing after an exhilarating sparring session at the Arena—a large earthen court surrounded by high stone walls. They had been running back and forth in teams, ducking behind rocks, jumping obstacles, and shooting at each other. The Arena was a specially scripted area for practice, so after each fight was over, they recovered their HP and ammo quickly to start another round without having to reload and eat to buff up. Each time, Arjun had been one of the first to go down, so he had spent most of the time watching the others fight from where he lay, writhing in a pool of his own blood, unable to get up.

Arjun had studied beforehand how the Virtual India weapons system worked, since each combat system (CS) was evidently scripted a little differently. Zurie had tried to teach him how to dodge bullets by using the 'always run' function (Ctrl-R) and running back and forth in unpredictable patterns. He was supposed to shoot just in front of a moving target to compensate for the time it took for the bullet to arrive, trying to run in the same direction as his target to make aiming easier. Arjun spent hours practicing these techniques at the chicken and monkey hunting grounds, kiting back and forth as his prey ran hither and thither while shooting as fast as he could. This had been good for his coin purse, but he wasn't sure how much his fighting skills had improved as a result.

Arjun's atman had even gone so far as to purchase a large gamer mousepad and a gaming mouse with a super-sensitive clicker and programmable buttons he had set to rapidly change between slower and faster mouse movements. Slower gave him a more precise aim for range (3-96 m), which was especially important because his mouse jiggled a lot when he clicked. He had practiced different speed-clicking techniques like 'jitter' and 'butterfly', and had repeatedly taken a 'clicking speed test', but had never reached more than about six clicks per second. Finally, he had gone online to research how to increase his FPS (frames per second) by adjusting his computer settings, lowering his graphics level, removing all unnecessary attachments, and so on.

Zurie had also helped Arjun practice melee (0-3 m) fighting with only fists and feet, which required the faster mouse movement setting and consisted mostly of either staying out of arm's reach or trying to run circles around her in unpredictable patterns in an attempt to get behind her while kicking and punching as fast as he could. Arjun was using the WASD keys to move, but his fingers kept getting tangled up and confused, so he would run in the wrong direction or freeze in place and get clobbered. So for homework, Zurie had told him to practice running in tight circles, first one way with WDSA, then the other way with WASD, over and over again until he could do it without thinking. That had helped a bit, but by the end of her lessons, he had fallen in a pool of his own blood so often that it no longer made him squeamish... well, at least not as much as before.

Zurie's instructions had all sounded logical and had even worked somewhat while practicing with her, but remembering and implementing them in the heat of battle had been another matter entirely. Arjun would get flustered, forget to draw his gun, stumble around with his fingers on and off the WASD keys, and in general make a fool of himself at the Arena. He had almost decided to throw in the towel when they had all been called together for a class discussion.

Arjun chuckles to himself wryly, "Well, at least sitting in class and taking notes is something I AM good at."

CARP and Powerplay

Mahir: /me claps his hands and beckons the group to gather around him. "Okay, okay... sit down, everybody. Time to talk about CARP."

They sit in a semicircle around him, half-naked bodies heaving and glistening with sweat, eager grins on their beaming faces—all except for Arjun, who sits glumly, nursing his wounds. Off to one side can be heard the metallic swish-clang of a couple engaged in melee fighting and, to the other side, the thwip-thunk of an archer practicing her aim.

Dorketta: looks up at the Mentor questioningly "What's all this talk about carp? I've only caught white and yellow fish in the river. Where do you find carp?"

Mahir: /me shakes his head and rolls his eyes, "CARP is short for CApture (and) RolePlay. It includes fighting, downing, capping (short for capturing), and all the associated roleplay. This can be done through metered combat using the scripted weapons and capping systems, better known as combat systems (CS), BUT..."

Arjun: /me interrupts, "Wait a minute, Mentor Mahir. You have said that each player emotes an action and that the next player decides what effect it will have. But with the fast pace of a fight with scripted weapons, how do you avoid power-play? Shooting or cutting someone with scripted weapons is immediate – BOOM! Action-reaction, right?"

Mahir: /me clears his throat, obviously struggling to keep his patience. "Right... As I was about to say when I was so RUDELY interrupted..." –he scowls at Arjun– "BUT... fighting with a CS is not true roleplay. It can be best described as real-time fighting, as opposed to text-based fighting.

"In text or turn-based fighting, also known as non-metered or roleplay fighting, you describe your movements and intentions in writing. Your opponent decides what effect your actions will have and takes the next step... within what is realistically possible, of course. Conventionally, each player gets two moves per post, such as one defensive action and one offensive action or two of either, although some sims have other rules."

In text or turn-based fighting, you describe your movements and intentions in writing.

Mamakie: /me interrupts, "One advantage of turn-based fighting is that I can emote drawing a gun and aiming it at you, regardless of whether the pixels show me holding a gun in my hand. You'll imagine what I'm doing and decide whether to raise your hands and try to appease me, run away, stand and fight, dance a jig, or whatever else your character would realistically do without being a twink.

"This is one of the two fields of roleplay—along with ERP—where it's especially important to avoid powerplay. For example,

> */me steps over to Mahir, grabs his throat with both hands, and forces him to the ground.*

"That's not acceptable because I'm deciding how my action will affect Mahir. But if I say...

> */me steps over to Mahir and throws her hands out TO grab his throat WITH THE INTENTION of forcing him to the ground.*

"...then this gives Mahir the freedom to decide what happens next."

Mahir: "So I can do this...

> */me sways on his feet to the left so that her hands miss his throat as he sticks out his right foot to trip her and brings his left hand around with the intention of grabbing her arm and using her momentum to throw her to the ground.*

"Or this...

/me chokes, his eyes bulging, his mouth gaping, his face turning purple, gasping for air as he claws at her fingers closing tightly around his throat. "Let me gooo..." he rasps.

"By choosing how the character Mahir will respond to the character Mamakie trying to grab his throat, I can change where the storyline will take us."

Mamakie: "Right. Now, although it's always up to the one receiving the action to decide what effect it will have, PLEASE don't always play the superhero. Be willing to take damage, and don't block or dodge every hit. In RL, you practically never finish a fight without at least a few cuts and bruises, even if you win. Think of *Batman v Superman: Dawn of Justice* and how many painful hits they both take before the denouement.

"Fights are supposed to be fast-paced, with short, action-packed emotes and brief, pithy descriptions. Refusing to take damage can make a fight go on forever. So let's say Mahir was successful using the first option:

/me loses her balance as he pulls her by the arm, tries to step forward to steady herself but trips on his outstretched leg and cries out as she tumbles face-first to the ground, tucking her head under just in time to roll and spring to her feet, whirling to face him again, fists up, seething with fury.

"All in all, RP is just that... I throw an idea out to Mahir, and he gets to decide what happens. He then gives me his next step, and I decide where to go from there. But it takes a good roleplayer to avoid crossing the line over to powerplay. Even Mahir makes that mistake with me from time to time, but I just let it slide and play along, unless I really don't feel comfortable with where the scene is going, and then I send him a friendly IM to let him know."

> Good roleplayers will let you hurt them in text-based roleplay. Others want to act invincible, a kind of godmodding.

Mahir: "Good roleplayers will let you hurt them in text-based roleplay, but some of the more competitive-minded beginners seem to want their characters to be invincible, which is a kind of godmodding. There is also 'passive godmodding,' where the character just barely avoids all attacks but without counter-attacking, until the attacker gets frustrated and gives up. You can resolve such cases using the 'Dice' option in your Karma HUD. For example:

Mamakie: /me swings her open hand at Mahir's cheek, her eyes full of rage and hurt

Dharma Guide: Mamakie throws the dice, which lands on 5

Dharma Guide: Mahir throws the dice, which lands on 3

Mahir: /rubs his stinging cheek and gapes at Mamakie. "What did you do that for???"

Mamakie: /me laughs, slinking an arm around Mahir's waist to pull him close. "So, in this case, my slap hits his face, and since five minus three is two, it landed with a force of only two on a scale from one to five, which is not really that hard." She smirks at Mahir.

Arjun: /me raises his hand and blurts out, "So for real RP fighting using text only, it doesn't matter whether I'm wearing a green or yellow Karma Tag, right?"

Mahir: /me snuggles closer to Mamakie, throwing an arm around her shoulders affectionately. "Yes, green tags can only use text-based fighting, as long as they don't have something like 'No aggression when green' in their RP limits. You can take scripted damage from red-tagged warriors when you're wearing the yellow tag but can only use text-based fighting against them, not scripted fighting."

Arjun: /me frowns, shaking his head in confusion. "Then why would anyone want to go yellow if they can receive damage from the scripted weapons system but not defend themselves with it?"

Mahir: /me strokes Mamakie's hair and tweaks her cheek, "Some people go yellow because they want their roleplay to be more realistic. In real life, most people carry no weapons, so are at the mercy of any baddies who do. Others just enjoy roleplaying captive scenarios. Everyone can fight using text-based roleplay, but only those who successfully complete the specialized warrior training can wear the red tag, which enables them to use the scripted weapons system to give damage to yellows and other reds."

Mamakie: /me lays her head on Mahir's shoulder and smiles, "Even trained warriors are sometimes not in the mood for CARP and can change to the green Karma Tag until they feel like fighting again. Other reasons may be that they're too laggy that day, their crappy computers can't handle the fast pace of a fight, or they just want to concentrate on their cooking for a while."

Competition versus Roleplay

Mahir: "Now then... I'm sure many of you have played first-person shooter (FPS) or 'ego-shooter' games, where the emphasis is on winning fights rather than teamwork and roleplay."

–Most of the students nod–

"Okay, well... if you want to roleplay a warrior in Virtual India, you will need to forget all of that. The primary goal of CARP is not to win but to roleplay with others and have fun together, and you can do that regardless of whether you win or lose."

The goal of CARP is not to win fights but to RP and have fun together, win or lose.

Mamakie: "Roleplaying requires developing a character, and all characters have strengths and weaknesses. We all want to be the best we can be, but nobody is born a superhuman warrior complete with invincible weapons—even in RL. Besides, your character needs to be built from the ground up, grow, and develop its potential. Nobody is born a hero.

"Instead of just trying to make your characters physically strong, consider showing their inner strength. You do this by making your character suffer. That's right—put them through hell. Then show how they overcome their physical, emotional, or other types of problems through their strength of character and how that leads them to grow even stronger inwardly.

"That will make for a much rounder, deeper character and a much more interesting, nuanced story than just winning fights. Players who fight only to win tend to find themselves alone very quickly. Nobody likes to roleplay with someone who is unwilling to lose as often as they win, or at least take a few scratches and bruises."

Nobody likes to RP with someone who won't at least take a few scratches and bruises.

Mahir: "Right, and pardon us for insisting so much on what may seem a simple matter, but it seems very hard for some people to grasp. If your idea of fun is limited to adding to your body count, then CARP is not for you. Go to a zombie region where you can shoot the walking dead to your heart's content with no need to roleplay and without bothering anyone else.

"Even when using the scripted weapons system, bear in mind that this is NOT a competition. It's about roleplaying and having fun together. And the sooner you get that through your *thick skulls*" –he scowls around at the group– "the sooner you'll discover that when everyone is having fun, everyone wins."

Eswaria: /me raises her hand, a confused look on her face, "But what's the point of fighting if you don't fight to win?"

Mahir: "Okay, well... think about what you just said. Everybody is fighting to win, and that's okay, nothing wrong with that. But if only those who have the best computer equipment, gadgets, technique, OR cheats..."

–Mahir stops to glare at some of the students, who cringe under his stare and glance around furtively at the others as if to see whether they have noticed that he had singled them out–

"...Yes, I see you know what I'm talking about... If those people always win, then what's the point of roleplaying fights for everyone else? Where's the fun for them if they never get the chance to roleplay being the captors? And we're here to roleplay, which should be fun for EVERYone. Got it?"

–Some students nod enthusiastically, but others more slowly, as if unsure–

Mamakie: "We should all be here for good roleplay, but too many put too little effort into it. This is especially true when it comes to CARP, where some just want to shoot their weapons and kill all the enemies they can. You need to realize that many who love roleplaying may have little or no interest in CARP. You can have good roleplay without CARP, but you can't have good CARP without roleplay."

Mahir: "In any case, fighting should be the exception, not the rule. It should be only part of a larger roleplay story. Avoid 'bubble play' or 'cubical play,' which centers on your own little corner of the story without considering the broader events unfolding around you. Just attacking people for no reason is not realistic unless you're a violent psychopath, in which case you should be locked up, not roaming the region freely.

"Even the most violent action films develop lots of plot before and after any battle scenes. If people just fought all the time in a film, we would leave the theater complaining about how boring the movie was—same thing with CARP. Don't be that shallow. Build a deeper plot. Develop an interesting story together."

Dorketta: "When you say we should tell a story, do you mean we need to agree on the plot beforehand and then act it out?"

–Some students start to snicker, but Mahir glowers at them, and they cringe under his fierce gaze–

Mahir: "Actually, that's an excellent question. Some roleplay regions have official 'Game Masters' (GMs) who pre-plan storylines like in D&D, but that's not the case in open RP regions like Virtual India. Here, anyone is free to propose a storyline for their roleplay partners or through the Virtual India group chat, but a group of creative roleplayers can also just go with the flow and develop the story ad-hoc."

When you play CARP, bear in mind that your IC 'enemies' are actually your OOC friends, or at least should be.

Mamakie: "When you play CARP, bear in mind that your IC 'enemies' are actually your OOC friends, or at least should be. The word 'frenemy' comes to mind, although that usually means an enemy who pretends to be your friend. In CARP, it's the other way around: your frenemies are friends pretending to be enemies. Gary Gygax, the co-creator of the Dungeons and Dragons roleplay game and founder of the Gen Con Gaming Convention, has said:

> Games give you a chance to excel, and if you're playing in good company, you don't even mind if you lose because you had the enjoyment of the company during the course of the game.[21]
>
> The essence of a role-playing game is that it is a group, cooperative experience. There is no winning or losing, but rather the value is in the experience...[22]

---

[21] Gary Gygax. GameSpy interview by Allen Rausch, Pt. 1, August 15, 2004.

[22] Gary Gygax. 2006 interview, quoted in "Gary Gygax, Game Pioneer, Dies at 69," The New York Times, March 5, 2008.

"In my humble opinion, if there is ANY competition in roleplay, it should be this: to be so convincing that the other players respond emotionally as though it were real, like when you see a good movie or read a good book and laugh, cry, or shiver with fright at a scene.

"Whoever among you can have this effect on your roleplay partners wins. In fact, your partners will also win because that's what we're all here for, right? And they will hopefully elicit a similar response in you. That way, everybody wins, and nobody loses."

Ambushes and Roleplay

Arjun: /me fidgets during the long silence that ensues after Mamakie's words, then finally clears his throat and blurts out, "Um... are people allowed to attack you without any previous roleplay?"

Mahir: "Well, some RP regions require you to post three good emotes before you attack anyone, such as this:

> */me unholsters his pistol and flicks off the safety with his thumb, his mouth twisted into a snarl.*
>
> */me raises his pistol to shoulder level with both hands and aims at the man, growling, "Hands up or I shoot!"*
>
> */me seeing the man reaching for his gun, shoots at the ground by his feet and bellows, "Last warning!"*

"However, other regions, such as Virtual India, allow people to attack without any preliminary roleplay. The rationale for this is that real-life ambushes DO happen, and for obvious reasons they're not announced beforehand. So here, if you're a habitual para-roleplayer, you may end up dead before you get one emote out. BUT... if there's no roleplay before a fight, there MUST be roleplay after it. What you must NOT do is just attack and leave without any kind of roleplay."

Mamakie: "That's why it's essential to read each region's rules before roleplaying in it. Another thing I do NOT want to see is anyone attacking others as soon as they log in, before they've had a chance to fully rez and get their bearings. This includes camping next to popular TP spots to down people as soon as they TP in. It's cowardly, discourteous, childish, and downright stupid."

Mahir: "That's another good point... Of course, if you chase after the ambushers, they can run away without emoting anything. They're under no obligation to hang around and get themselves killed, but they must escape legitimately. No teleporting out or logging off in those cases."

Student: "Some avatars seem to have super-speed. You can't catch up with them when they run away, and you can't get away from them when they chase you. They can even outrun fast animals, like cheetahs."

Chiptag: "There can be a few reasons for that. One may be lag, in which case your computer skips frames, and things seem to move faster. Another problem is crossing sim borders, which can slow you down. The third reason is that they may be using a 'speed HUD' to run faster, which is illegal here and in most CARP-enabled regions because it gives them an unfair advantage."

Mahir: "Personally, when I see people using speed HUDs, I just leave them to themselves and look for a roleplay partner who doesn't need to cheat to win. Of course, you could file a complaint about them with the region's authorities, but how can you prove it? You could also open an IM and tell them why you prefer not to roleplay with them, but that could invite an argument.

"It's better just to ignore them. At some point, they will hopefully realize that cheating is not the best way to encourage people to roleplay with them. But whatever you do, never respond to cheating with cheating. They're not your teachers. Set a better example for them."

Never respond to cheating with cheating. They're not your teachers. Set a better example for them.

Mamakie: "Speaking of complaints, don't freak out if someone reports you to the authorities. They are aware that many complaints are bogus, and they tend to ignore the obvious ones or turn around and challenge complainers on their own actions. Some people are just paranoid and will obsessively complain about anything and everything, even things that are clearly not cases of cheating.

"So, it's not the end of the world if you're reported. Just be sure to keep all transcripts in case the issue becomes serious. It's also useful to take quick snapshots of certain situations to use as evidence of misbehavior or cheating if you plan to report someone."[23]

Mahir: "Warriors can actually be demoted if they break the CARP rules. It's a three-step process. At the first offense, they are only admonished and reminded of the rules, but at the second offense, their warrior's powers are taken away for a week. At the third offense, they are put in jail for a month and assigned a mentor to work with them on the issue during that time. Finally, at the fourth offense, they are demoted from the warrior class and have to start their training all over again, which is much more rigorous the second time around."

Chiptag: "About jail, this might not be the right place to mention it, but if you roleplay criminal activities like breaking and entering, burglary, arson, etc., leave an object with a giver script and a notecard containing clues, such as what evidence can be found, whose fingerprints are on it, and so on. This will enable the owner or the authorities to hunt you down for a good CARP scene and maybe even a court trial roleplay. If you're the one playing the investigator, let the truth

---

[23] To learn how to take these snapshots, see wiki.firestormviewer.org/fs_snapshot.

be revealed gradually as events unfold. Don't just jump to a conclusion right away; squeeze all the roleplay juice you can from it."

Capturing a Prisoner

Chiptag: "Okay, Mentor Mahir has asked me to explain the technical aspects of capturing ('capping'), and then he will do the roleplay part. Gobs of technical tips are available online for maximizing your computer's performance, and I'm available for any specific questions you might have, so for now, I will just talk about the Virtual India system.

"While you're downed, anyone who clicks on your Karma Tag will get a menu with a 'Bind' option. Clicking on that will attach a binding bracelet to your wrist. They can then click on the bracelet to get a menu with several options such as Leash, Yank, Handoff, Post, and Unleash.

"The Leash option will make a chain rez between their bracelet and your hand, and they will not be able to move more than a few meters away from you. 'Yank' will shorten the leash to about an arm's length. 'Handoff' and 'Post' will give you lists of nearby players or objects where you can pass or tie the leash. Finally, 'Unleash' derezzes the leash and frees your captive.

"If your fight has been in text-based and you lose, you can attach the binding bracelet to your own wrist by clicking on your Karma Tag and choosing 'Bind.' This will put the binding bracelet on your wrist to let your captor leash you. Alternatively, people will sometimes pass you copy/transfer handcuffs, blindfolds, gags, hoods, or other props to use as part of the roleplay scene, or you can get your own from the Marketplace for when you need them."

> You have a few minutes before they recover, so take your time and roleplay exactly what you're doing.

Mamakie: "Yes, or they can just emote it without needing the actual object as a prop. Bear in mind that this kind of prop isn't necessary for the actual roleplay. Granted, good visuals are great for inspiring better roleplay, but they are still OOC elements until emoted, so you should roleplay putting them on anyway, not just click the menu. Once you emote that you have bound their wrists behind their backs or in front, tied up their ankles, put a blinding hood over their heads, clamped a gag in their mouth, or whatever, those things exist for roleplay purposes, even if no props are used."

Mahir: "Right. Now let's talk about the roleplay aspect of capping. First of all, when capturing someone, be aware that leashing them doesn't stop them from attacking you with any weapons you haven't emoted taking away from them, or melee punching or kicking you if you haven't emoted tying up their hands or feet, or at least tied them to a post and moved out of their melee distance.

"You have a few minutes before they recover from the downing, so take your time and roleplay exactly what you're doing. If you do it carefully, they won't be able to legitimately attack you once they recover. For example, you could emote something like:

> */me takes two lengths of rope from his bag and stands over his victim, bends down, and taking advantage of the man's weakened state, twists his hands forcibly behind his back, tying one rope tightly around his wrists and using the other to lash his ankles together.*
>
> */me bends down and takes the man's knife from his belt, tucking it into his pack for safekeeping. Picks up his bow, takes out his hunting knife, and cuts the string, rendering it useless, then unholsters the man's pistol, empties the chamber of all bullets, and puts these into his pack.*
>
> */me pats him down, looking for any other hidden weapons and communication devices, and, finding none, clips a leash to the handcuffs and stands back with a mirthless chuckle, "Sohohooo, you've finally fallen into my hands. I guess now it's payback time, huh?"*

"Of course, you can create 'gestures' for this purpose to avoid having to write it out every time, which is especially useful when involved in a multi-player fight and you're in a hurry. BUT… it's NOT enough just to emote '/me takes their weapons.' That's godmodding, and serious roleplayers won't accept it. Using gestures at all is considered bad roleplay, so use them sparingly and only in emergencies. Under normal circumstances, it's better to type out your own posts in response to specific situations."

Phobos: /me, a small, mousy student, raises his hand timidly and says in a high-pitched voice, "I don't like fighting, partly because I always lose…"

–laughter around the group–

Phobos: /me grins around at his classmates as if wondering whether they are laughing WITH him or AT him, then clears his throat and continues, "…but once I downed and capped a suspicious-looking man who was hanging out in the village square. I emoted taking away his weapons and communication devices, then leashed him to a post.

"But then he said I hadn't done it exactly right and attacked me with the same weapons I had taken away from him. He was such a prick about it that I blocked and muted him. I don't want to roleplay with someone who is more interested in winning at all costs than in having a good time."

Mamakie: /me wobbles her head in agreement. "Exactly. Good example, Phobos. Technically, he may have been right about your faulty capping technique. But if he'd been more interested in roleplaying than in winning a fight, he might have graciously accepted defeat but then explained how you should do it next time. That way, you both would have been happy with the outcome, and you wouldn't have muted him.

"When people fight only to win, real roleplayers get fed up and start blocking them, which means they lose in the end. They lose good people to roleplay with, and precious time arguing about rules."

Mahir: "Right. Now, once you've captured an opponent, there should normally be a follow-through roleplay. You may have to continue the fight with other characters before returning to your prisoners, and those captured should take that into account and be patient. Captors may also transport prisoners to a secure location such as their camp before continuing the roleplay, but at some point, the roleplay must continue.

When people fight only to win, in the end they lose: good people to RP with, and precious time arguing about rules.

"If prisoners are left captive without roleplay for a long time, they're allowed to leave, especially if they have put a maximum time without RP in their limits. But first, they should tell their captors OOC why they're leaving. Of course, it's much better to be patient and wait for your captors to finish whatever they're doing so that the roleplay can continue.

"Before you start the captor roleplay, check your captive's RP limits to be sure you don't do anything against them. The captured CHARACTER will most likely complain and struggle IC during the roleplay, but that doesn't mean the PLAYER is opposed to what you are doing. However, if at any time they tell you OOC, such as in IMs or ((between brackets)) in Local Chat, that they feel uncomfortable with what you're doing, change direction immediately. Don't try to force your wants and likes on others."

Urstud: "I was once hypnotized and ordered to rape a girl, but after I had downed and capped her, she IMed me saying she didn't feel comfortable with rape, so I answered that she should attack me in melee to wake me up. She did, and when I came out of the trance, I didn't remember having downed her and was horrified when she said I had been about to rape her."

Mahir: "That's a great example of seeking IC solutions to an OOC problem, Urstud. Also, it's not permissible to down someone again once you have capped them. You can emote hitting and injuring them, but don't down them again using the scripted weapons system.

"Also, don't blindfold, gag, or tie your captive so tightly that they're unable to do any roleplay. It's common sense, but you'd be surprised how many people make that mistake. Finally, if you run out of roleplay ideas, you can always just release your prisoner, especially if you have other captives."

Mamakie: "Some experienced roleplayers advise against paying ransom because it can start a vicious circle with ransoms growing larger over time as each side demands more than the other until it gets out of hand. Another solution is just to emote paying the ransom without any actual exchange of coin. That tends to solve the problem" *chuckles*

Mahir: /me laughs, "Right. Bear in mind, too, that whatever you do to your prisoners can come back to bite you in the ass later. If you tickle them and joke with them, they will probably be softer on you the next time you're their prisoner. But if you torture and rape them, you can expect similar treatment when it's your turn to be the captive."

Mamakie: "This is especially true when women capture men. Some guys with macho hang-ups cannot accept defeat at the hands of a female warrior and will seek revenge to reassert their superiority. So ladies, watch out for those types."

Caring for Each Other's Feelings

Mahir: "As in the case of ERP, CARP can also evoke intense emotions IRL. It can be thrilling for a player to win a fight, especially a difficult one with a good opponent, while the losing player may be ashamed, embarrassed, frustrated, or angry. The captor can feel a sense of power and be tempted to gloat, while the captive may feel powerless, helpless, or anxious. The fight and capture are virtual, but the feelings are very real.

"Much of the drama arising after fights seems to spring from these emotions. The vanquished tend to want to justify their loss, claiming they had a low FPS, that the winner cheated, or whatever, and victors tend to justify their win by minimizing or refuting any arguments. This can also lead to hard feelings OOC that carry over into RL.

> Showing that a friendly player is behind the enemy character will enrich your RP over the long haul.

"As we said before, the ideal is that your 'enemies' should actually be your 'frenemies.' That can help avoid the kind of OOC drama that often follows a fight. But even if you have never dealt with a player before, making your IMs courteous and friendly, accepting both defeat and blame where due, can help show that a friendly player is behind the enemy character, which will enrich your roleplay experience over the long haul."

Mamakie: "Speaking of feelings, there is a special kind of powerplay so subtle that it rarely gets discussed. It relates to taking serious consequences on one's own character due to other characters' actions, i.e., making your character suffer severely because of what another character does, without discussing it with them first OOC. This can be annoying to some and emotionally disturbing to others, so it's important to identify this kind of powerplay and avoid it.

"For example, a domme put her captive onto a milking machine, telling her it would feel good and that it even made some women orgasm. But the captive, not wanting to play a sub, emoted pain and bruising as a result. She went so far as to wear severe breast bruises afterward and complain to others that the domme had mistreated and tortured her. In this way, she forced her captor into an abusive role that she didn't want, which is why I say it's a kind of powerplay. Of course, this upset the domme's player IRL, who had wanted to give her captive pleasure, and tainted the friendship between the two players.

"In another case, a man attacked a woman during a raid, unaware that she was IC pregnant, and continued to attack her after she had been downed. This upset the woman IRL, so she roleplayed aborting as a result and went around carrying her still-born baby and accusing her attacker of its death. This was disturbing for the man, who had experienced the pain of losing a child IRL. He IMed her that the roleplay had saddened him, asking her to stop. She complied and apologized profusely OOC, thereby saving the relationship between these two frenemies."

Student: "I don't see the problem. You said that each player is free to choose how other characters' actions affect theirs. After all, one of roleplay's basic principles is that 'IC actions have IC consequences', right? Doesn't that mean the two women had the right to respond the way they did?"

Mamakie: "Well, strictly speaking, yes. According to roleplay convention, both women were free to decide how the actions of the other characters would affect them, but turning the story around to blame the other characters for severe consequences could also be seen as a subtle kind of powerplay, or perhaps we should call it 'reverse powerplay' because it forced them into roles that they had not and would not have chosen: those of sadist and baby-killer, respectively.

"In such cases, the principle of basic courtesy should take precedence, and the 'victims' would be well-advised to open a friendly IM and consult with their captors before imposing such extreme consequences on them. Otherwise, such reverse powerplay could be taken as a kind of emotional bullying. Remember that rule number one of roleplay is that it should be fun for all players involved. Abusing your prerogatives can make it less than fun for other players, so we should try to be sensitive to their wishes."

CHAPTER EIGHTEEN

CAPTURE ROLEPLAY – II

The CARP class had already gone over two hours, so the group decided to continue the next afternoon. Arjun spent the following morning practicing text-based fighting with Zurie and enjoyed it much more than the scripted weapons system. He still lost more than he won, but by choice. He found it was just as fun to lose as to win, especially when Zurie made him pleasure her for his release.

What Are You After?

The group was waiting for the last stragglers, chatting about capturing versus being captured, when Eswaria said, "When I'm captured, I have LOTS of roleplay ideas, but I don't know what to do with a captive. I don't like the ransom/torture/rape scenarios most seem to favor, so I usually just bring them to the Arena and have them spar with me and teach me all their tricks." -laughs-

> In real life, only sickos engage in wanton, senseless violence. Go deeper and think about your character's goals.

Mahir: /me chuckles and waggles his head, "I know what you mean. Demanding ransom and torturing/raping victims have gotten old and boring. One way to move beyond that is to think why you fight and build your roleplay around that."

Arjun: /me raises his hand. "You said all characters should have a goal—isn't it the same with a villain? Raiders say if you're not one of them, you're their enemy, and they shoot people for no reason. That's ridiculous. Even pirates, guerrillas, human bombs, and the CIA Jackals have better reasons for violence than that."

Mahir: /me nods begrudgingly at Arjun, "Some people enjoy pew-pew games, like the 'Cowboys & Indians' or 'Cops & Robbers' we played as kids, and that's okay if everyone agrees and enjoys it. But yes, even in CARP you should have a 'driver'—something you're trying to achieve beyond shooting and capturing others. It can be as simple as looking for 'bad guys' to put them in jail or seeking revenge on an attack, but it can also be much more nuanced and complex.

"In real life, only sickos engage in wanton, senseless violence. Yes, you can roleplay a violent psychopath, but try going deeper and think about your character's goals. Otherwise, simply downing, capping, torturing, and ejecting people for no reason is piss-poor roleplay.

"Think about your backstory. What motivates you to fight? Are you a highway robber? Are you trying to recover something stolen or defending your village? Are you seeking revenge, or were they hitting on your lover? Are you looking to capture a slave, or do you enjoy making your captives fight each other, promising to set the victor free and feed the loser to your pet crocodile?

"Your character can be driven by IC prejudices or hatred against stereotypes. Or maybe you're just lonely and want someone to share a cigarette and chat with. You should have a reason for downing someone, even if it's just because they're a member of an enemy group and you want to down them before they get you.

"Anything goes, as long as everyone accepts and it's fun for all. In your case, Eswa, I assume you were fighting just because you enjoyed it, so taking them to the Arena for some sparring would make sense. But next time, think of something more closely related to your backstory and roleplay story."

Mamakie: "Everyone's ideas and preferences should be taken into account, even if they are your 'enemies.' So you could work together with them on developing a story, too, without trying to force others to act out the one you have in mind."

Eswaria: /me bobbles her head from side to side and chews on the inside of her cheeks, looking up and to the right as if thinking, a sparkle in her eyes.

Being Captured

Mahir: /me looks around, then clears his throat. "Okay, looks like everyone is here. Yesterday we talked about roleplaying as a captor, and today we'll discuss being a captive. You may go into a fight expecting to defeat your opponent, but sooner or later, we all find ourselves on the other end of the binding leash. Being downed and capped wasn't in your plans, so now what do you do?"

Dorketta: shifts nervously and grins sheepishly, squeaking, "It scares the sh*t out of me to get downed and captured. I freeze up and don't know what to do"

Mahir: /me chuckles and waggles his head, "Yes, it can be scary. Some captors can be abusive, with vicious insults and highly graphic descriptions of cruel acts. Naturally, that can pull on your emotional strings or trigger unpleasant memories of something that happened to you or a friend IRL. That's understandable.

"If you ever feel upset or distressed with the direction the roleplay is going, just tell your captors OOC. If they don't stop, you have every right to TP out, and if they repeatedly ignore your limits, report them. We're here to have fun, not to feel abused. But don't adjust your RP limits to every situation. That won't fly."

Mamakie: "People sometimes confuse threats with real RP actions. If threaten a potential thief, it's to scare them off. If someone threatens to torture you, don't assume they're actually going to do it.

"But of course, if you ARE worried, send them a friendly IM saying, 'Sorry, but I hate torture RP.' More likely than not, they will say it's just a threat, so don't waste a good roleplay opportunity without checking with them first."

Eswaria: /me shrugs, grinning and squirming excitedly in her seat, "Being captured gives me an adrenaline rush. I try to squeeze all the RP juice I can from it. Once I seduced a captor into setting me free by offering him sexual favors. He had taken my weapons, so as soon as he fed and untied me, I attacked him in melee with fists and feet. That took him by surprise, so I downed and capped him."

Arjun: /grins mischievously, "A man once capped me, took my weapons, and tied my hands, but I was able to wriggle out of my binds, picked up a knife from the floor and stabbed him..." He hangs his head and mumbles, "...but then he downed me again and made me regret it, so that didn't turn out so well."

Mahir: /me chuckles, "Yes, you can try to sweet-talk them or bribe your way out. You can cringe like a coward, wet yourself and beg for mercy, be stubborn and unyielding, fiercely proud and defiant, yell and curse, strain and struggle in your binds, or threaten to get revenge.

"If you pull out a concealed weapon, you should emote pulling it out before using it to give your partner a fair chance to respond. Not to do so would be cheesing, which is against roleplay convention. Whatever you do should be in keeping with your character and the roleplay situation. AND it should be realistic; I mean, don't pull a bazooka out of your ars... I mean, your 'rectal storage facility'."

Cry out, groan, curse, or try to stop your bleeding, but whatever you do, don't just drop to the ground and stop roleplaying.

Mamakie: /me laughs out loud. "I sometimes add some humor to the situation by complaining that they've messed up my hairdo, broken a fingernail, or made my mascara run."

Mahir: "Yes, be creative and try new things, but whatever you do, don't just drop to the ground and stop roleplaying. I mean, you CAN faint, but EMOTE it and then regain consciousness and keep roleplaying. For example:

> */me collapses, clutching his wounded leg as blood spurts through his trembling fingers until his vision goes black and he lets out a long, tremulous moan, slumping back helplessly and losing consciousness.*

Fading and Voiding

Dorketta: Is that what 'fade to black' means? Losing consciousness? Fainting?

Mahir: "Not necessarily. Fade to black (FtB) is where players agree how a scene ends without roleplaying it through. It's a time-skip, like when the curtain drops on an ongoing scene and you're left to imagine how it plays out.

"You can request an FtB if a scene is taking too long, if you have to log, or you feel uncomfortable with it, such as torture/rape. The other players must then summarize how it ends without any details, and conclude the scene. This doesn't 'void' the scene as if it never happened; it just skips all the gory details.

"Anyone can request an FtB, but overusing it can be frustrating. Some roleplayers use FtB whenever they don't like where a scene is going, just to end it and not even assume it continued behind the dropped curtain. This illegitimate use is why some regions penalize FtB by saying that all players involved must leave the region and/or not roleplay with the same characters for X amount of time."

Mamakie: "A lighter version of Fade to Black is 'Fade to Gray' (FtG) – a shorter time skip intended to move things along. If your character leaves to go grocery shopping, you can emote, '/me returns two hours later, her arms full of shopping bags, and sets them on the kitchen counter, then starts putting them away...' to avoid having to include all the dull details of the actual shopping."

Arjun: /me raises a hand, "Excuse me, Mentor Mahir... You mentioned voiding. What is that and how is it different from fade to black?"

Mahir: /me nods slowly as if thinking, "Well... FtB is to avoid seeing something that hasn't happened yet, but will be understood to have happened, such as rape. Voiding, nullification or erasure strikes out a something that already happened. The participants decide to act as if it never took place, like deleting a sentence, paragraph, or chapter from a novel, which has already been written."

Arjun: /me raises his hand "Is that the same as 'retconning'?"

Mahir: /me blinks at Arjun. "I haven't heard THAT in a while. Retcon or 'RETroactive CONtinuity' is from the world of comic books. It originally meant changing a character's backstory without altering past events but just changing their meaning. In roleplay it's changing any aspect of what has happened, which could be voiding, but is more often a small adjustment due to some mistake.

"About voiding, the most common case is deleting a single post or action, maybe because you failed to read a post that would have changed what you wrote, or because someone powerplayed. For example:

Mahir: /me headbutts Chiptag's nose as hard as he can

Chiptag: ((that's powerplay :P))

Mahir: ((You're right. Sorry. Scratch that.))

Mahir: /me throws his forehead as hard as he can toward Chiptag's nose

"Sometimes an entire sequence of interactions—or scene—is voided because it was based on metagamed information that put players at an unfair disadvantage, especially if it 'took on a life of its own' and started to spread IC. An example might be a rescue operation when there was no IC way for the rescuers to have known that their mate was captured, as we will see later.

"Voiding is NOT acceptable just because things didn't go the way you hoped, or because you divulged info IC by mistake. That's life—suck it up and deal with it. Voiding is also unacceptable due to an OOC falling out. If an IC father and son have an OOC fight, they should invent a creative way out, like discovering that he was not the father after all, before going their separate ways.

"Voiding entire scenes, storylines or plots should be avoided when possible, as it can impact many players with other storylines branching off from them, who may resent having wasted so much time and effort on them.

"Try to find other options, or just accept whatever happened and enjoy the unexpected turn of events. Is playing by the book so important that you would disrupt the roleplay for one little broken rule? BUT... if there really is NO other alternative, inform all affected players and explain the rationale for the decision."

Fading to black or gray and voiding can be disruptive, so try to find other options.

Chiptag: *holds a bloody rag to his broken nose and speaks in a nasal voice* "If I may add something about being capped, it's NOT allowed to sit down so that your captors can't move you—unless they're trying to do something against the rules, like dragging you off with an eagle...

"Instead, if they've tied your ankles or if you've fallen to the ground, use the 'crouch' function to sit or lie down because that way they can still drag you. To crouch, simply hit Ctrl-C, and the same to stand up again.

"You can easily make your own AOs (animation overdrives) for situations like being captured using a HUD like the ZHAO (animazooanimations.com/zhao-ii) or loading your animations into the lag-free Firestorm AO (see how to do this here: wiki.phoenixviewer.com/animation_overrider)."

Rescue Roleplay

Mahir: "Speaking of not allowed, I mentioned rescue roleplay. It can make for an interesting scene, but it's amazing how often people go to rescue friends when they had no way of knowing about it in-game, such as hearing about it from an eye-witness. That's metagaming, as is locating them using the mini-map.

"You can't just IM your friends and say, 'Hey, come rescue me. I'm in the meanie bunker.' Of course, if you're wearing a communication or 'comm' device and your captor hasn't confiscated it or tied your hands, you can roleplay using that and then IM your friends. But to avoid cheesing, the comm should be visible so that your captor will know to take it off, and its range should be limited to a single sim. Alternatively, if your friends are within shouting distance and your captor hasn't gagged you, you could shout for help."

Chiptag: *interrupts* To shout, hold down the 'Ctrl' key while hitting 'Enter,' or start your post with '/shout.' If you want to just roleplay shouting for help without actually being 'heard' by anyone outside chat range, use all caps like this: "/me cries out SOMEBODY! PLEASE! HELP ME!!!"

Some captives don't want to be rescued because they're enjoying the RP or don't want you to risk your IC hide for them.

Mahir: "Bear in mind that some captives don't want to be rescued, either because they're enjoying the roleplay or because they don't want you to risk your IC hide for them. So even if you see them being dragged away, IM them first before barging in. I wouldn't want someone to run in, pistols blazing, just as a gorgeous female warrior was about to take advantage of me" –grins and winks at Mamakie–

Mamakie: /me scowls, elbows him angrily and humphs

Arjun: "The other day, I IMed Zurie to propose a scene that involved her capturing me. But when she attacked me, another friend tried to save me and got downed and capped too. Then they started arguing about rules. I had to beg them to stop arguing, saying that I didn't care about the rules, and could they PLEASE just get on with the roleplay."

Mahir: "Yes, that's called 'white-knighting' – riding in like a knight in shining armor to save the day when someone is attacked, downed, or captured. The 'no white-knighting' rule means that you don't get to decide whether a friend needs saving. If they shout for help, you might take that as an invitation, but even so, IM both parties to ask whether it's just part of the scene or they really want you to roleplay a rescue attempt.

"Otherwise, you could very well be interfering with a preplanned scene that everyone is fine with, like in your case, Arjun. So yes, technically, your friend made a mistake by white-knighting, but on the other hand, if you—being the prey—didn't mind, it didn't matter. I commend you on choosing to continue the roleplay instead of fighting over rules. That said, maybe next time you could give any nearby friends a heads up about the scene you've planned."

Urstud: "Yeah, people waste too much valuable RP time and energy squabbling about rules. It takes a lot of the fun out of it. I'm not just fighting to win; I'm fighting to RP, win or lose. So demanding that others follow my own interpretation of the rules of engagement is not an issue for me. I'd like to see more tolerance, less quarreling, and more roleplay."

Mahir: "Well said, Urstud. When competition is the most important thing, the rules will always be in question, but when your goal is to roleplay, you can be more lenient, patient, and forgiving of other people's blunders, and they with yours. And we shouldn't be too quick to assume that other people's mistakes are intentional cheating. We ALL mess up sometimes."

Giving up Control

Mahir: "Okay, now… Once you have been defeated and captured, you give up a certain amount of control to your captor. You're relatively weak and defenseless, tied up and at their mercy. You accept that possibility the minute you change your Karma Tag from green to yellow or red. You can't be yellow or red and have something like 'No taking me prisoner' in your RP limits.

"However, good roleplayers will avoid powerplay even as captors. Instead of posting, '/me heaves him to his feet and throws him onto the rack,' they will be careful to word it to avoid powerplay, which doesn't necessarily mean saying, 'Please get on the rack for me,' although that's a possibility. Rather, they might write, '/me wraps her arms around his chest to heave him to his feet and throw him onto the rack.'

"In this case, you have to comply, but you have the choice either to flop back on the rack like a rag doll and crack your head open on the iron frame, or to kick and scream, trying to wriggle out of her grasp.

"However, there are other ways of giving up control. If your RP partners are willing, you can introduce novel RP elements by using hypnosis or injections to force their characters in some way so that they will have to roleplay it out until the effect wears off. But even then, you cannot emote how your victim will respond to your forcible actions. For example, you can push them to the ground but not say that they then fell into a limp heap—that is up to your victim to decide.

Hypnosis and injections take away your control, so can only be used with your consent.

"Hypnotic suggestions or descriptions of injectable drugs can be as general or detailed as you like. They can turn friends into enemies or enemies into friends, ramp up or turn off sexual desire, or even make a character take on an entirely different personality, act like a clown, or be unable to speak for a day. The sky's the limit, as long as everyone agrees to roleplay it out.

"Hypnosis and injections take away the victim's control, so they can only be used with their consent, making sure you don't ask them to do anything against their RP limits. Once accepted, the effects of hypnosis or injections shouldn't be ignored, but you can be as creative as you like in how you play them out."

Mamakie: "Urstud has already given us a good example of how he thwarted a hypnotic suggestion to rape someone. Does anyone else have any other creative examples?"

Arjun: /me raises his hand "I once attacked Zurie 'by accident,' and she gave me an injection. This is what I did to RP it out, with all OOC messages indented:

> *Zurie: ::chuckles darkly and pulls him toward her, her lips curling into a sneer:: You aimed your bow at me, boy. I'd never have shot you if you hadn't. I heard the damn arrow sliding against the wood of your bow ::crosses her arms and glares down at him:: I'm not amused.*
>
> *Arjun: /me cringes under her glare, looking up at her with puppy-dog eyes, "Please don't hurt me, Zurie. I'd never have shot at you if I'd known it was you. Honest!"*
>
> *Zurie: ::narrows her eyes at him and purses her lips:: I won't hurt you, Arjun, but I AM going to have to punish you. Hold out your arm.*
>
> *Arjun: /me hesitates, rubbing his arm as though it had already been hurt, then, seeing her earnestness, closes his eyes and turns his head, wincing, and holds out his arm hesitantly, as if to pull it away at her slightest movement.*
>
> *Zurie: ::takes his wrist gently, turning it so the palm faces up as she reaches into her satchel for her syringe:: Open your eyes, Arjun. Don't look away from me.*
>
> *Arjun: /me opens one eye, the other squinted, and looks at her sideways, cringing with fear, a deep trembling starting in his stomach and growing out to his arms and legs as he holds his breath in horrid expectation of what is to come. When he sees the syringe she is holding, he opens both eyes wide with fright, crying out, "No, Zurie. Please. Not that. I can't stand injections. No! Pleeeeez!!!"*
>
> > Zurie: Is this a limit of yours?
> >
> > Arjun: No, 'needles' to say, I'm just RPing being afraid :P
> >
> > Zurie: Good, just making sure :D
>
> *Zurie: ::shakes her head at him and sighs softly, her grip on his wrist tightening:: Shouldn't have shot at me, Arjun. This should remind you never to do so again ::She shakes the syringe and holds it up to the light, flicking away the air bubbles and depressing the plunger until three drops of the purple liquid leak from the tip, sliding down the needle's length::*
>
> *Arjun: /me watches her in horror, knees shaking and lower lip trembling. "Please, Zurie, I lov... I like you a lot... I'd never hurt you on purpose. It was all a terrible mistake. I'm no fighter. I just got scared when someone flew over me on a bird like the Mafia does, and I started shooting like a mad man. PLEASE believe me."*
>
> *Zurie: ::raises an eyebrow at him and steps closer, shaking her head, her voice low:: And this will remind you never to draw your bow on someone again without a damn good reason ::She gives him a pointed look and slips the needle into the soft skin of his upper arm, her hand clenched tight on his*

wrist to keep the arm steady as she presses the plunger, sending the liquid directly into his system, then slips the syringe back into her pocket and rubs soothing circles on the pricked skin, watching his face, a slight smirk on her lips::

> Rampatol @ 300 mg: Makes host incredibly horny, unable to think or do anything else (hunt, fight, etc.) until they have had sex [minimum 30 min. of ERP] and an orgasm. The urge grows worse as time passes. Rational thought and previous personality traits do not manifest if they stand in the way of getting what is needed. Lasts until the host has had sex (not oral; must be full anal or vaginal penetration).

Arjun: /me watches in shock as the needle approaches his arm, then clamps his eyes and mouth shut, his whole face screwed up. He turns his head away, crying out as the needle sinks into his arm, "Nooooo, pleeeeez. I HATE needles. Ooooowwww! Damnit Zurie, that huuuurts!"

Zurie: ::grins, almost chuckling, at his whine and raises his arm to her mouth as she presses feather-soft kisses up and down it, her lips just grazing his skin:: How you feeling?

Arjun: /me cringes at her approach then slowly straightens as a strange look creeps over his face and he gazes at her lasciviously, licking his lips, his manhood pressing uncomfortably against his bulging loincloth. He reaches out his bound hands to grasp her top and pull as if to tear it off or pull her closer, and growls in a much deeper voice than usual, "How do I feel? Oooooh, like I could fuck you right here and now, hottie."

Zurie: ::chuckles darkly and ruffles her hand through his hair, lightly pulling at the strands before stepping away, twisting his hands off her top as she speaks softly:: Now, I'm going to have to tie you to the table so that you'll have to look elsewhere for help with your 'issue,' hmm? ::She locks his leash to the examination table, tosses the keys under the wooden bench, and turns to go:: Good luck, boy...

> EXP leasher: Zurie ties your leash to Examination Table
>
> Zurie: You okay with the RP?
>
> Arjun: Yeah, so what happens now?
>
> Zurie: Now you RP out the injection :P

Arjun: /me gasps as he feels his leash pulled and locked to the table, then turns to see her leaving and calls out after her, "Zuuurrriiieee, where are you going? Come back here..."

Zurie: ::laughs:: No, no, you aimed your bow at me. You get the consequences. You're gonna have to find someone to help you with your li'l problem, eh?

Zurie leaves chat distance, so the rest of the RP is done in IMs:

Arjun: /me lies down and stretches his foot toward the bench, but can't reach the keys, then looks around like a crazed person and sees the mock skeleton on a stand, tears off a leg, and tries to reach the keys with that, but still no luck. He gets behind the heavy table and pushes with all his might, his muscles almost bursting from the effort, an uncommon expression of fierce determination on his face, finding a strength he never knew he had, and moves it a couple of feet before taking the leg bone again and fishing the keys out from under the wooden bench. He quickly unlocks the bind, then goes to the red trash bin, finds a used scalpel, and cuts the plastic zip-ties from around his wrist. His blood is boiling, his head spinning, his body sweating, his breath heaving, and his heart pounding in his chest as he steps out into the twilight like a feral beast seeking its prey. Suddenly, from somewhere deep in his subconscious, he hears a voice from his childhood advising him... teaching him... and he sets out at a brisk trot for the swamp.

Zurie: good boy ;)

Arjun: /me, arriving at the swamp, looks around like a crazed person, not sure what he is doing there, but feels the voice in his head drawing him to the muddiest, most stagnant part, where he lies down and sinks his body into the mud, making sure his head rests safely out of the water. Soon, he feels painful bites all over his body, as if dozens of little teeth were tearing at his skin. Looking down, he gasps, "Leeches!" as his vision starts to darken, and he slowly slips into unconsciousness...

Zurie: Good god! You have zero survival skills *shakes head*

[Here there is a Fade to Gray as Arjun sleeps, but he didn't mention it at the time]

Arjun: /me, at first light, opens his eyes and looks around, trying to get his bearings, squinting through the haze... Then suddenly, it all comes back to him—the terrible mistake of shooting at Zurie without first being sure of who it was, her anger, the needle, the painful erection that wouldn't stop, his wild dash through the forest, the LEECHES. He looks down and sees dozens of them floating dead around him, red splotches all over his skin where they had latched onto him, sucking out the poisoned blood. He grins now, remembering his mother's advice: 'Son, if you're ever poisoned, run to the swamp and let the leeches suck out the poison. You're strong, and your body will produce fresh, new blood to replace it.' She had even made him practice it to make sure the lesson stuck. He grins to himself mischievously, then laughs out loud to nobody in particular, "Ha! I'll bet Zurie would never have thought of that one." He stumbles to his feet, staggers to a clean part of the swamp to rinse off, then drags himself out to forage for his breakfast.

Zurie: Damn, gotta hand it to you, wild boy!

Arjun: Hahaha

Zurie: That was smart. Hell!

Arjun: Hey, you're the medical staff. You should have guessed :D

Zurie: ::grumbles::

Arjun: /me sticks out his tongue at you and grins impishly

Mamakie: /me claps her hands and glows "Good work, Arjun. What a story!"

IC Killing and Dying

Mahir: /me laughs out loud "Yes, but now we all know Arjun's secret and can use it against him." Then he clears his throat and becomes serious. "Okay, our last topic is about killing and dying, which is important because different RP regions have different rules about this.

"Some only require a 'dead time,' meaning that those killed have to refrain from fighting for a given length of time. This usually doesn't mean you can't roleplay, only that you must remain a non-combatant for the prescribed amount of time. However, your killer must clearly emote actually killing you, such as '/me sees that the victim is still alive and shoots him in the head, putting him out of his misery.' Once you have been clearly killed IC, you must obey the region's rules and stay out of the battle until your time is up.

"Other regions have stricter rules, such as saying that if your character has died, you can no longer roleplay as that character. How will the admins know? You can be sure that other players will complain if your character sticks around after death. The only options to continue roleplaying in such regions are: 1) change your character's display name and profile, and start roleplaying as a completely different character, albeit with the same account; or 2) return to the region through an alt with a completely different name, profile, and character."

Mamakie: "Obviously, both options are highly disruptive and can undo weeks, months, or even years of avatar design, character development, networking, and storylining. People put a lot of effort into developing their character's profile and appearance—shape, skin, hair, outfits, even down to the curve of the eyebrows, which can take time, money, and effort. That's why most people prefer to include 'no permadeath' in their RP limits.

Mahir: "Needless to say, this is a highly controversial issue. Some defend each roleplayer's right to choose whether to accept or reject permadeath. Others say that surviving multiple mortal wounds is unrealistic and should not be allowed. They claim it's a form of metagaming to put your character at unreasonable risk because you know OOC that nobody is allowed to kill you. They say that if you don't want your character to die, you shouldn't place it in situations that any reasonable person wanting to survive would avoid.

"In the case of Virtual India, it's your choice whether your character will die as the result of an attack, but you should put it in your RP limits. If you've grown tired of roleplaying in a certain group or region, you can stage your own death as one of several possible reasons for going instead of just disappearing. You should be clear—and make clear to others—who is dying: the entire account or just the character. Will you be coming back with a different display name and avatar design, or will your account leave the region for good?

"On the flip-side, if you plan to kill another character, you should open a friendly IM, explain why you think it's essential to the overall storyline, and nicely ask whether they would accept an IC death. The final decision is up to them, of course. However, be warned that by doing so, you are also agreeing to the possibility that your own character may end up dying in the attempt to kill theirs.

> If your character dies, stick around to let other players develop some scenes around the death.

"If your character dies and you can stay inworld a little longer, stick around to let other players develop some scenes around the death. The medical personnel may try to save or resuscitate you, and you can emote how your lifeless body responds to their attempts. Law enforcement officials may search your body and clothing for clues as to who you were, how you died, or 'whodunnit,' and you can IM them about any identification or clues they can find on your body.

"If there's an undertaker, they will finally have a job to do. Friends may want to mourn your character's loss and even hold a wake and burial. If the roleplay region allows it, you may want to come back as a ghost or zombie. The players could also decide to leave your corpse on long-term display—as a prop, of course. As in all RP situations, squeeze as much juice as you can from your death."

Mamakie: "Bear in mind that in some cultures, especially in Western countries, the whole question of death is taboo. Some players may also find it disturbing for other reasons. So be sensitive to the fact that some players may not want to have anything to do with death-related scenes. Bear in mind what we discussed yesterday about caring for each other's feelings. It could be very troubling for the other player to be made forcibly responsible for your character's death."

The class ends on that happy note, and since this has been an introductory session there is no exam this time. The more Arjun learns about CARP, the less attractive being a warrior seems to him. Anyway, he can roleplay fights in text as much as he wants without needing the red Karma Tag. He knows that the scripted weapons system ultimately favors whoever has the best, most expensive technology and lives nearest to San Francisco for the best 'ping times.'

There is still the introductory course for prospective healers, so Arjun has that to look forward to. He logs out for the night as a little voice whispers in his head:

Why are you here, Arjun?

To make sure everybody wins, even those who lose.

CHAPTER NINETEEN

HEALING ROLEPLAY

Arjun: /me groans and opens his eyes a slit to see Elaine bending over him. "Who… where… what happened?" he murmurs weakly, his thoughts a blur.

Elaine: /me coos softly, a compassionate expression on her face. "Hey, there you are. We thought we had lost you, Arjun. I was finally able to stop the worst of your bleeding, though. How do you feel?"

Arjun: /me tries to move but cries out in pain and slumps back. "I hurt all over," he manages to gasp. "Even my hair hurts."

Elaine: /me smiles and would gently dab his face with a cool, damp cloth. "Well, at least you haven't lost your sense of humor. Now just try to relax while I bandage you up." She sprays some disinfectant onto a gauze pad and would start to clean his wounds with it, gently dabbing and brushing the dirt away.

Arjun: /me soon realizes that the key word had been 'try,' as she starts scrubbing his wounds with something that burns so badly, he writhes in agony and tears chunks of sod from the ground with his hands, wondering whether he hadn't been better off without her healing.

Elaine: /me chatters cheerily as she opens sterile packets of gauze and smears them with antiseptic ointment before attempting to press them gently to his open wounds. "You took quite a beating out there, Arjun. It was a valiant thing you did."

Arjun: "You should have seen the other guy…" he seethes between clenched teeth, "…not a scratch on him." He tries to chuckle, but it comes out sob. Then it all comes back to him—how the prospects had invited the warriors to a mock battle, how he had foolishly accepted to take part, and even more foolishly had offered to draw enemy fire so the others could sneak around and attack from the rear. The last thing he recalls is having fallen, writhing in a pool of his own blood. "Did they… did we… how badly did they… did we lose?" he groans as a wave of anxiety washes over him.

Elaine: /me laughs as she would tape a large gauze bandage to a particularly nasty wound on his thigh. "Lose? No, the plan worked—your team won thanks to you. You're a hero, Arjun!" She would start to spread salve on his scrapes and an ointment on his bruises.

Arjun: /chuckles mirthlessly, "Well, at least I'm a LIVE hero and not a DEAD one... there's that..." then nibbles thoughtfully on his lower lip as the medicine starts to take effect, and he finally gets some relief. "I don't think I'm cut out to be a warrior, Elaine," he says in a remorseful tone. "I suck at fighting, and I hate violence and bloodshed. It makes me feel sick at heart."

Elaine: /me nods understandingly as she wipes her fingers clean, then would take his face gently between her hands, smiling sadly into his eyes. "I know what you mean, Arjun, and there's no shame in that. You have a kind, sensitive heart, and that's a good thing. It's one of your many strengths." She hesitates to take a deep breath then murmurs softly, "Have you ever thought that maybe you were cut out to be a healer instead?"

Arjun: /me looks up into her kind eyes and feels a strange strength flowing from his healer friend as she holds his throbbing head between her cool palms and her words caress his aching soul like a soothing balm. He realizes he had only wanted to be a warrior to be close to Zurie and Eswa, who had both chosen that route. But it had never been his own path, and he knows that now. "Maybe you're right, Elaine," he murmurs, then hesitates and stammers, "Um... will you... would you mentor me? I mean... only if you have time and are not too..."

Elaine: /me interrupts with a broad smile, "I would be glad... honored to mentor you, Arjun. I'll be meeting with a group of new prospects tomorrow afternoon at the Sanjay Health Clinic." She winks at him with a twinkle in her eye and a playful smirk on her lips. "Do you think you'll be well enough to join us by then?"

The Health Clinic

Early the next morning, Arjun takes the short stroll from the Landing to the Sanjay Health Clinic. It is a cluster of one-room, whitewashed brick structures arranged around a central garden with a fountain in the middle and shade trees all around. Unsure where the class would be held, Arjun decides to explore a little when he sees Healer Mentor Elaine with a patient and sits nearby to watch.

Elaine: /me would hold her wrist to take her pulse, feel her throat, then take the thermometer from her mouth and squint at it, murmuring, "Hmm, no fever; that's good." Then she peels the sterile wrapping from a tongue depressor and holds it to her mouth, "Open your mouth wide and say 'ahhh,' please."

Patient: /me sneezes and blows her nose into her hanky, blinks tears from itchy eyes and coughs, then opens her mouth "AHHH."

Elaine: /me shines a small flashlight on the back of her throat while pressing down her tongue and nods. "Well, no infection yet, but you need to take care of that cold before it gets worse." She goes to the counter, measures some medicinal herbs into her mortar and uses a pestle to grind them together into a fine powder, adds distilled water and mixes well, then pours the mixture into a small glass and hands it to the lady. "Drink this please" ((eat it as if it were food)).

Patient: /me takes the glass and sniffs it, pinches her nose with the other hand, throws her head back, and downs the liquid with one swallow. She makes a sour face. "Yuck, that tastes terrible"

Elaine: /me chuckles as she puts away her supplies and washes her hands. "I know, right? But it should clear up your nose and throat right away. Be sure to rest, drink lots of liquids, and avoid getting cold, okay?"

Patient: /me gets up to leave, "Thank you, doctor. I feel better already," and goes out to look for her family.

Elaine: /me steps out of her office and sees Arjun. "Is it that time already? Come with me, and I'll show you where the classroom is."

Being Healed

Five healer prospects sit in the clinic's little classroom, surrounded by a skeleton, two dummy avatars—male and female—and several anatomical posters on the wall. They are talking excitedly in hushed voices, while Elaine sits on the examination table in front of the class.

Elaine: /me clears her throat to bring the class to attention. "Today, we will be going over the basics of healer roleplay. Afterward, if you decide to continue with this specialty, you will be assigned a Healer Mentor to teach you the more technical aspects of healing.

"As you know, the Virtual India system will make you sick periodically. You can also drown, be attacked by animals or humans, or even roleplay any health problem. When the Karma Tag gives you an illness, it puts a message in Local Chat about it, and your HP starts to go down. For example, one message looks like this:

> Karma Tag: You have caught the flu and start to lose health. You need to find a healer and roleplay getting treated. Please do so IC and in Local Chat. Do NOT look for healing via IMs. This is an RP opportunity. Take advantage of it.

"These messages tell you enough to roleplay your sickness, but it's up to you what signs and symptoms to emote. Maybe you start sneezing, your eyes and nose are itchy and start running, and your throat feels sore. Then maybe you will start coughing, your bones will ache, and you will run a fever. Be creative.

"After the initial notice, periodic messages will tell you how many HP lost to the sickness. The whole purpose for getting sick is to enable you to roleplay getting healed and give the healers a chance to roleplay their specialty, so don't be in a hurry to get cured by any means possible."

Dorketta: raises her hand "What if we ARE in a hurry and don't have time?"

Elaine: "Then just log out. When you log back in, your sickness will start where you left off. You can live with a disease indefinitely as long as you keep eating, so no hurry. The only drawbacks are the HP notices and needing to eat more.

"Don't just IM a healer saying, 'I have the flu; please send me the medicine.' If they complied, they would be demoted. They are instructed to respond that you must look for a healer and roleplay with them in Local Chat. So, if you're sick, find a healer or have somebody find one for you, and roleplay the hell out of it.

"How to roleplay being sick? You can try to brave through it, be a hypochondriac, or scream in pain. You can be humble and accepting or tell the healers how to do their job and question or criticize them. You can offer to pay or capture a healer and force them to treat you. You can quarantine yourself to avoid spreading a disease or spread it on purpose. It's up to you.

Once you find a healer, describe your signs and symptoms and let them take their time diagnosing it. Let them roleplay it out.

"Once you find a healer, don't tell them your diagnosis and demand a cure. Rather, describe your signs and symptoms and let them diagnose it. Inversely, don't say, 'You're the healer—you figure out what I have.' That will not fly and could even work against you if your healer gets annoyed at you."

Chiptag: "Anyone who clicks on your Karma Tag can see what illness you have. You can, too, by clicking on 'Status' in your Karma Tag. Your stats will show something like this in Local Chat:

Name: Chiptag
Level: 29 - Mentor
Ammo: 24
Illness: None
HP: 13.53"

Dorketta: hides a snicker behind her hand, murmuring almost inaudibly to the student nearest her "And he scolds me whenever I let my health drop to 15"

Elaine: /me grins at Dorketta's remark and continues, "But remember, that's OOC information, and using it in your roleplay would be metagaming, so please don't. Remember that your sickness is not just a nuisance to be solved expeditiously. It's a rare roleplay opportunity for you both, so build an interesting story around it and squeeze all the RP juice you can from it."

Healing Others

Elaine: "What if you're the healer? Rule number one: never heal yourself. It's against the healer code and would waste a chance to learn from other healers' roleplay. Besides, since you're sick, you might make it worse."

"All healing must be done IC in roleplay, not through IMs. You'd be surprised how many people IM us asking for distance healing or saying we are needed at such-and-such a place. Answer that this is a roleplay region and they need to go themselves or send a friend to look for a healer and roleplay it out.

"Always ask permission before reviving someone to make sure you don't interfere with their plans. If they are downed and capped, ask their captor, but if no-one is in sight or the problem is drowning or starvation, ask them directly. The Karma Tag has a 'Revive' option next to 'Bind,' which will activate the revival process with animations and all.

"Remember that green healers can only revive other greens, while yellow and red healers can revive anyone. That doesn't apply to healing with potions, only to reviving downed people. A green healer could roleplay reviving a yellow and red in text, but it wouldn't reverse their scripted downing. For that matter, even non-healers can roleplay healing someone in text, although they cannot heal any scripted sicknesses.

Roleplay everything: gathering herbs and utensils, diagnosing patients, making medicine and healing them.

"Otherwise, roleplay everything: gathering herbs and utensils, diagnosing patients, mixing potions, and healing them. If you're caught handing out potions or reviving people with no roleplay, or if you use pre-made gestures instead of writing different posts for each instance, you WILL lose your healer status. You never know who's behind the avi you're healing. The only exception is when sparring for practice, in which case you don't have to roleplay the reviving.

"Don't let anyone rush you. This is your show, so own it and shine. If your patient gives you a hard time, you can refuse to heal them, give them the wrong medicine, or even poison them. Unprepared herbs are poisonous, so I bundle them with fruit and keep them on hand for that. Just rez a set of herbs and a fruit, select them all with the fruit last, then take them up as a bundle."

EyeCandey: "Wait a minute, Mentor. We were told healers are supposed to follow high standards, but now you're saying we can give our patients the wrong medicines or even poison them? I'm confused."

Elaine: "Yes, healers are expected to keep a high standard of ROLEPLAY, but that doesn't mean you have to be a perfect HEALER. You can fumble and make mistakes on purpose, diagnose and prescribe incorrectly, come to work stoned or half asleep, or drop and break things.

"What kind of healer you will be depends on your character. Bring out its personality. Sure, that may be kind, caring, and sensitive, but it may also be gruff, rough and grumpy; cold, cruel, and sadistic; arrogant, condescending, and critical; rational, calculating, and insensitive; sultry, sexy, and erotic; bumbling, stupid, and forgetful, or anything else that goes best with your character.

"When examining your patient, ask yourself how your character would do it. Ask your patient questions, including personal, intimate, or stupid ones. Check their pulse and take their temperature in strange, unusual ways. Feel their lymph nodes, but not only the ones at their throat. Test unusual reflexes, use your stethoscope in uncommon places, probe their orifices and other parts, and so on.

"Once you diagnose the malady, it's time to prescribe the remedy. As a healer, you will have an extra 'Potion' option in your Karma Tag that will ask you to rez the right herbs for the medicine you want to make. This will give you a bottle of potion to 'Share' for your patient to 'Eat' like any other food. If they tell you the wrong signs and symptoms, follow their lead and give them the wrong potion."

Student: "Does that mean that healer roleplay always consists in preparing potions for their patients and giving them the bottle to drink? Wouldn't that limit our roleplay options?"

Elaine: "That's the way the scripted system works, but it doesn't mean that your actual ROLEPLAY must always involve mixing herbs and giving them a bottle of potion. Not all illnesses are healed by drinking something, and you don't have to follow medical canon. You can roleplay curing them in any way imaginable while still passing them the potion OOC for the scripted healing.

"You can use herb teas, IV bags, injections or inhalations, menthol for a cold or poultices for a sprain, bloodletting or sucking out poison, massages, hot/cold baths and physical therapy, bone setting and casts, prayer and shamanism, eroticism and sex, even cutting off limbs or members if that's not against their RP limits.

The only constraints are the limits of your imagination.

"The only constraints are the limits of your imagination. Well, I take that back—there IS one restriction: being a healer or shaman does NOT give you magical powers, so don't use any kind of magic. And no, praying to the gods to bless the patient or the remedy is not considered magic."

Eswaria: "Does that mean we can use any other props besides the herbs and potions?"

Elaine: "Absolutely, but bear in mind that you don't need to have a prop in your Inventory to roleplay using it. You can write anything into existence, but even if you do have the actual prop, you should still emote using it. It should not be used as a substitute for the actual roleplay.

"If you have your patient lie down on an examination table, emote how you do it. If you have them wear a tourniquet, emote putting it on and tightening it. Whatever prop you use, even if it has the most realistic animations and scripting, emote it as if it were not in the pixels. That way, your patients will be able to respond accordingly in their own posts.

"Okay… Let's see… other creative ideas… Oh, yes, side effects. You can tell your patient that the medicine you gave them has a crazy side effect, such as enhanced sexual appetite, a craving for certain foods, an inability to see or hear or speak for 24 hours, losing their hair and having to grow it back again, raging against a certain person or group, or whatever else you can come up with.

"If you're roleplaying a stupid healer, you can add extra ingredients 'by mistake,' such as 'human catnip' to make them dash around the region for an hour or 'horny goat weed' to make them sex-crazed. OOPS!" –laughs– "If you're especially wicked, you can give them an injection to make them do something they weren't expecting. Or, if your patient shows a liking for BDSM in their profile, you can be rough and make them like it.

"The healing roleplay doesn't even have to end once they are healed. You can tell them to come back in a week or the next day for a follow-up, or look for them to ask how they're doing and give them a checkup. There are not that many opportunities to do healer roleplay, so squeeze all the juice you can from it."

Healing an Animal

Arjun: "What about wildlife? I understand animals can also get sick, but since they can't speak, how do they roleplay a sickness, and how do healers roleplay curing them?"

Elaine: "Yes, animals do get sick the same as humans and need the same healing, but they can't speak in Virtual India. They can only emote, which makes it harder for both them and the healers.

> Animals can't speak but only emote, which makes it harder for both them and their healers.

"They need to come into chat range of a healer or someone else who can bring a healer and emote being sick, hurt, or in pain. If a healer sees an animal growling, whining, limping, lying down and panting heavily, licking its wounds, or so forth, they need to be sensitive to that and check their Karma Tag to see what disease they have, then decide how to roleplay treating it.

"In this case, an additional difficulty is that wild animals can be dangerous and tend to be even more so when they are hurt or sick. Even domestic animals can snap when they are hurt, especially if they don't know and trust the healer. Non-dangerous animals can hurt themselves if they struggle to break free so a healer will often have to lasso or trap an animal first or use a poison dart to roleplay shooting it with a sedative, then bind its paws and muzzle it to avoid getting clawed or bitten, or to keep it from hurting itself by struggling.

"Healing an animal can involve injections, force-feeding medicine by pushing a pill down its throat, or inserting a tube through its mouth to pour in a liquid, scrubbing and binding wounds, pulling or cutting out a sting or arrow, setting and casting bones, and so on. Once an animal has been treated, you can take off the binds and move out of range. When the sedative's effects have worn off, it should run away, but if it decides to attack, you need to be prepared to defend yourself.

"Let's look at a sample healing roleplay I had with Wendi, who, being a deer doe, is a relatively peaceful animal. She had high BP, and as you will see, I found a way to cure her without using sedatives, bindings, or muzzles.

Wendi: /me groans, her breathing labored, her heart beating hard and paining her

Elaine: /me notices the doe on the ground in front of her. Listening, she notices her erratic breathing and approaches with caution

Wendi: /me's instinct is to run away from this place of humans. She tries to get up and escape, but her strength fails her, and she collapses back, eyes wild, her fear worsening her symptoms

Elaine: /me squats down to seem less threatening and looks the doe over from closer up but sees no visible wounds or disfigurements. She scratches her head for a moment, going over all the possibilities in her mind, then kneels, pulls some herbs and a mortar from her bag, and starts preparing some medicine while murmuring gently to the doe, "All your signs seem to point to high BP, but how to be sure? Well, if I end up killing you, at least I can use your meat and hide"

Wendi: /me eyes the human warily, trembling with fear, but then her squatting down and murmuring remind her of the soft, soothing manner of the one who sometimes brings her fruit, and she relaxes, somehow aware that this human may be her only chance of getting well

Elaine: /me finishes mashing the herbs into a paste, digs the core from an apple, and presses the paste into the hole. She then places the apple on the ground in front of the doe and watches to see if she will eat it.

Second Life: Elaine gave you 'Potion against high BP.'

Wendi: /me watches her as she works, looks from the fruit to the woman and back again as if undecided, then slowly stretches out her neck and warily sniffs the apple. The fruit smells good, and the herb paste is not unpleasant either.

Elaine: /me stands up and moves back but continues watching the doe

Wendi: /me nibbles at the apple, tasting it cautiously. Then, convinced that it is good food, takes larger bites until it is all gone

Karma: You have been successfully healed.

Elaine: /me sighs in relief and murmurs softly, "Well, I've done what I could for you, but it was purely guesswork. You'll either die or recover and move away. If you're here later, I'll put you out of your misery."

Wendi: /me's head starts to clear, her breathing becomes less labored, and her heart starts beating more regularly

Elaine: /me approaches the doe to see if she will move at all, then gently taps her rear with the side of her foot

Wendi: /me struggles to find her feet but is still barely able to sit

Elaine: /me chuckles to herself and murmurs, "Well, you sat up and seem to be breathing less erratically than at first, so that's an improvement. I'll let you rest some more and see"

Wendi: /me struggles to find her feet again and is finally able to stand on wobbly legs

Elaine: /me laughs, "Oh, you're on your feet. Maybe I'm a good guesser after all. I was starting to have my doubts"

Wendi: /me gathers all her strength to limp away from this place of humans, looking back once at the woman as if to thank her before disappearing into the forest

Whacky Healing

Elaine: /me looks around at the class with a mischievous smile curving her lips "Well, if there are no further questions, some of our healers have prepared a fun little show for you... Please follow me."

The class follows her out of the classroom to the next building, where they see an old, red-faced, balding doctor wearing an ancient brown leather overcoat and aviator goggles. He stands over an examination table where a man lies with a large pressure gauge screwed into his heart. The needle on the indicator is in the red, and an emergency release valve on top has steam hissing out of it. "High blood pressure," Elaine explains.

In the next building, a naked man lies in a hot tub in the arms of a voluptuous woman wearing only a tiny nurse's cap. He holds a marijuana joint to trembling lips with shaky fingers, and the nurse runs her hands slowly up and down his body, murmuring sweet nothings in his ear. "Anxiety," Elaine says as she closes the door softly, and they move on.

Farther down, a woman writhes face-down on the examination table while the doctor drives a large cork into her anus with a rubber mallet. "Let me guess," says Arjun. "Diarrhea," everyone says in unison, and they laugh.

Next, an Incan shaman wearing multicolored feathers, beads, and bands of gold on his arms and legs, a rattle in one raised hand and a smudging stick in the other, stands over a man with a black, swollen ankle, apparently from a scorpion sting, chanting in a high, wailing voice.

They quickly pass by the room where a pretty young lady kneels in front of a doctor, his britches around his ankles, his cock in her mouth. "Nothing like a daily dose of fresh, non-oxidized semen to cure the thirst sickness," Elaine explains with a gleam in her eye.

The next room makes the students stop in their tracks, mouths gaping in surprise. A gaunt man, his pale white skin stretched dry and taut against his bones, lies on the examination table. A rubber tube sticks out of his arm, the other end in a bucket overflowing with blood. A girly-girl in a nurse outfit perches on a stool, busy filing her nails and chewing bubble-gum, swaying to music from huge earphones on her head, apparently oblivious of her patient. "Um... Cutiepie," Elaine says, tapping her shoulder, "I think he's done." The nurse looks up, gasps, and squeals in a silly high-pitched voice, "Oh... my... God. A little OVER-done, actually." Elaine rolls her eyes as they move on. "Bloodletting for an infection," she sighs.

In the last room, a toothless hag shows an elderly man to the door. "Oh, I forgot to mention the side effects," she says. "For the next three days, you will have an insatiable craving for fresh tiger or snow leopard meat."

Arjun: /me shakes his head incredulously. "This place is a madhouse..." he says, then a broad grin spreads across his face. "I LOVE IT!"

Healer Training

That very day, Arjun signs up for the Healer Training under Mentor Elaine, thereby leveling up to 26 – Healer Prospect, and spends the next week doing the Herbalist quest. He finds all the places to collect the different medicinal herbs and adds them to his map. He then learns each of the herbs' properties and how to mix them to prepare the potions for each disease in Virtual India.

Once he learns all that, reaches level 27 – Herbalist, and starts on the actual Healer quest. Over the next week, Elaine makes him practice healing several people for the different diseases. He gets sick almost every day and complains to Elaine, who explains that it is actually a blessing in disguise because it enables him to observe several people's healing methods from a patient's perspective. He keeps the transcripts of these healings and studies them but adds his own humorous touch to his practice sessions, which earns him quite a reputation.

Why are you here, Arjun?

To do things I always wished I could do in RL.

CHAPTER TWENTY

THE GRADUATION

> Dharma Guide: Congratulations. You have completed the "Healer" Quest and advanced to Level 28 - Healer. You are cordially invited to attend the Graduation Ceremony at the Gir Ashram on Friday at 2:00 pm SLT.

Arjun grins at the excited, expectant faces around the Ashram auditorium. Urstud holds EyeCandey in his lap, Eswaria has her head on Chris's shoulder, and Chiptag—Arjun does a double-take—with Dorketta? Who would have guessed?

The ever-frowning Mahir and the motherly Mamakie sit at the front table. Beside them is elderly Platistotle, followed by dignified Janus, and finally Pujari Arjuna in his yellow robe. Arjun turns to smile at Zurie, who is squeezing his hand, and is about to whisper something in her ear when...

Mahir: /me stands and clears his throat loudly. "Welcome, students, friends, and ineluctable frenemies to this formal graduation ceremony. This semester's graduates have worked hard and done an excellent job, as you will all attest. Before handing out the diplomas, it's my pleasure to ask our dear Platistotle and Janus to share some words of wisdom with us all."

The Power of Words

Platistotle: /me struggles to his feet and stands as straight as he can, despite the weight of age and worry. He nods to Mahir "Thank you, Mentor" then turns to the assembly and unfolds some notes

"You ask for a few words, and words are precisely what I want to talk to you about—not just because our art uses a lot of them, but also because our words have the power to define our reality. They make us believe that our way of seeing the world is the 'real' world when it's actually only one way of perceiving it.

"For example, the term 'virtual world' has created a false dichotomy between VWs and the so-called 'real world.' When the Lindens named their virtual world

'Second Life,' it invited objections such as why you need a second life unless you have no first life. Virtual worlds such as InWorldz, Avination, Kitely, OpenSim, and Sansar usually do not spark that kind of comment because their names do not create the impression that they are in any way opposed to 'real life.'

"I read on someone's profile: 'This should never have been called Second Life, but rather a participatory, immersive artistic endeavor, a unique opportunity to give fuller expression to special facets of who we are, a space for global encounters, a place beyond place that transcends geographical distance and obstacles.'

"I agree entirely. If Bell had named his invention 'virtual talk,' it wouldn't have detracted from our 'real talk' any more than it has by being called a 'telephone,' although it may have raised more debates. If the 'television' were called 'alternate reality,' it wouldn't have invaded the world any more or less than it has.

If Bell had named his invention 'virtual talk,' it wouldn't have detracted from our 'real talk' any more than it has by being called a 'telephone.'

"All technologies are tools, and as such, can be used to constructive or destructive ends. Virtual worlds are no exception: some use them to escape from reality or waste time, but they can also enable people to meet, share, and enrich each other's lives in ways they could never have achieved without this revolutionary technology.

To wrap up, I would like to quote Tom Boellstorff, an anthropologist who has conducted ethnographic studies in Second Life. He says,

> ...To call the physical world 'real life' is the number one problem in the study of technology. A lot of what happens online is real. If I learn German online, I can use it when I go to Berlin.... When people talk about Second Life versus real life, the assumption it contains is that everything physical is real, yet some things in the physical world AREN'T real. You can read a novel in the physical world, or you can act in a play. What is the meaning of the word 'real'? I wish I had the answer to that. I don't, but what I do know is that virtual worlds... give us a wonderful way to think in new, fresh ways about that question... As these things keep changing and emerging, we really want to make them serve the cause of good as much as possible. And that's in our hands, not in the hands of the technology."[24]

Platistotle: /me folds up his notes and smiles. "Congratulations to those graduating here today, and to those who have been around longer, because you are at the cutting edge of this technology and of developing innovative exciting ways to use it." He performs an Anjali mudra to the students, gestures to Janus, then sits slowly, folding his hands on his lap.

---

[24] The Drax Files: World Makers [Episode 31: Tom Boellstorff]: youtu.be/zhrE5MYbeOs.

Are Virtual Worlds Games?

Janus: /me stands, thanks Mahir and Platistotle, then turns to the students and smiles. "It seems my brother Platistotle and I have been on the same wavelength because my talk will hopefully support and supplement what he has just said.

"Virtual worlds are commonly referred to as games, but are they only that? True, in computer jargon, virtual worlds are categorized as such, but must this limit the way we see and use them? I think not. You can play in a virtual world and in the 'real world,' but that doesn't make either a game. Serious endeavors can also be undertaken in both, from education and training to artistic creation.

"The dictionary defines a game as 'a form of play or sport, especially a competitive one, played according to rules and decided by skill, strength, or luck.' Games are often seen as lacking any practical, productive purpose other than just relaxing and having a good time.

"But virtual worlds can be much more than that. Many of us take them as seriously as we do our 'first life.' Tom Boellstorff also says, 'Second Life is not a game... like a soccer stadium isn't a game; you can play a game in it... but you could also have a rock concert in it... It's a space... not the game itself.'[25]

> A virtual world can provide a place to play, but so can real life. We all know people who treat their entire life as a game.

"We all know people who treat their entire life as a game, but even roleplay can be so much more than that. Gary Gygax, the 'father of RPGs,' said:

> Many games are mere pastimes, but RPGs are enjoyable pursuits of a sought-after nature and are hobby-like, rather than pastime creations aimed at filling an otherwise empty period of leisure. While some games are aimed at rainy afternoons or social gatherings that might bring boredom, role-playing games are designed for and should be played under far different circumstances. Participants engage in playing such games because they have an active desire to do so. This is because games of this nature provide fun, excitement, challenge, social interaction, and much more on an ongoing basis.[26]

"Virtual worlds also offer opportunities to form deep, lasting friendships with people from all over the world, safe places to share joys and sorrows, venues for teaching and learning, spaces that enable fuller, richer expressions of creative talent, chances to give and receive support in times of need, peaceful environments to meditate and pray alone and with others, and so much more. Carrie Tatsu, pioneering virtual baby designer in Second Life, says,

---

[25] Our Digital Selves: My Avatar is Me [full feature film]: youtu.be/GQw02-me0W4.

[26] Gary Gygax, quoted in paizo.com/threads/rzs2nmqv.

> The word 'roleplay' implies 'I'm pretending,' and I don't think that's true. People really like to care for things; they like to nurture things. Human connection is human connection. We have human connection when we meet people face-to-face, and we have human connection virtually. Both are valid. I don't think we should make assumptions about how people want to spend their time in virtual worlds, that it's just an avenue for play. I see it as a space where people can be creative. It removes isolation... We're just regular people who want to connect with other human beings across the world.[27]

"Just as many of us feel we are in the physical world to learn and grow spiritually, we can also use virtual worlds to seek spiritual development. Both worlds challenge us to become more loving and kind, more tolerant and forgiving, more empathetic and compassionate. These qualities are latent within our beings just as a tree's beauty lies dormant in the seed. It's through experiencing these worlds that the hidden is brought to light, making us more fully who and what we are.

"I hope that you will persevere along this path, open new vistas along the way, and, as you become mentors, patiently accompany others in their efforts to do the same. Congratulations, graduates." He gestures to Mahir and takes his seat.

Learning with our Avatars

Mahir: /me stands and bows to Janus and Platistotle. "Thank you very much, friends. You have given us much to think about. Finally, I would just like to add that we all make mistakes and we all learn something new every day. That's why we don't see beginners as 'newbies' in Virtual India but as potentially great roleplayers. We're not here to judge each other but to help each other have the best experience we can.

> We all make mistakes and learn something new every day. Don't see beginners as 'newbies' but as potentially great roleplayers.

"We hope our classes and mentoring have helped you, and believe they have, because you have all made incredible progress over these past months, even those who were total flops in their first roleplay regions..." *he winks at Arjun* "...it's always wonderful to see new roleplayers learning and growing into this art. Thank you for being so patient with us. It has been fun working with you, and we hope you will all continue to flourish.

"One last word. This graduation is not the end of the road; it's only the beginning. You now have the tools and resources to carry your roleplaying to new levels. There are more quests ahead—much more challenging than any you have

---

[27] The Drax Files: World Makers [Episode 49: Zooby]: youtu.be/hMjEQ81ogOQ.

completed. Anyone can also propose new quests for others, and you can set yourself your own quests. Challenge and stretch yourselves and each other continually. And most importantly, remember rule number one: HAVE FUN!"

Mentoring Others

It is getting late as they all file out of the auditorium, diplomas in hand, but just out of curiosity, Arjun opens his Karma Tag, clicks on 'Quests,' and reads:

You have a new quest available: Mentoring [Accept] [Cancel]

Intrigued, he accepts the quest, and a message appears in Local Chat:

Dharma Guide: You have accepted the quest "Mentoring." To complete it, read the instructions that have been sent to your Inventory. Good luck.

Arjun checks his Inventory and finds a new notecard titled 'Mentoring Quest Instructions,' which says he is supposed to accompany a new arrival through their quests. It includes a chart summarizing the different levels, skills, quests, and powers, as well as advice on how to help newcomers without telling or showing them too much.

Arjun is to help them adjust to life in the region while learning and practicing roleplaying skills. He can ask them guiding questions, nudge them in the right direction when needed, and even give them little hints, but never tell them directly how to complete their quests. The idea is to keep it challenging and fun for them. Most of all, he should encourage them and celebrate their achievements. Arjun recalls one mentor who had seemed incapable of saying anything encouraging to anyone and actually determined to foil his efforts to succeed. "I should thank him for giving me such a good example of how NOT to be a mentor," he murmurs to himself with a sour grin.

This quest is also designed to help him review everything he has learned so far since "to teach is to learn twice." His mentee should give regular reports of his assistance on notecards that Arjun will then take to the Temple of Knowledge. This is a long quest that may take him several weeks or months, depending on how quickly his mentee progresses, and he will have to start over if his mentee drops out of the process.

Arjun: /me glances at Chris's Karma Tag, which reads 'Level 29 – Mentor,' and eyes him suspiciously, "Sooo... I guess this means that all this time, I've just been part of your Mentoring Quest, right?"

Chris: /me frowns at the insinuation "Well, at first, maybe... but then we became good mates, didn't we?" His expression softens "I mean, I think of you as a mate, at least. We've had some good times together and gotten to know each other pretty well..." He grins "You turned out to be an okay bloke... smart... except when you've done dumb things, funny… except when your jokes have sucked… but anyway, I've enjoyed doing this with you, and I hope we'll stay mates."

Arjun: /me grins "Yeah, I guess you turned out not to be a complete asshole after all… at least less of a jerk than I thought you were at first." He opens his arms to Chris for a hug, "Thanks for being an awesome mentor and friend, Chris."

Chris: /me gives Arjun a big hug and claps him on the back "Maybe that's one of the reasons for this quest—so people can make friends. Actually, all the quests seem designed to get to know people and roleplay with them so that we can really form a roleplay community here…"

Just then, Mamakie comes up to Arjun and asks, "So, how has it gone with the other quest I gave you? Have you decided why you are here yet?"

Arjun: /me is about to respond but then hesitates. He had found so many answers to that question over the past months. Which one should he give her?

Mamakie: /me interprets his hesitation as doubt and answers her own question with a twinkle in her eyes "To have fun, right?"

Arjun: /me returns her gaze and smiles into her soft brown eyes "In part, yes, Mamakie, but mostly to challenge myself and others to learn and grow."

When Arjun logs in the next day, he sees a group gathered around a newcomer, and goes to get a closer look. The center of attention is a young woman about Arjun's age, with mascaraed chestnut eyes adorning a picture-perfect bento face, auburn rigged mesh hair in two long braids that fall over her ample bosom. She wears a cowgirl outfit straight out of some old Western movie, complete with silver spurs on crocodile boots, two six-shooters holstered at her curvy mesh hips, a red bandana around her perfectly shaded neck, and a pheasant feather in her black Stetson hat. She certainly knows how to put together a splendid avatar, albeit not exactly themed for Virtual India. However, to judge from her posts and profile, she apparently has no clue how to roleplay.

Mahir: /me lays a hand on Arjun's shoulder. "There you are, Arjun. Just in time. Why don't you show our newcomer around, teach her the ropes, and help her get adjusted," he says in what sounds more like a command than a question.

Arjun: /me frowns up at him, "Do I have to?" then whispers, "*She's such a noob.*"

Mahir: /me scowls down at him "You DO want to finish that quest, don't you?" he asks sternly.

Arjun: /me sighs in resignation and shrugs, "Oh, alright, Mentor," then turns to the girl and looks her up and down curiously before reaching out his hand to shake, saying, with a cheery voice and a smile, "Hi, I'm Arjun. What's your name?"

AFTERWORD

Status: Mentor
Level: 29
HP: 25.0

This book is not finished. Even now, as I continue to roleplay, I learn something new practically every other day that I wish I had included. But all things must end, and books must get published, so we'll have to wait for a second edition (or maybe a sequel?) to add the new lessons learned, hopefully including constructive feedback from you, dear reader. Have I said anything you disagree with? Have I left out something you would like included? Please contact me inworld or go to the discussion page at Panniepaniscus.com.

Writing this book has taken several years, which were mostly *not* spent doing bibliographical research. Literature on the subject was very scarce—primarily a few blog posts and instructions by roleplay region admins, aside from the many inworld classes I attended. What made it such a long, drawn-out process was all the 'field research'—actual roleplaying experience—that went into it.

I (Arjun's atman speaking here) have lived vicariously through various 'incarnations' (alternate accounts or alts) in several roleplay regions. Actual roleplaying has been so fascinating and absorbing that weeks have gone by without getting much book writing done. I hope this treatment of the subject—relatively extensive but by no means complete—will be a solid jumping-off point for your own roleplay and that you will learn your own lessons through actual, hands-on-keyboard experience.

The roleplay involved in learning enough to write a book about it has been challenging but exciting, soul-stretching but satisfying. I hope you will find the same sense of fulfillment in your roleplay. And who knows? Maybe someday we will roleplay together. You may not know it's me, and I surely won't know it's you, but who cares? The important thing is that we will be enriching each other's lives.

GLOSSARY [28]

Action RP: Using simple emotes and actions interspersed with dialog.

AFK: An abbreviation of 'away from keyboard.'

Aggro: An abbreviation of 'aggravate.' To attract hostile attention from a mob (mobile NPC) to attack you.

Alt: An abbreviation of 'alternate account' as opposed to a different avatar or character using the same account.

Animation: A series of poses that simulates movement in thirty-second cycles. Animations that appear longer than thirty seconds are actually two or more animations placed in a chain.

ARP: An abbreviation of 'adult roleplay,' which involves strong language, violence, and sex. ERP and CARP, among others, are subsets of MRP. Also known as 'mature roleplay.'

Atman: In this book, the player behind the screen, managing the avatar, also known as 'typist' or 'mun'—short for mundane—in other contexts.

Augmentationist: A person who treats virtual worlds as extensions of their real life, as tools to achieve their ends. Also, an activity in a virtual world reflecting such a view; the opposite of 'immersionist' (see below).

Avatar / Avi / AV: A character's virtual body or visual representation within the virtual world. One same account can have various avatars for different uses or characters, saved as 'Outfits.'

Backstory: The history of a character preceding and leading up to the plot, also known as 'background story.'

BDSM: A combination of the abbreviations B/D (Bondage and Discipline), D/S (Dominance and Submission), and S/M (Sadism and Masochism and/or Slave-Master). Can include a wide range of activities that usually involve a dominant partner (the 'dom(me)' or

---

[28] Definitions may vary by medium or region but are given here as used in this book.

'top') and a submissive partner (the 'sub' or 'bottom').

Brackets: Used to indicate OOC messages, usually double brackets ((...)) but sometimes (...) or [...].

BRB: An abbreviation of 'be right back' or sometimes 'bathroom break.'

Bubble play: Centering one's attention on one's own little corner of the story without considering the broader events unfolding around it. Also known as 'cubical play.'

Canon: Official lore from the primary source on which a region, character, and/or storyline is based, such as Gor, Hogwarts, Lord of the Rings, Star Trek, and so on, as opposed to 'fanon.'

Canon character: A roleplay character based on a character from a novel, movie, comic, and so on, with the qualities set by the canon story. The opposite of 'original character' (see below).

CARP: An abbreviation of 'CApture (and) Role Play.'

Chain-posting: Posting more than once at a time or out of turn. Also known as multi-posting. See 'machine-gun posting' and 'cross-posting.'

Character: The fictional persona (human, animal, or fantasy) who appears in a roleplaying story. Can be a player character (PC) or a non-player character (NPC).

Character definition: Outlining a character's backstory, appearance, personality, quirks, ticks, speech patterns, and other characteristics. Not to be confused with 'character development' (see below).

Character development: The way characters change, grow, mature, and acquire new characteristics over time as a result of the experience they gain and the challenges they overcome. Not to be confused with 'character definition' (see above).

Character relationships (CRs): The short, medium, and long-term relationships that exist or develop between and among roleplay characters, through which a story evolves.

Character tag: A hovertext, also known as a 'titler', that provides vital information such as name (if different), rank or title, accent or unusual speech, current mood and appearance, and others.

Chat-boxing: Limiting a post to dialog without using any emotes or other narration, not considered acceptable in most roleplay communities.

Chat replacer: A script that makes it possible to post under another name, also known as 'text replacer' or 'name replacer.' Often used for doubling (see below) and to post for NPCs.

Cheesing: Bending the planned or expected outcome of a scene to one's favor by invoking a 'fact' not previously mentioned IC or OOC. The adjective is 'cheesy.'

Closed region: A roleplay region requiring an application and invitation to join and/or enter.

Crash: To lose connection to the virtual world, also known as a punt. Requires logging back in.

Cross-over: Taking a character from one roleplay setting and inserting it into a different one with little or no adjustment.

Cross-posting: Posting out of turn in a roleplay group. See 'posting order,' 'post round,' and 'chain-posting.'

Cross-region roleplay: Also known as cross-sim roleplay. Playing the same *character* in more than one roleplay region. Does not include using the same avatar and/or account to portray a completely separate character in a different region.

CS (combat system): A scripted weapons system such as OCS, VICE, SPD, G&S, DCS2, GM, Zcs, Unity Empire/Maxim, or Amazonia.

Cubical play: Centering one's attention on one's own little corner of the story without considering the broader events unfolding around it. Also known as 'bubble play.'

D&D: An abbreviation of 'Dungeons and Dragons,' a popular fantasy tabletop roleplaying game.

Dialog: The speech element of a post, set apart from narrative by using quotation marks, asterisks, dashes, or other signs.

Double-brackets/parentheses: ((...)), used to indicate OOC messages, usually in Local Chat.

Doubling: Temporarily taking over another character's roleplay, *at the request* of their player while the latter is AFK, often using a 'chat replacer' (see above).

Drama: When not IC drama, refers to creating personal OOC issues with other players.

Drama-llama: A person who shows a penchant for creating OOC drama.

Dual-Boxing: Running two instances of a viewer simultaneously to have two accounts inworld at once.

Economy system: A scripted system such as G&S or Amazonia for the exchange of cash and goods as a roleplay support.

Emoting: Describing a characters' appearance, emotions, context, actions, and other narration in a post, as distinct from and in support of dialogue.

Erasure: See 'voiding.'

ERP: An abbreviation of 'erotic roleplay'—a subset of 'adult roleplay'—where characters participate in erotic and/or sexual acts, from cuddling and love-making to BDSM and rape. Not to be confused with mere cyber-sex or pixel-sex.

Fade to Black (FtB): Skipping over an event that players do not wish to roleplay out but that is then assumed to have taken place, such as sexual relations or torture. The scene picks up again after the skipped event is assumed to have ended.

Fade to Gray (FtG): A jump ahead in time to avoid having to write all the details of a quotidian event such as sleeping, shopping or spending the day at work.

Facebooker: A derogatory term referring to those who use a virtual world like a type of social media.

Fanon: Non-canon roleplay with characters and/or scenes created by the players themselves, not based on an existing work of fiction.

Flat character: An entirely predictable persona having consistent, unvarying attitudes and behaviors, as opposed to a 'round character' (see below).

Fluffing: Lengthening posts unnecessarily with descriptions and internal dialogs ('fluff') that have little or no relevance to the actual story or plot, also known as 'post stuffing.'

FPS: 1) An abbreviation of 'frames per second'—the screen update rate; 2) An abbreviation of 'first-person shooter'—a type of video game.

Freestyle roleplay: Using para, semi-para, and one-line posts indistinctly or in combination. Not to be confused with freeform roleplay (FFRP), which is roleplaying with few if any rules or guidelines.

Ghosting: Simply disappearing from a roleplay or even from a virtual world without informing RP partners first. Deemed cowardly, disrespectful, and very bad form in the roleplay community.

GM: An abbreviation of 'Game Master' ('Dungeon Master' in D&D), who organizes and oversees a roleplaying game and outlines the story.

God mode: 1) Originally a video-game cheat using scripts or codes that confer invincibility or other powers not available to other players; 2) Playing as though a character had powers akin to a god, such as omnipresence, omnipotence, omniscience, or omnicompetence; 3) An umbrella term that comprises metagaming, god-modding (double 'd'), powergaming, and powerplay.

Godmodding / God-modding: Comes from 'god moderating' but now refers to: 1) Controlling other players' characters without their consent (also known as powerplay or powergaming); 2) Playing an all-powerful, invincible character like a god; 3) Doing things that would be impossible, particularly for your character; 4) Writing events into a story without permission from the GM or moderator. Not to be confused with god-moding (single 'd').

Griefer: A player who deliberately irritates and harasses other players through language, behavior, or scripts.

Group chat: Can be one of two kinds—the chat function in a group such as the Virtual India group, or a multi-party IM.

Hiatus: Absence from a roleplay for a relatively extended period, which should be announced to the other players and preferably integrated into the storyline.

Hitbox: A box-like area, normally invisible, that counts a 'hit' when touched or penetrated.

HP: An abbreviation of 'health points' or 'hit points,' which are buffed up by eating and lost with time, work, or some sort of damage.

HUD: An abbreviation of 'head(s)-up display,' which can easily be seen without taking one's eyes off the screen.

ICA = ICC: An abbreviation of 'In Character Actions = In Character Consequences,' meaning that IC actions have IC consequences that must be accepted and dealt with IC.

IM: An abbreviation of 'Internal Message,' as opposed to 'Local Chat.' Also known as a 'Private Message' (PM). Usually reserved for OOC messaging.

Immersionist: A person who views a virtual world as a discrete 'place' separate from the 'real world.' Also, an activity in a virtual world that reflects this view, such as roleplay. Also known as 'lifestyler.' The opposite of augmentationist (see above).

In character (IC): A state in which you have stepped into the personality of one's character to speak, act, and respond as your character would do. Usually posted in the third-person present tense.

Interests: A tab in an account profile for indicating your interests, skills, and language(s).

Internet shorthand: Also known as internet slang, cyber-slang, netspeak, chatspeak, 133t, lolspeak, and so on. Abbreviations commonly used in chats, which should be avoided in roleplay.

IRL: An abbreviation of 'In Real Life.'

Kiting: A maneuver to get an aggroed (NPC) enemy to chase after you (like a kite on a string), staying just out of range of it while causing damage to it.

Lag: The delay between an action and its result in an online environment, often due to low computer capacity or internet speed, high graphics settings, or heavy network traffic.

Level up: To move up to the next level in a merit system, which often earns additional powers, skills, HP capacity, and so on.

LI: An abbreviation of 'land impact'—Second Life's way of calculating how many sim resources an item uses, which is more useful than the earlier measurement of 'prims.'

Lifestyler: A immersionist who treats roleplay almost as a parallel life, not just a story or game with a beginning and end.

Limits / RP limits: A roleplay action that a *player* feels uncomfortable with, as communicated in a Profile Pick and in OOC/IMs, as distinct from what the *character* itself may feel uncomfortable with. Must not be invoked to avoid the IC consequences of IC actions.

Local Chat: A public chat seen by all within chat range, as opposed to an Internal Message (IM). Also known as 'nearby chat' or 'general chat.' Usually used for IC posts in roleplay.

Lure: An IC post, often sent out as a group IM, describing a scene or situation framed as a roleplaying idea, accompanied by an OOC invitation for others to participate.

Lurking: Observing a roleplay scene from within chat distance without taking part in it. Usually has no negative connotations but rather is positively seen as being part of an 'audience.'

Mary Sue / Gary Stu or Marty Stu: A character that is too perfect in every way. Often used as a pejorative, as it is widely held that all characters should have flaws.

Machine-gun posting: Spreading a roleplay post among several short, consecutive posts instead of grouping the whole message in a single post. See 'chain-posting,' 'cross-posting,' and 'posting order.'

Machinima: The genre and method of producing animated films using digital 3D media such as virtual worlds and other real-time computer graphics engines.

Main character syndrome: Seeking to be the center of attention, make everything about oneself, and/or actively try to make the story revolve around one's character. Also known as 'protagonist syndrome.'

Metagaming: Using OOC knowledge (that the character could not have obtained in-game) to solve IC problems in roleplay—for instance, bringing OOC information into an IC situation.

Mob: An abbreviation of 'mobile,' usually referring to NPCs or scripted creatures that can be interacted with, such as predators or prey.

Moderator (Mod): A person in charge of designing, suggesting, and coordinating storylines in certain roleplay regions. May also be assigned to watch over roleplay forums and accounts.

Mood post: A descriptive post meant to set the mood or context for a scene, tie the story together, or move it forward.

Mouselook: Enables adjusting the view by moving the mouse, as though you were looking through your avatar's eyes. Most commonly used for aiming and striking or shooting.

MRP: An abbreviation of 'mature roleplay,' which involves strong language, violence, and sex. ERP and CARP, among others, are subsets of MRP. Also known as 'adult roleplay.'

Multi-para roleplay: Posting multiple paragraphs at a time, often three or more, also known as 'novella RP.'

Multi-posting: See 'chain-posting.'

Mun: An abbreviation of 'mundane,' also known as player, typist, or, in this book, atman—the person behind the keyboard/screen.

Murderhobo: A player character that comes into a roleplay region for the sole purpose of killing, looting, and terrorizing others with little or no consideration for—or interest in—the storylines unfolding there.

Name replacer: see 'chat replacer.'

Nearby chat: A public chat seen by all within chat range, as opposed to an Internal Message (IM). Also known as 'local chat' or 'general chat.' Usually used for IC posts in roleplay.

Notecard: An inventory object used for writing, storing and sharing text.

Novella RP: See 'multi-para roleplay.'

NPC: An abbreviation of non-player character—a character not directed by a specific player (as opposed to PC—player character). Can either be a scripted/dummy avatar or be written into existence by a player as needed. As a verb, to use or impersonate an NPC in roleplay.

Noob: An abbreviation of newbie or noobie—a beginner roleplayer and/or poor or default avatar design.

One-line RP: Posting a single sentence or line of text at a time, sometimes referred to as 'action roleplay,' wherein simple emotes and actions are interspersed with the dialog.

Opener: An initial post in which players describe their characters using appositive phrases. Also known as 'starter.'

Out of character (OOC): 1) A state/post from a player's perspective and not their character's, usually written in the first person, to be limited to IMs or among brackets in Local Chat; 2) Acting in a way that is contrary to or an inaccurate portrayal of a character's definition.

Out of game (OOG): A variant of OOC posts that are in no way related to the roleplay. This kind of post is usually frowned upon in roleplay regions.

Open region: A roleplay region that allows anyone to enter/join, although some require an application and/or test before granting full membership.

Original character (OC): A roleplay character defined entirely by the player and not based on a 'canon character' (see above).

Outfit: The set of clothing, HUDs, and other attachments an avatar is 'wearing.' Each outfit can be given a name and saved to enable changing easily and quickly from one to another as needed.

Para-RP: Posting in complete paragraphs, usually four or more sentences long.

Perma-death: The final death of a character, which forces a player to create or use an entirely new character to continue roleplaying, albeit on the same account.

Picks: A tab in an account's profile, comprising a title, image, and text.

Pixel-sex: A derogatory term for sexual scenes that involve little or no actual written narrative or 'emotes,' also known as pixel porn. Not to be confused with true erotic roleplay.

Player: The person behind the keyboard/screen controlling the character. Also known as 'mun' or, in this book, 'atman.'

Player character (PC): A character controlled by a human player, as opposed to a non-player character (NPC).

Pose: A script that places an avatar into a static or unmoving posture (as opposed to an 'animation,' which is dynamic or moving).

Post: A text written by a player, usually in Local Chat, from the start of typing to when 'Enter' is hit.

Post round: When roleplaying in a group, one complete round of posts, preferably respecting a 'posting order.' Also known as postround.

Post stuffing: Filling posts with details that do little or nothing to further the two main purposes of revealing one's character and moving the story along. See also 'fluffing'.

Posting order: The order in which the participants in a group roleplay session present their posts. Following a posting order ensures that everyone has a chance to post and avoids the confusion that cross-posting can cause.

PbM: An abbreviation of 'play-by-mail,' a form of text-based, character-driven roleplay. Also known as 'play-by-post' (PbP).

PbP: An abbreviation of 'play-by-post,' a form of text-based, character-driven roleplay. Also known as 'play-by-mail' (PbM) when posts are mailed to a Game Master or coordinator.

Poseballs: An old system still in limited use in Second Life, often in the form of small colored balls such as blue for males and pink for females. 'Sitting' on them puts an avatar into a static pose or dynamic animation. They have been largely replaced by including poses and animations directly in furniture itself in an effort to achieve greater realism.

Powerplay/powergaming: 1) Presuming that an action by one's character toward or against another character is successful without giving them the freedom to decide how your action will affect them or how they will respond to it (also known as 'godmodding'); 2. Claiming extreme political and/or physical power for one's own character (known as 'bunnying' in Tumblr RPGs).

Prim: Short for 'primitive' shape such as a cube, sphere, cylinder, and others, which can then be stretched, cut, twisted, and in other ways 'tortured' into many different shapes.

Profile: 1) An in-depth character description or bio, initially written prior to commencing roleplay but also further developed throughout the roleplay; 2) A window containing information on an account, with sections such as Groups, Web, Interests, Picks, and 1st Life.

Protagonist syndrome: Seeking to be the center of attention, make everything about oneself, and/or actively try to make the story revolve around one's character. Also known as 'main character syndrome.'

Purple prose: Writing focused more on detailed description than on actions that move the plot forward, often rich in metaphor and simile. Widely used as a derogatory term.

PVP: An abbreviation for player-versus-player, where players fight each other, not with NPCs.

Quest: A goal-oriented activity created to further the story, raise a character to a new level, or obtain some resource.

Real-time: An activity that is not turn-based but in which each player acts simultaneously with others. Often involves using a scripted combat/economic system. Opposite of 'turn-based' (see below).

Region: A virtual area designed for roleplay, the size of which can go from part of a sim to several sims.

Retconning: Modifying something that occurred in the past, usually a minor adjustment due to some mistake made, from 'RETroactive CONtinuity.'

Reverse powerplay: Turning a story around to blame other characters for more severe impacts of their actions on one's own character than they would have chosen or are willing to accept.

Rez: Originally short for 'resurrect'—for instance, logging back into a game after dying. In this book, it refers to making an object or avatar appear in a virtual world by creating it, dragging it from Inventory, or logging in.

RL: An abbreviation of 'real life.' Also referred to in character as 'Ar-El'—an alternate reality that characters sometimes go to.

RLV: An abbreviation of 'Restrained Love Viewer' (aka 'Restrained Life Viewer')—an optional feature enabling in-world scripts to control an avatar, used on sims to create 'experiences.'

Round character: A persona that evolves and can evince apparently incongruent attitudes and behaviors, as opposed to a 'flat character' (see above).

RP: An abbreviation of 'roleplay'—a social activity in which players assume fictional characters that interact with each other through scenes and stories.

RPF: An abbreviation of 'roleplay fighting,' also known as 'text-based' or 'turn-based' fighting, which usually does not use a scripted combat system but only descriptive posts.

RPG: An abbreviation of 'roleplaying game' or, less commonly, 'roleplay group,' in which participants assume character roles and play out stories collaboratively.

LitRPG: An abbreviation of 'Literary Role-Playing Game,' also known as 'RPGlit'—an abbreviation for 'Role-Playing Game Literature'—a genre of fiction literature created or framed within or through a role-playing game (RPG).

Scene: A sub-set of a storyline: 1) A single roleplaying session within the same setting; 2) A single IC situation, which may span across multiple RP sessions, such as a battle that takes several sessions to play out.

Self-insert: A character modeled after the real-life persona, roleplayed practically as though the character were its mun.

Semi-para RP: Posting two to three sentences at a time.

Setting: 1) The virtual environment in which roleplay takes place; 2) Adjustment of a variable in a menu such as Preferences or Options.

Sim: An abbreviation of 'simulator'—the basic programming unit used when building a virtual world, which makes it possible to add both avatars and 3D 'objects,' textures, scripts, sounds, environments, experiences, and other elements. It is called 'simulator' because it enables users to 'simulate' (create a virtual version of) a real-life or fictitious scenario. In Second Life, each sim is 256m x 256m (65,536 m^2).

SL (Second Life): An online virtual world developed and owned by Linden Lab since 2003. SL can also be an abbreviation for 'storyline.'

SLT: An abbreviation for 'Second Life Time' or 'Standard Linden Time,' the real-world time zone of Linden Lab, which is equivalent to PST/PDT (Pacific Standard Time/Pacific Daylight Time).

Sparring: Fighting for practice purposes, often in a no-damage area or state.

Spoofing: Using a chat/name/text replacer to impersonate another player's character without their express permission.

Starter: An initial post in which players describe their characters using appositive phrases. Also known as 'opener.'

Storyline: The overall story covering several scenes and involving all characters in the roleplay, like the plot of a novel.

Stuffing: Lengthening posts unnecessarily with descriptions and internal dialogs that have little or no relevance to the actual story or plot, also known as 'fluffing out a post.'

SWRP: An abbreviation of 'Star Wars Role Play.'

Text replacer: See 'chat replacer.'

Titler: A hovertext, also known as a character tag, that provides vital information such as name (if different), rank or title, accent or unusual speech, current mood and appearance, and others.

TP: An abbreviation of 'teleport.'

Trigger: Something that upsets or harms a person's mental or emotional well-being.

Turn-based: Roleplay that advances as players take turns posting, as opposed to 'real time' (see above).

Twinking: Acting nonsensically from an IC perspective, grossly violating realism and believability. The adjective is 'twinky' and the noun, 'twink,', is a derogatory term for such a character.

Typist: The person behind the keyboard managing the avatar, also known as 'player,' 'mun,' or 'atman' in this book.

Voiding: An OOC agreement in which all players involved decide to proceed as though a scene or IC event never took place, also known as 'erasure.'

WASD: The W, A, S, and D keys used like arrow keys to control avatar movement.

White-knighting: Rescuing a character that has been attacked, downed, and/or captured without first asking the players involved for permission.

Wolfspeak: An invented accent and/or set of invented words used by some players to make their (often animal) characters distinctive. This practice is generally looked down upon within the roleplay community because it makes posts hard to read and rarely adds much of anything useful to the roleplay.

INDEX

About the Author

In Second Life, Pannie is the CEO of "Paniscus Industries" specializing in Adult Furniture Guidebooks and other virtual books such as the "10 Commandments of Erotic Roleplay" (marketplace.secondlife.com/stores/217863).

Pannie's various reincarnations (alts) have been involved in virtual worlds for over a decade as event hosts, estate managers, builders and, of course, roleplayers and supporters of roleplay regions.

In real life, their mun has worked in dozens of countries on five continents as a researcher and entrepreneur, trainer and consultant, linguist and author/editor of both fiction and non-fiction works.

www.ingramcontent.com/pod-product-compliance
Ingram Content Group UK Ltd.
Pitfield, Milton Keynes, MK11 3LW, UK
UKHW041643190726
13854UKWH00006B/2672

9 789942 387257